Turner and Beard

Men are the product of history, but history is made by men.

EDWIN R. A. SELIGMAN

> No systematic thought has made progress apart from some adequately general working hypothesis, adapted to its special topic. . . . To venture upon productive thought without such an explicit theory is to abandon oneself to the doctrines derived from one's grandfather.

ALFRED NORTH WHITEHEAD

Turner and Beard

AMERICAN HISTORICAL WRITING RECONSIDERED

BY LEE BENSON

THE FREE PRESS, *New York*

COLLIER-MACMILLAN LIMITED, *London*

Collier-Macmillan Canada, Ltd., Toronto, Ontario

Library of Congress Catalog Card Number: 60-10890

FIRST FREE PRESS PAPERBACK EDITION 1965

Second Printing August 1966

For JAMES C. MALIN

A scholar with whom I have sometimes disagreed,
but from whom I have always learned.

18418

PREFACE

◇◇

IN RECENT DECADES a tendency has developed to view
Frederick Jackson Turner and Charles A. Beard as though their
seminal ideas derived from, and represented, radically different
theories of history. This book challenges that view and argues
that their surface differences should not obscure their fundamental similarities.

Searching for an overarching scheme that would help them
comprehend and summarize American experience, Turner and
Beard both drew upon European models. Both adopted eclectic
approaches that inconsistently combined concepts taken from
the "economic interpretation of history" and from economic

determinism. Consequently, they both presented theses that are ambiguous and self-contradictory.

Before we can restate and reappraise either the Turner thesis or the Beard thesis, we must try to untangle their contradictory elements and remove their ambiguities. The essays collected here are designed to contribute to that process. Since they were written ten years apart, they vary in form and content. But an underlying theme unites them: the impact upon American scholarship of European theories of economic determinism and economic interpretation of history.

In 1949, I became intrigued by the similarity between Turner's and Beard's ideas that one-to-one relationships existed between economic developments and other phases of American life. And I became intrigued also by the similarity between their ideas and those of Achille Loria, an Italian economist whose system of "economic sociology" received international acclaim during the late nineteenth and early twentieth centuries. Some provocative questions suggested themselves:

Did the frontier thesis owe more to Old World theory than to New World experience? Had Loria's theory of "free land" tended to misdirect the course of American historiography? Would it be accurate to describe both the "Turner thesis" and the "Beard thesis" as versions of the "Loria thesis?" Could the difference in their intellectual milieu help to explain the difference in their emphasis, Turner's upon geographic place and Beard's upon economic class?

The essay on Beard and his critics is published in this book for the first time. The two essays on Turner and Loria were published in *Agricultural History* and are reprinted here, except for minor changes.

It is a pleasure to acknowledge that the Beard essay benefitted from critical readings by my wife, Eugenia Singleton Benson, by Daniel Aaron, Carl Auerbach, Daniel Bell, Merrill Jensen, James C. Malin, and Robert K. Merton, and from the stimulating company of Fellows at the Center for Advanced Study in the Behavioral Sciences, 1958-1959. I am also grateful for the resources made available to me by the Director of the Center,

Ralph W. Tyler, and by its other administrative officers, Preston S. Cutler and Jane A. Kielsmeier. And I am also grateful to Mary Hurt for her patience and skill in translating a handwritten scrawl into a typewritten manuscript.

I am indebted to many people, but particularly to Dr. Leland C. DeVinney and the other officers of the Rockefeller Foundation who recommended generous support of an exploratory study designed to adapt to historiography procedures developed in other disciplines. The study has been carried out at the Bureau of Applied Social Research and the Beard essay is the first of a series of publications reporting upon its results.

Bureau of Applied Social Research
Columbia University
November 1959

CONTENTS

◇◇

[xi]

Part III
A Critique of Beard and His Critics

Part One

*A*CHILLE LORIA'S INFLUENCE ON AMERICAN ECONOMIC THOUGHT: *Including His Contributions to the Frontier Hypothesis**

◇◇

IN RECENT YEARS a mantle of obscurity has fallen over the name and reputation of the Italian economist, Achille Loria. Yet, in the last two decades of the nineteenth century, his system of "economic sociology" was of primary importance, and contemporary observers placed him among the foremost academicians of the time. His theories concerning the role of land in the social process profoundly influenced both European and American thought. Thus there is a warrant for attempting to rescue him from an undeserved obscurity.

---

* Reprinted from *Agricultural History*, 24:182-199 (October 1950).

A.
Loria's Career, the Origin of His Ideas, and His General Influence

Loria was born in Mantua, Italy, on March 2, 1857, and his long life, ending on November 6, 1943, was marked by an amazing literary productivity.[1] A bibliography of his publications up to 1932 alone comprised some 884 separate titles; and numerous others appearing thereafter could be listed. Receiving the degree of doctor of laws in 1877 at the University of Bologna, he continued his schooling under two leading contemporary Italian economists, Luigi Cossa at Pavia and Angelo Messedaglia at Rome. After being sent abroad by the Italian government to pursue advanced studies at Berlin with A. H. G. Wagner, C. L. E. Engel, and August Meitzen, he later climaxed his researches in the British Museum. There, in the summer of 1882, indefatigable reading in little-known English books, tracts, and pamphlets of the eighteenth and early nineteenth centuries resulted in a system of thought, based upon land, which was to pervade all his subsequent work.[2]

Upon returning to Italy from Berlin in 1881, Loria taught at the University of Siena, later at Padua, and from 1902 to 1932 he was professor of economics at the University of Turin. In the course of a long career, numerous honors were bestowed

1. Convenient summaries of Loria's early career with biographical and bibliographical details may be found in Johannes Conrad and others, eds., *Handwörterbuch der Staatswissenschaften* (ed. 3, Jena, 1910), 6: 522-523; J. Espasa and Sons, eds., *Enciclopedia universal ilustrada Europeo-Americana* (Barcelona, n.d.), 31: 258-262. The obituary of Loria by Luigi Einaudi, his close friend and literary executor, in the *Economic Journal* (London), 56: 147-150 (March 1946), gives further data and an excellent summary of Loria's views.

2. *Ibid.*, 147-150; and "Personal Notes," American Academy of Political and Social Science, *Annals*, 2: 371 (November 1891). Luigi Einaudi has kindly sent me a copy of a letter by Loria's son, dated Apr. 28, 1950, which supplies the information concerning Loria's study at the British Museum.

upon him, among them appointments as Italian correspondent of the Royal Economic Society of London from 1896 to his death, fellow of the Academia dei Lincei at Rome, 1901, and honorary fellow of the American Economic Association, 1926. He contributed a multitude of articles and reviews to American, English, French, German, and other periodicals, and many of his books were translated into foreign languages. One in particular, *La teoria economica della costituzione politica*, scored a tremendous international success. First published in Italian, 1886, it soon appeared in French, 1893, German, 1895, and English, 1899.[3]

Several of Loria's articles, written for British and American publications during the nineties, give an excellent picture of the intellectual atmosphere in which he matured.[4] Describing the evolution of economics in Italy, he traced the developments which led from the relatively optimistic, laissez-faire views of Francisco Ferrara, the founder of the modern school on the Peninsula, to the rise of Loria's own school, called "the landed property system of political economy." True to his concepts, he showed how the material conditions peculiar to Italy had at every step determined the course of economic theory. Thus, in his view, the conflicts of interest in that country, from the struggles over unification to the eventual dominance of capitalist property relations, were inevitably reflected in political economy.

Loria spelled out this process in detail, beginning with the initial period of Franco-American influence (prior to 1870) symbolized by Ferrara, through the application of English classical doctrines, and the subsequent impact of German scholarship. At all points, he thought, these transformations, conflicts, and advances, occurring in his lifetime, corresponded to the changing structure of the Italian economy. However, with

---

3. *Ibid.,* 371; Einaudi, in *Economic Journal,* 56: 150; Conrad, *Handwörterbuch,* 6: 522.

4. Achille Loria, "Political Economy in Italy," *Economic Journal* 7:450-459 (September 1897); "Italian School of Economics," in R. H. Inglis Palgrave, ed., *Dictionary of Political Economy,* 2: 460-470 (London, 1896); and "Economics in Italy," American Academy of Political and Social Science, *Annals,* 2: 203-224 (September 1891).

capitalism now sovereign (1891), the necessary conditions had at last been achieved for economic theory to attain a final and permanent definition.[5] This climax was of first importance, he concluded, not only for Italian but world economics.

> Upon the economists of Italy who have already had experience of the scientific impotence of the schools that will not consider the question of landed estate; upon those whose constant object of thought and of study is the constitution of landed proprietorship; upon them it is incumbent to follow in the path so successfully traveled by their great predecessors, and to confront the economic theories beyond the Alps, which are the science of darkness, with an economic theory eminently Italian, which, based on the analysis of landed proprietorship, shall illumine the entire social fabric.[6]

Loria's own thinking shows traces of all the various influences he enumerated as affecting Italian economic thought generally. Although essentially in the classical tradition and strongly marked by the Malthus-Ricardian doctrines of population and rent, the imprints of other schools are clearly visible. However, as Luigi Cossa pointed out in appraising Loria in 1893, his system stemmed from numerous diverse sources, from all of which he borrowed but with all of which he disagreed. Among others, David Ricardo, Karl Marx, the German historical school, and the evolutionists such as Herbert Spencer, are found in Loria, but so, too, are his serious criticisms of each one in turn.[7] The judgment of Loria, delivered in 1897, that Italian economists as a whole "adopt, and temper by an intelligent eclecticism, methods and systems of the greatest disparity" would certainly apply with great force to himself.[8]

---

5. These views are present, more or less, in all the articles listed in the preceding footnote, but see in particular the *Annals*, 2: 218-224.

6. *Ibid.*, 224.

7. Luigi Cossa, *An Introduction to the Study of Political Economy*, tr. by Louis Dyer (London, 1893), 510-511.

Loria's great emphasis upon free land appears to have been essentially derived from acquaintance with the works of Benjamin Franklin, Gibbon Wakefield, Herman Merivale, and Henry George. In addition, the authors of numerous pamphlets, tracts, and travel accounts of the seventeenth, eighteenth, and early nineteenth centuries might well be added to this list of precursors.

8. Loria, in *Economic Journal*, 7: 451.

In a word, Loria was a "Lorian"; he was *sui generis*, a school by himself, and an attempt to classify him as a devotee of any established school would be doomed to failure. Almost every appraisal made by contemporaries familiar with his work laid stress on this aspect. Thus, Cossa, under whom Loria had studied, cited him as "a man whose mind puts him on a par with any one hitherto named [contemporary Italian economists] and whose original genius places him above all the rest."[9]

B.
Resumé of Loria's System

If the intellectual influences upon Loria are difficult to separate out without distorting his ideas, the essentials of the system itself are fortunately clear and unmistakable. He subscribed to a rigidly deterministic economic interpretation of history. Its fundamental proposition was that the relationship of man to the amount of "free land" available for cultivation holds the key to human history. A corollary to this axiom was the Hegelian concept of the unfolding of world history in a series of stages, leading at last to a final stage of society. Loria's version of that final society, however, differed radically from that of the German philosopher.[10]

Faced with the necessity of demonstrating the validity of his system, and writing at a time when the deductive-inductive methodological argument was at its height, Loria hit upon the idea of using modern colonial countries to verify his abstract conclusions. According to him, these modern colonies of European powers recapitulated all the past stages of human experience. In his renowned work, the lengthy *Analisi della proprietà capitalista*, volume 1 demonstrated his system theoretically and

---

9. Cossa, *Introduction*, 510.

10. See the summary of Loria's views that follows. The footnotes in his *Analisi della proprietà capitalista* (Turin, 1889), 2: 8-15, make clear his debt to Hegel. For a translation of this important chapter, see the appendix at the end of this essay.

deductively, and volume 2, based upon an intensive analysis of American development, proved it historically and inductively.[11]

The ideas embodied in Loria's system, particularly as worked out in the *Analisi* of 1889 and in later works, were but the development of a schematic plan embodying underlying principles which he had formulated a decade earlier.[12] The brief outline which follows is vastly oversimplified and should be read with that caution in mind.[13]

The sad state of affairs that exists today (1889) in the civilized world under the system of capitalism is not the inevitable result of conditions organic to human nature; it is merely the outcome of certain historical tendencies that will disappear at a later stage of social evolution. All economic phenomena, and even in a general way all social evolution, are due to one sole cause, namely, agricultural conditions as historically determined by the varying degrees of density of population. The relationship between the productivity of the soil and the density of the population is the ultimate factor in determining the various historical periods of the economy of nations.

As long as free lands exist that can be cultivated by labor alone, and where a man without capital may, if he chooses, establish himself upon an unoccupied area, capitalistic property is

---

11. *Ibid.*, 2: 1-7.

12. The letter from Loria's son to Luigi Einaudi referred to in footnote 2 states that the system was worked out in embryonic form in 1876. Fitting together the information in Einaudi's 1946 article, and that contained in the 1950 letter, it is apparent that the summer of 1882 is the probable date when Loria specifically hit upon "free land" as the fundamental key to a much more elaborate version of his system. By 1885, he formally employed it in his *Profitto del capitale*, which won for him the Royal Prize of the Academia dei Lincei.

13. This outline has been pieced together from numerous sources. See, in particular, Ugo Rabbeno, "Loria's Landed System of Social Economy," *Political Science Quarterly*, 7: 258-293 (June 1892), especially 258, 269, 276-282; and Achille Loria, *The Economic Foundations of Society*, tr. by Lindley M. Keasbey (London, 1899), 1-9. Keasbey's translation was made from the second French edition, 1893, which in turn was a revision of the original Italian edition of 1886. See also the chapter in the appendix below.

In this outline an attempt has been made wherever possible to keep the flavor of the original. For a proper understanding of Loria and his influence, the reader should examine Rabbeno's article in full.

out of the question. No laborer is disposed to work for a capitalist when he can labor on his own account upon *land that costs him nothing*. Evidently, therefore, while such conditions prevail, the laborers will simply take possession of the free lands and apply their labor to the soil, adding to this the capital they accumulate. Neither interest nor profit can exist, and only a relatively simple economy can prevail under these conditions. Access to free lands must be cut off in some way before capital can produce profits. If, because of the sparsity of population, the soil itself cannot be entirely appropriated, access to the free lands can only be prevented by subjugating the laborers themselves. Thus slavery is introduced, but later on, when the declining productivity of the soil has to be offset by labor with a higher degree of efficiency, a milder serfdom supplants the more brutal slavery. Eventually, the increasing population and the diminishing fertility of the soil ends the era of free lands cultivatable by labor alone. Then the era of capitalist production relations begins, and man, though legally free, actually loses his freedom.

Colonial countries, where free lands abound, offer striking illustrations of these propositions, and anyone who has rightly comprehended the development of these interesting lands must recognize the truth of the above assertion. The evolution of colonial economies and institutions under our very eyes enables us to grasp the entire course of human development. The history of the United States, from its first beginnings as an English colony to the present time (1889), furnishes an excellent illustration of this principle.

In the beginning of the English colonies in America, a most fertile free soil existed which could be cultivated without capital, hence no wage class could exist, and the population was dispersed. The existence of fertile uncultivated lands rendered improvements unnecessary, and the isolation of the producers rendered them impossible. Although as a result of these conditions the population was lethargic, a general feeling of comfort prevailed. This state of affairs could not last owing to the increasing population and the diminishing fertility of the soil.

Since wages were incompatible with free land, a system of compulsory association was necessary to secure increased efficiency. Slavery was introduced, but though it is more efficient than isolated cultivation, after a while the increased efficiency is overbalanced by the continuing exhaustion of the soil. Indentured servants were then introduced because as long as free land existed it was impossible for a capitalist to get free men to work for wages. During all this period the reward of free labor was very high because the only other form of production apart from forced labor was the small industry, where the entrepreneur was at the same time a workman. Thus the beginning of the nineteenth century in the United States marked a golden age of the laborer. In time, the increase in population again demanded a more efficient form of production, property tended to become concentrated, large farming superseded small farming, and the demands of an increasing population acted as incentives to industrial inventions.

In the United States during the nineteenth century a movement took place similar to the enclosure movements of Europe during the sixteenth and seventeenth centuries. It was caused by the same phenomenon, the cessation of free land cultivatable by simple labor. Today (1889), small landed properties are more characteristic of those States where population is scanty and industries are little developed. However, in the regions where population is relatively dense and industry flourishes, the ownership of the soil shows a threatening and ever-growing concentration, a situation accelerated by injudicious grants of government land.

Once this stage is reached, all the economic and social evils of Europe are reproduced. Although at a slower rate, these conditions are now also developing in America (1889). It is noteworthy that in America this economic transformation goes hand in hand with a political transformation. The cessation of economic freedom, because of the total occupation of the soil, is destroying democratic methods, the glory of early American times. The Congress of great democrats, which once characterized the era of independent producers, is being superseded today by a Congress of plutocrats and railway magnates, which is the parliamentary expression of an era in which capital predominates.

Interestingly enough, these fundamental ideas, roughly outlined by Loria in his work on agricultural rent, completed in 1879 with the title, *La rendita fondiaria e la sua elisione naturale*, coincided in time almost exactly with Henry George's *Progress and Poverty*, which also focused attention upon the role of land in society. However, not only has it been established that Loria did not know of George's work in 1879, but it is a fact that there are fundamental differences in the Italian economist's treatment of land.[14] As noted above, Loria was generously eclectic, and it is possible, with but a little difficulty, to ascertain the numerous sources upon which he drew. His fundamental conceptions are to be found in earlier writers, and he made constant use of the works of these predecessors, with detailed comment and explanation. E. Benjamin Andrews paid tribute to his "astonishing mastery of economic literature, whether standard or recondite, old or recent. In [this] . . . respect . . . [he] is second to Roscher alone." Andrews also commented on the fruits of his long study in the British Museum,[15] as did Luigi Einaudi in his obituary of Loria, published in the *Economic Journal:* "I never met a man who could quote from memory so many forgotten English books, tracts and pamphlets of the eighteenth and of the first half of the nineteenth centuries."[16]

---

14. Rabbeno, in *Political Science Quarterly*, 7: 259 n. 1, 262, 266, also n. 3. The date of publication of Loria's *La rendita fondiaria e la sua elisione naturale* is frequently given as 1880, but the preface is dated Oct. 29, 1879. The earlier year is used in Conrad's *Handwörterbuch*. It is quite possible that Loria saw George's book by 1882, the year when he first became aware of the importance of free land.

15. Review by E. Benjamin Andrews of Loria's *Analisi* in the *Political Science Quarterly*, 5: 717 (December 1890). In a most flattering review of another work by Loria in the *Economic Journal*, 4: 82 (March 1894), James Bonar placed Loria *above* all others as "thoroughly conversant with the literature of his subject in almost every European language."

16. Einaudi, in *Economic Journal*, 56:148.

Loria's own contribution was to combine and fuse the ideas, suggestions, philosophies, and methods of extremely diverse thinkers into an elaborate, minutely worked-out, historical system in which the evolution of human societies was traced upon strikingly novel lines. It is not that he originated the ideas of economic determinism, free land, and stages in human history, nor that he alone promulgated them at the time, but his application and fusion of these concepts resulted in a system peculiarly his own. This point, almost universally acknowledged by contemporary reviewers, needs to be emphasized because of its importance in assessing Loria's impact upon subsequent economic thought. Otherwise, the inadequacies of the brief sketch given above may mislead modern readers familiar with the fact that numerous writers dealt with much of the same material in the last quarter of the nineteenth century.[17]

C.

Introduction of Loria to American Scholars

In the decade of the eighties, following his volume on agricultural rent, Loria published three more works which rounded out his description of the economic basis of political, social,

---

17. Despite the fact that many others dealt with these subjects, Loria's role in promulgating such concepts received wide recognition. Some notion of this may be gained by the fact that Edwin R. A. Seligman, in his famous series of articles on "The Economic Interpretation of History," found it necessary to chastise the "many critics in England, France and Italy . . . [who] have hailed Loria as the originator of the doctrine of economic interpretation. Even Professor Keasbey [American translator of Loria's work] is not entirely free from this error." *Political Science Quarterly*, 17: 297 n. 1 (June 1902). At an earlier date, 1893, Seligman came close to, if he did not actually commit, the same error himself; see *ibid.*, 8: 751-755 (December 1893), particularly 752. The degree of originality attained by Loria in all phases of his work was also attested to by men of the stature of Luigi Einaudi, Luigi Cossa, Ugo Rabbeno, James Bonar, E. Benjamin Andrews, Frank W. Taussig, and Henry R. S. Seager; others might be named. For specific citations of their views, see footnotes 1, 7, 13, 15, 38, and 52 of this essay.

literary, and religious ideas and institutions. This series of books culminated in the massive *Analisi della proprietà capitalista* (1889), a work which won for its author widespread acclaim. In Italy the zenith of his influence was accordingly in the nineties, and Luigi Einaudi is authority for the statement that no young student of economics in that decade neglected to read the *Analisi*.[18] By 1896, Loria could list as partial or thoroughgoing adherents of the "landed property system of political economy" at least twelve well-known Italian academicians.[19]

Nor was Loria's influence limited to the Peninsula. Despite the grave handicap that none of his major works was translated out of the original Italian until 1893, his theories received widespread attention on the Continent in the eighties.[20] When *La teoria economica della costituzione politica* (1886) was revised and translated into French in 1893, it reached a much larger audience and created even more of a stir than had the original.[21]

The man probably most responsible for bringing Loria to the attention of American scholars was Edwin R. A. Seligman of Columbia University. As early as 1886, he pointed to the increasingly important role played by Italians in economic theory, and his interest in them continued thereafter.[22] An

18. Einaudi, in *Economic Journal*, 56: 148.

19. Loria, in Palgrave, *Dictionary*, 2: 469.

20. In the 1893 revised edition of his 1886 work, Loria wryly pointed out that his theory had at least the merit of calling forth numerous objections from eminent critics. See "In Answer to Some Objections," in his *Economic Foundations*, 355-379.

21. See the reviews of this work by Edwin R. A. Seligman in the *Political Science Quarterly*, 8: 751-755 (December 1893); and by James Bonar in the *Economic Journal*, 4: 76-82 (March 1894).

Although I hesitate to appear guilty of exaggerating Loria's influence unduly, I wish to call attention to the close parallel between the ideas in Loria's books and Charles A. Beard's economic interpretation of history as expounded, for example, in his *The Economic Bases of Politics* (New York, 1922). Compare part 3, "The Economic Foundations of Politics," in Loria's *Economic Foundations* (1899), with Beard's work. Of particular interest is Loria's chapter on "Property and Politics" and Beard's chapter on "The Doctrines of the Philosophers." See also pp. 96-100 of this book.

22. Seligman's review of *Giornale degli economisti*, in the *Political Science Quarterly*, 1: 704 (December 1886). Support is lent to this supposition by a letter from Henry R. S. Seager to Richard T. Ely in 1893,

excellent linguist, Seligman frequently reviewed Italian books for the *Political Science Quarterly*, of which he was an editor. As a result of a flattering review in 1889 of one of his books, an Italian, Ugo Rabbeno, wrote to Seligman in January 1890, expressing a desire to correspond regularly.[23] Seizing this opportunity to get an authoritative article on recent developments in Italian economics for his *Quarterly*, Seligman obtained a promise from Rabbeno to do such a review.[24] Originally it had been scheduled for publication in 1890, but Rabbeno's personal affairs intervened and it was not actually printed until September 1891.[25] During the course of their correspondence, Rabbeno indicated his great enthusiasm for Loria,[26] and particularly his *Analisi*, but Seligman expressed reservations concerning aspects of the Lorian system. As a result of this interchange Rabbeno wrote a long critique, printed in the June 1892 *Quarterly* under the title, "Loria's Landed System of Social Economy."

This critique was not the first to present Loria's work favorably to the American audience. Possibly as a result of the Rabbeno-Seligman correspondence, E. Benjamin Andrews had already reviewed the *Analisi* in the *Political Science Quarterly* for December 1890. No author could hope for a better notice.

Italy has long been giving us much of our best economic literature, and this is her masterpiece. Already well known . . . Loria now presents his *magnum opus*. . . . The broad scope of the *Analysis* affords space and occasion for review of every cardinal topic in political economy,—population, value, money, interest, taxation,— and upon none of them does Loria fail to show himself a master.[27]

---

quoted in footnote 52 below, as well as other material presented in this essay.

23. Rabbeno to Seligman, Jan. 16, 1890, in the Seligman Papers at Columbia University. All Seligman correspondence cited hereafter is in this collection.

24. Rabbeno to Seligman, Feb. 22, 1890.

25. Ugo Rabbeno, "The Present Condition of Political Economy in Italy," *Political Science Quarterly*, 6: 439-473 (September 1891). Seligman translated the article from the Italian.

26. Rabbeno to Seligman, May 3, 5, 1891.

27. Andrews, in *Political Science Quarterly*, 5: 717.

Pointing out that "Loria's main thesis is that profits arise solely from the suppression of free land," Andrews proceeded to summarize the first volume, but gave little notice to the second except to comment that it was "a most valuable addition to economic history." This flattering review appears to be the earliest analysis of Loria's ideas in an American scholarly journal.

The next year Loria's views on the history of the United States were presented even more forcefully to American scholars. Not only did Rabbeno's piece appear in the *Political Science Quarterly* with a statement that his colleague's work was important enough to warrant a forthcoming separate article, but, in the same month, September 1891, the *Annals* of the American Academy of Political and Social Science carried Loria's own description of "Economics in Italy," including a brief discussion of his system.[28] Immediately thereafter, the October issue of the *Quarterly Journal of Economics* appeared with a short article by Loria on "The Landed Theory of Profit."[29] This contribution had been elicited in response to the highly polemical discussion raging in that periodical on the then "burning question" of profit and capital, in the course of which James Bonar had called attention to Loria's work upon those topics.

In capsule form, Loria presented his views on American history, seeking to justify the position that social classes were not the product of human nature but the result of historic factors.

. . . it is especially to researches in the economic development of the United States that I owe this conviction. In fact, the study of this marvelous development has shown me that, so long as there is free land which can be cultivated without capital, profit is impossible. . . . Profit, then, is only the corollary of the lack of free land, which takes away from the laborer all option and establishes economic servitude.

All Americans who know the history of their enchanting land

---

28. Loria, in *Annals*, 2: 203-224.
29. *Quarterly Journal of Economics*, 6: 108-111 (October 1891).

will readily recognize that it gives a striking illustration of these views.[30]

And Loria went on to show how the landed theory of profit explained the democratic features of the United States, the existence of slavery and the behavior of the planter aristocracy, and to indicate that American protectionism, the indirect system of taxation, and many other developments could easily be explained by his doctrines.[31] Thus, in the space of two months, the three leading American scholarly periodicals had all brought the Italian economist to the attention of their readers.

Despite this effective publicity, it was probably in 1892 that the details of Loria's system became really well known in the United States for the first time. The April number of the *Quarterly Journal of Economics* carried a short article paying tribute to Loria's free land theory, but terming its postulates exaggerated,[32] and in June, Rabbeno's second paper—a 36-page exposition and analysis—appeared.[33] When the intense interest in the land question at this time, and the importance of the *Political Science Quarterly* as a scholarly medium, are kept in mind, the generalization is warranted that few careful, up-to-date students were unaware of Loria's views thereafter.

The next year was to see Loria's stock boosted even higher, for it was marked by the appearance of the French edition of the 1886 work dealing with the explicit relationships between economic and social history. Entitled *Les Bases économique de la constitution sociale*, it was hailed by Edwin R. A. Seligman in the *Political Science Quarterly* with these striking sentences:

This is a most remarkable book. In the original Italian edition it made a considerable stir. In its present form it is destined to make far more of a stir; for it is bold and original, and deals with the most fundamental of all questions—that of human progress.

---

30. *Ibid.*, 108-109.
31. *Ibid.*, 110.
32. C. A. Conigliani, "Professor Loria's Theory of Profit," *ibid.*, 6: 344-346 (April 1892).
33. "Loria's Landed System of Social Economy," *Political Science Quarterly*, 7: 258-293 (June 1892).

Professor Loria really makes two points: first, that the growth of law, politics and morals is based primarily on economic relations; second, that the evolution of economic relations is the simple working out of one cause—the suppression of free land.[34]

Seligman's review was, however, by no means an unmixed panegyric. Emphasis upon the economic basis of social relations and the erudition displayed in working out the details of this process won lavish praise, but Loria's concept of the role played by free land in the discussion was dismissed as immature and unproven. However, Seligman concluded by noting that an English translation was underway, and "If any work of the last decade deserves this distinction it is surely that of the talented and erudite Paduan professor."[35]

Actually, it was not until 1899 that Lindley M. Keasbey was finally able to publish his translation, entitled, *The Economic Foundations of Society*. Fortunately, some letters of the Seligman-Keasbey correspondence relative to the translation have been preserved, and they help to reveal the importance attached to Loria's work by leading economists. Thus, despite Seligman's reservation on free land, he maintained the book was so important that "we *must* get this English version out," and his feelings on the matter were essentially shared by Simon N. Patten and Jeremiah Jenks.[36] It is important to note, however, that even Keasbey, who extravagantly admired Loria's work, found it impossible completely to accept his views on land and expressed some criticism in the preface to the translation.[37]

---

34. Seligman, in *ibid.*, 8: 751-752.
35. *Ibid.*, 755.
36. Keasbey to Seligman, Nov. 10, 1895.
37. Loria, *Economic Foundations*, ix. T. N. Carver, reviewing this edition in the *Political Science Quarterly*, 15: 143-147 (March 1900), acutely observed (p. 145) that Loria's views, despite wide reading, were derived mainly from observations based on his native environment where landed property operated in somewhat the manner described by the Italian economist. Edward A. Ross, in his "Recent Tendencies in Sociology," *Quarterly Journal of Economics*, 16: 552-553 (August 1902), also pointed out that Loria's exaggerated notion of universal laws stemmed from Italian experience.

Similarly, in 1895, Frank W. Taussig, reviewing one book by Loria, and another by his disciple, Rabbeno, put forth a mixture of grave doubts with high praise:

To the present writer [Taussig] the theory of pristine equality and of free land, which is the foundation of this new philosophy, seems untrue to history and weak in logic; the application of that theory to the explanation of all economic and social development, seems forced and artificial. . . . It is inevitable, therefore, that he [Taussig] should dissent. . . . But such dissent is not inconsistent with a high respect for the learning and the ability of the author, or a cordial appreciation of the brilliant talents which he has again shown. . . .[38]

And referring to Rabbeno's application of free land to American tariff history, Taussig wrote:

The boldness and brilliancy of Professor Loria's work, and the suggestiveness and ingenuity of his generalizations, not unnaturally tempt to emulation. But it may be doubted whether the keys to the understanding of the industrial development of the United States have been found by either the leader or the disciple.[39]

One further quotation from a review by E. Benjamin Andrews in 1899 might fairly well summarize the general American reaction to Loria at the end of the decade:

The great value of Loria's contribution to economic science is his demonstration of the vital part played in human history by men's relation to the land. This, his central thesis, may be said to have been pretty successfully made out, and his work upon it entitles him to a permanent and high place among economic thinkers. But that men's relation to the land takes effect in the precise ways fig-

---

38. Taussig's review of Loria's *Problemi sociali contemporanei*, in the *Political Science Quarterly*, 10: 538 (September 1895).

39. Taussig's extended review of Ugo Rabbeno's *American Commercial Policy*, in the *Quarterly Journal of Economics*, 10: 108 (October 1895). This work by Rabbeno is an excellent example of the application of Loria's system to a phase of American economic development. As such it helps make up for the handicap of not having Loria's *Analisi* in English, and it is worth the attention of those readers whose curiosity has been aroused by the necessarily oversimplified sketch of the Italian's system.

ured out by Loria is far less clear, despite the mass of apparent evidence with which he seeks to substantiate his analyses.[40]

D.
Loria's Influence on Richard T. Ely

At least one outstanding American economist was greatly influenced by Loria's free land theory. A comparison between Richard T. Ely's *An Introduction to Political Economy* of 1889 and his 1893 *Outlines of Economics* unmistakably reveals the power of Loria's fine Italian hand. The contrast between the two works is definite and sharp, and as Ely himself pointed out in the preface, although his original intention had been merely to revise the *Introduction* (1889), the result was virtually a new book.[41] Fortunately, Ely's papers have been preserved, and by using them it is possible to reconstruct some of the events that lay behind this development.

As a result of a disagreement with President Daniel Coit Gilman over his future status, Ely left Johns Hopkins University in 1892 to assume the directorship of the newly created School of Economics, Political Science, and History at the University of Wisconsin.[42] Among the graduate students in his first seminar that fall was H. H. Powers, a former professor of French at Oberlin College who had resigned from that position

---

40. E. Benjamin Andrews' review of Achille Loria's *La costituzione economica odierna*, in the *Political Science Quarterly*, 14: 719-720 (December 1899).

41. Richard T. Ely, *Outlines of Economics* (college ed., New York, 1893), v-vi.

42. Richard T. Ely, *Ground Under Our Feet: An Autobiography* (New York, 1938), 175-176. A valuable discussion of this development and the role played by Turner in bringing Ely to Wisconsin is found in Merle Curti and Vernon Carstensen, *The University of Wisconsin, A History* (Madison, 1949), 1: 630-639.

because of a growing interest in economics and sociology.[43] Powers' grasp of these subjects must have impressed Ely because he was asked to assist the latter in revising the 1889 *Introduction*. According to Ely, he had only anticipated help which could be passed over perfunctorily in the preface, but the total aid received was so great that it became necessary to make particular acknowledgement of it and to declare the product a joint effort.[44]

It is possible that one element of Powers' aid lay in giving Ely a better picture of Loria's system than he could have obtained by merely reading the article in the *Political Science Quarterly*. Just prior to joining Ely's seminar in the late summer of 1892, Powers, already a gifted linguist, had spent several weeks in Italy traveling with Emory R. Johnson. Loria's system was then creating something of a sensation, and possibly they heard it referred to during their stay there.[45] However that may be, the minutes of Ely's seminar reveal that at the October 12, 1892 meeting, a student named Samuel Edwin Sparling gave a review of the article on Loria in the *Political Science Quarterly* for June 1892.[46] Hence it is clear that Ely, and all his graduate students present that day, became acquainted with the theories of the Italian economist, at least as early as October.

---

43. Powers to Ely, May 1, 1893, in the Ely Papers at the Wisconsin State Historical Society. All Ely correspondence hereafter cited is in this collection.

44. Ely, *Outlines*, v-vi.

45. Emory R. Johnson to Ely, Sept. 4, 1892. Johnson did not mention Loria in the letter, but American graduate students abroad in those years almost invariably attempted to become familiar with the views of leading economists in each country visited.

Support is added to the above speculation by the following facts. Upon returning to America in 1892, Johnson was made coeditor of the book department of the *Annals*. David Kinley and H. H. Powers of the University of Wisconsin were listed as cooperating in the work. *Annals*, 3:vi. The next year, with Johnson becoming sole editor, the list of cooperators was expanded to include, among others, Achille Loria. *Annals*, 4:vi. Johnson received his M.Litt. from the University of Wisconsin in 1891 and had been at Johns Hopkins University in 1890-91. He was greatly impressed with Powers' ability, and in a letter to Ely on Sept. 4, 1892, he recommended that Powers be given a fellowship in economics.

46. Economic Seminary Minutes, 1892-1893, p. 7, in the Ely Papers.

It was probably due to Powers' linguistic abilities that Loria's theories came to play so large a role in the 1893 edition of Ely's *Outlines of Economics*. The letters from Powers to Ely show that he actually wrote the greater part of the revised edition, although this writing was done under the general supervision of Ely. The same letters also indicate that the book was written in the early months of 1893, following the seminar discussion of the *Political Science Quarterly* article.[47] Indisputable evidence exists that Powers could read Italian at the time, and Loria's untranslated work on agricultural rent, *La rendita fondiara e la sua elisione naturale* (1879), is listed in the bibliography of the college edition.[48]

Unfortunately, no footnotes were employed in the *Outlines*, but the transformation from the 1889 edition would alone appear to be convincing testimony as to the impact of Loria's doctrines. The differences in the treatment of the two key subjects of wages and rent are particularly pertinent because these topics are standard, fairly precise, and are defined at some length. In the 1889 version, Ely gave the classical definitions of Ricardian rent, and "the iron law of wages," using those exact words in referring to the latter.[49] The 1893 book introduced a most important change in the wages question. There is no longer any mention of the iron law of wages operating in the United States. On the contrary, the view is given that the American workingman had been more fortunate than his English cousin:

Through our industrial history to the present he has been able, by going a reasonable distance, to find cheap or free land where

---

47. Powers to Ely, Feb. 3, 4, 6, 16, Apr. 5, June 14, 1893, Jan. 3, Oct. 4, 30, 1894.

48. Sometime after graduation from the University of Wisconsin in 1882, Powers studied French and Romance philology for 26 months in Paris. Powers to Ely, May 1, 1893. That Powers could read Italian is evident from his review of a book in that language for the *Annals*, 3: 658 (March 1893).

It is interesting that the University of Wisconsin, so far as can be learned today from a study of the university library records, has never possessed a copy of Loria's *La rendita fondiara*. This suggests that Powers or Ely probably owned a copy personally.

49. Richard T. Ely, *An Introduction to Political Economy* (New York, 1889), 215-216, 221-225.

he could earn an independent living. Under such circumstances it has been impossible for the pressure of competition to work out its natural results in manufacturing industries. It is *free land* [italics added] rather than a protective tariff which has kept up the wages of labor, and if that resource, which has thus far tempered the asperities of the struggle, once disappears we may look for different results unless new safeguards take its place.[50]

The analysis of rent shows equally significant modifications. In fact, in the later book, a chapter is entitled "Rent With and Without Free Land," and there is no suggestion of this factor in the 1889 *Introduction*.[51] Hence, despite the lack of direct citation, there seems to be little doubt that Loria's doctrines were of considerable importance in the writing of a textbook which did so much to shape the course of economic thought in the United States. This conclusion is reinforced by the knowledge that in later life Ely often quoted from Loria's works and corresponded on occasion with him.[52]

---

50. Ely, *Outlines*, 56. See also 54-59, 180-185. In this book Ely's treatment of stages in history is somewhat different than in the 1889 edition and appears to have been influenced by Loria. Compare Ely's *Introduction* (1889), 42-54, with his *Outlines* (1893), 14-24.

51. Compare Ely, *Introduction*, 215-216, with his *Outlines*, 168-178.

52. James Washington Bell of the economics department at Northwestern University is authority for the statement that Ely frequently quoted from Loria. Letter from Jens Nyholm, Northwestern University librarian, to the author, Apr. 25, 1950. Mario Einaudi of Cornell University, who knew Loria as a colleague and close friend of his father, Luigi Einaudi, informed me of the Ely-Loria correspondence. I am also indebted to Einaudi for much helpful information concerning Loria and his system. Another indication of Ely's familiarity with Loria may be inferred from a letter to him by Henry R. S. Seager, dated Rome, May 11, 1893. Seager maintained that in spite of the boom Seligman and others were trying to give to Italian economic literature it was only a feeble reflection of English and German work. However, "Loria stands alone and seems really worthy of careful study. He has an original and consistent system." In Ely's *Ground Under Our Feet*, 191, there is an intriguing statement which might also indicate Loria's influence. On Wisconsin's pioneer role in developing land economics, Ely wrote: ". . . I am confident that very soon after I came to Wisconsin in 1892 we began a systematic treatment of what is now called Land Economics. I treated the whole subject under the awkward title, 'Landed Property and the Rent of Land.'" This wording smacks a good deal of Loria's and Rabbeno's phraseology, particularly the latter's article, which Ely read in 1892.

E.

Frederick Jackson Turner's Debt to Loria

An even more striking transformation in the same period is apparent in the work of Ely's young Wisconsin colleague, Frederick Jackson Turner, then a professor of history at Madison. In this respect, the publication in 1938 of Turner's early essays is of the greatest value in tracing the indirect role played by Loria in the formulation of the frontier thesis.[53] Although Turner acknowledged the influence of the latter's work in his famous essay of 1893, the brevity of the citation there given has to date effectively prevented discovery and recognition of the great debt owed by him to the Italian economist. Yet, reading the early Turner essays in sequence, against the background of Loria's prominence in the early nineties, and recognizing the penetration of the free land doctrine into the work of Ely—Turner's then colleague, friend, and former teacher—the existence of the debt would appear to be unmistakable. Fortunately, in addition to a brief quotation from Loria by Turner, an abundance of internal evidence exists to clarify the relationship.

As early as 1889, the young Wisconsinite, Turner, in a review of Theodore Roosevelt's *The Winning of the West*, had definitely indicated his awareness of the importance of westward expansion in American history.[54] Nevertheless, despite such awareness, and despite the fact that, as James C. Malin has put it, ideas concerning the importance of free land were clearly "in

---

53. *The Early Writings of Frederick Jackson Turner*, with a list of all his works compiled by Everett E. Edwards and an introduction by Fulmer Mood (Madison, 1938).

54. *Dial*, 10: 71-73 (August 1889). In numerous articles, Fulmer Mood has presented an excellent analysis of Turner's early writings, and the frontier concept generally, which are indispensable for a proper evaluation of Turner. I have greatly benefited from studying them and from Mood's generosity in making available to me unpublished research notes of the highest value.

the air,"[55] the crux of the matter is that, as late as the fall of 1891, Turner had far from crystallized his thinking on what later came to be known as the frontier thesis. In October and November of that year, he published an essay titled "The Significance of History."[56] Although the germs of some later formulations can be traced to it, and to earlier work, this essay makes clear that Turner was quite uncertain and unassured in his grasp of the historical development of the United States. Though American history was often alluded to, there was no discussion of the stages of growth, its importance as a laboratory for social science, the landed basis of American democracy, etc. On the contrary, Turner was somewhat dissatisfied and pessimistic concerning the ability of scholars to understand American history. In context, if not otherwise, the following quotation tends to support this judgment:

The story of the peopling of America has not yet been written. *We do not understand ourselves* [italics added].[57]

However, when we turn to the very next essay in the volume, first published on November 4, 1892, and probably written in late October,[58] a completely different situation obtains. The tone of "Problems in American History" is definitely unlike its predecessor's. In the 1892 work, the thirty-one-year-old Turner is now boldly assured, self-confident, unequivocal. The

---

55. James C. Malin, "Space and History," *Agricultural History*, 18: 67-68 (April 1944).

56. *Early Writings*, 43-68.

57. *Ibid.*, 64. See also Rudolph Freund, "Turner's Theory of Social Evolution," *Agricultural History*, 19: 78-87 (April 1945). This article first called my attention to the pessimistic note in Turner, as well as to the idea stated below that he did not see the census bulletin before 1892.

58. *Early Writings*, 71-83. I am indebted to Fulmer Mood for the information suggesting that the essay was composed in late October. Turner's opening words refer to a recent conversation with a leading State Senator. A special session of the Wisconsin legislature was called for Oct. 17, 1892, and this session probably brought about the meeting. Several other facts tend to reinforce this conclusion—chief among them being Turner's characteristic habit of putting off writing until the very last, and the tremendous amount of his time consumed earlier in the year arranging for Ely's coming to Wisconsin and the creating of the new school.

essay is filled with sweeping and unqualified generalizations, and some previous judgments are completely reversed. For example, he was now highly scornful of Hermann Eduard von Holst's study of the Constitution, whereas, in 1891, he had flatteringly referred to von Holst, along with James Bryce, as having "shown us a mirror of our political life in the light of the political life of other peoples."[59]

Nothing resembling the following declaration had appeared in the earlier essay:

In a sense, American history up to our own day has been colonial history, the colonization of the Great West. This ever retreating frontier of free land is the key to American development.[60]

Fulmer Mood's comment upon these sentences is of the greatest significance:

In this reference to free land, Turner for *the first time in print* [italics added] put his finger upon the material cause, the fundamental economic factor, that he was to stress in his interpretation of our history.[61]

What had wrought the great transformation? How had Turner discovered that the "ever retreating frontier of free land is the key to American development"? Sufficient evidence now exists definitely to rule out the possibility that the famous census bulletin was responsible. For one thing, Turner, in the essay itself, clearly revealed that he could not possibly have seen the bulletin, announcing the end of the frontier, in time for it to have affected his thinking.

Study the maps in *Scribner's Statistical Atlas* in which the settled area is colored for the various census periods, and you will perceive that the dark portion flows forward like water on an uneven surface; here and there are tongues of settlement pushed out in advance, and corresponding projections of wilderness wedged into the advancing mass. The map for the next census will show gaps filled in, and *the process repeated on a new frontier line* [Italics added].[62]

59. *Early Writings*, compare 61 with 71-72.
60. *Ibid.*, 72.
61. *Ibid.*, 37-38.
62. *Ibid.*, 75.

Moreover, the publication by Wendell H. Stephenson in 1945 of some correspondence between Turner and Woodrow Wilson demonstrates the validity of the interpretation.[63] Turner sent Wilson a copy of his "Problems in American History," published on November 4, 1892. The latter followed the doctrine of this essay closely in an extremely critical review of Goldwin Smith's work on American politics, which he published in the *Forum* for December 1893.[64] In this review, Wilson specifically stated that the frontier still existed. Thus, Turner clearly could not have made any marginal comment, if he had learned, subsequent to completing his article, that the frontier was gone.

If not the census bulletin, what then was responsible for the transformation in Turner's essays? Could it have been the result of his learning about Loria's work? Even if no other evidence existed than the material presented in the preceding pages, the presumption would be quite strong that this was the case, unless a most astounding coincidence had occurred. Fortunately, it is unnecessary to depend upon such circumstantial logic to sustain the point. Turner himself specifically pointed out that the "Problems" essay was the foundation for the more famous "Frontier" paper of 1893,[65] and this celebrated essay contains a most important quotation from Loria, which is not only a fundamental part of the paper, but furnishes the basis for the entire section on the frontier as a field for "comparative study of social development."

In addition, a plethora of internal evidence exists in *both* essays which clearly establishes the close relationship between the Italian economist's free land system and Turner's own views. Taken in conjunction with still other data, there appears to be little reason to question the assertion that Loria was, if not *the*

---

63. Wendell H. Stephenson, "The Influence of Woodrow Wilson on Frederick Jackson Turner," *Agricultural History*, 19: 253 (October 1945).

64. Woodrow Wilson, "Mr. Goldwin Smith's 'Views' on Our Political History," *Forum*, 16: 494-495 (December 1893).

65. *Early Writings*, 185 n. 1.

most important, at least *a* most important influence upon the Turner hypothesis.[66]

As noted above, positive written evidence exists that Loria's system was being seriously discussed on the Wisconsin campus by Richard T. Ely. In view of the extremely close relation between the two professors (Turner having been very influential in bringing Ely to Wisconsin) and the equally close relations between the history and economics departments generally,[67] it seems unlikely that Turner would fail to share some of Ely's interest in Loria. In addition, it is more than likely that Turner read the *Political Science Quarterly*, since at that time it was the sole scholarly periodical which regularly carried articles and reviews on American history, and that therefore he read, or soon heard of, the article by Rabbeno.[68]

These speculations aside, the opening paragraphs of "Problems in American History" reveal, to this writer at least, unmistakable evidence of Loria's views. Turner began the essay by repeating almost word for word some observations made by him in the 1889 review of Roosevelt's *The Winning of the West* concerning the importance of territorial expansion and the failure of Eastern historians to recognize this factor.[69] But something new was then added. Von Holst, praised the year before, was now held up to censure because in his treatment of slavery he had failed to take "note of the evolution of political and constitutional institutions resulting from this [territorial] expansion."[70] This new note corresponds closely to Loria's emphasis that political and governmental institutions in the United States, during the period of slavery and indentured servitude, differed from

---

66. An interesting aspect of this relationship is revealed by the fact that in later life Turner spoke of Loria as an important figure in social science. Merle Curti of the University of Wisconsin has been kind enough to give me this information.

67. Ely, *Ground Under Our Feet*, 179-180; and Curti and Carstensen, *Wisconsin*, 1: 630-641.

68. This statement is based upon a fairly diligent survey of the contents of these journals published from 1886 through 1893.

69. *Early Writings*, 71; and *Dial*, 10: 71-73 (August 1889).

70. *Early Writings*, 71-72.

those of all other countries with similar economic forms, precisely because of the vast territorial extent of the country.[71] In his *Quarterly Journal of Economics* article of October 1891, Loria had pointed out that Americans employing his system would easily be able to understand "the historical necessity of slavery [in the United States] as the only means of obtaining a profit in the epoch of free land. . . ."[72] Further, the *Analisi* of 1889 contains a long, detailed analysis of the economic, political, and institutional results of slavery at different times in American history, depending upon the amount and quality of free land available.[73]

Immediately after the criticism of von Holst in Turner's 1892 essay came the famous statement that the "ever retreating frontier of free land is the key to American development."[74] It was precisely this very feature of American development which Loria had already emphasized in pointing to the United States as a recapitulation of man's social and economic development. Turner was clearly aware of Loria's concept, and was impressed by it, because in the "Frontier" essay he quoted the Italian's dictum that the United States held "the key to the historical enigma."[75]

In his 1892 essay, Turner called for a study of the vital forces that lay behind American institutions. The leading role played by the frontier was used by him to highlight the suggestion that the American commonwealth be studied as a developing organism.

---

71. Loria, *Economic Foundations*, 141-142. Of course Turner could not have seen this edition because it was published in 1899. However, Loria's *Analisi* of 1889, from which Turner quoted, was the volume in which the Italian economist gave his views on American evolution in great detail. The entire book elaborated upon the theme of free land's consequences and used America as the prime example.

72. Loria, in *Quarterly Journal of Economics*, 6: 110.

73. Loria, *Analisi*, 2: 55-119, *passim*. No impression is intended that I read Italian. I have been fortunate in securing a summary of these chapters from George Banfi, of the Italian Department at Cornell University.

74. *Early Writings*, 72.

75. *Ibid.*, 198.

The institutional framework of the nation may be likened to the anatomy of the body politic; its physiology is the social and economic life molding this framework to new uses.[76]

Compare these statements with Loria's formulations:

The colonies really are . . . a political animal from which social physiology is able to garner treasures; they are for economic science what the mountains are for geology, since if the latter make the primitive stratifications of the earth accessible to modern science, the colonies enable us to read, in the book of the present, pages torn from social history.[77]

There is little doubt that Turner's biological phraseology came from Loria because in the "Frontier" essay he also used both the "mountain" illustration and the "page in history" illustration. It might be well at this point to reproduce Turner's discussion of Loria, exactly as he gave it in 1893.

Loria, the Italian economist, has urged the study of colonial life as an aid in understanding the stages of European development, affirming that colonial settlement is for economic science what the mountain is for geology, bringing to light primitive stratifications. "America," he says, "has the key to the historical enigma which Europe has sought for centuries in vain, and the land which has no history reveals luminously the course of universal history." He is right. The United States lies like a huge page in the history of society. Line by line as we read from west to east we find the record of social evolution. It begins with the Indian and the hunter. . . .[78]

The citation that Turner himself appended after the name "Loria" in the first line read simply: "Loria, *Analisi della Proprieta Capitalista*, ii, p. 15." No place or date of publication was given. This citation was not amplified in any edition of the "Frontier" essay with which Turner was directly concerned.

This passage, thus cited, has many interesting aspects. Chief among them for our immediate purpose is the question as to how Turner was able to abstract these sentences from a massive,

---

76. *Ibid.*, 73.
77. Loria, *Analisi*, 2: 8. For a translation of the entire section, see the appendix of this essay.
78. *Early Writings*, 198.

complicated, two-volume, economic treatise in a language then quite unfamiliar to him.[79]

In view of the close relationships existing among members of the School of Economics, Political Science, and History at the University of Wisconsin, it is highly probable that Turner, as well as Ely, profited from H. H. Powers' translation of Loria's work. Direct evidence on this point is not available, but it is certain at least that Powers, who minored in history at Wisconsin, knew Turner more than casually. In a letter to Ely, dated January 3, 1894, Powers, then teaching at Smith College, wrote that the offer to have him return to Madison was tempting and he would again like "to work with Ely, [William A.] Scott, and Turner."[80] Furthermore, Ely's preface, dated June 1893, makes it clear that Turner was asked to read and criticize the early chapters of the 1893 *Outlines, before publication*,[81] and we know that those chapters were written by Powers.[82] Still another fact tends to indicate the close-knit nature of the Turner-Ely-Powers relationship. The University of Wisconsin has never possessed a copy of Loria's *Analisi*, from which Turner quoted, but Ely did, and his copy, purchased by the John Crerar Library in 1902 along with other books, now reposes in Chicago.[83]

The passage in Loria given above, and the sentence immediately preceding it in the "Frontier" essay, also demonstrate that the Italian theorist was the direct source of two of Turner's most important ideas, *i.e.*, American evolution recapitulates all the stages of man's social and economic development, and the

---

79. I am indebted to Fulmer Mood for the important information concerning Turner's unfamiliarity with Italian in 1892 and 1893. Two letters by Turner to his mother from Italy, dated Nov. 18, 1900 and Jan. 1, 1901, describe his Italian lessons and indicate that he was quite innocent of any prior knowledge of the language.

80. Powers to Ely, Jan. 3, 1894.

81. The Chautauqua Literary and Scientific Circle edition of Ely's *Outlines*, v. The college edition was issued later and contained additional material.

82. A letter from Powers to Ely, Apr. 5, 1893, informed Ely that the first nine chapters were finished.

83. Louis Kaplan of the University of Wisconsin Library is authority for the first statement, and a letter from the librarian of the John Crerar Library, Herman Henkle, informed me of the second.

corollary that this recapitulation offers an invaluable scientific laboratory for the study of the past.[84] The importance placed upon these ideas by Turner can be readily grasped by the space and emphasis given to them in the 1893 version and in a subsequent revision made by him in 1899:

> The history of the United States finds its chief claim to attention in its value as a field for the scientific study of social development. The speed of settled society into these continental wastes, and the free development of a democracy in relation to unoccupied lands, constitute the peculiar features of our national life.[85]

Turner's brief citation of Loria, quoted above, needs amplification if the Italian's influence on him is to be properly understood. In actuality, the paraphrased figures of speech, *i.e.*, the "mountain," "political animal," and "page in history" figures, occur on page 8 of volume 2 of the *Analisi*, and only the sentence directly quoted by Turner is on page 15. But this span, pages 8-15, includes Loria's entire chapter titled "The Historical Revelation of the Colonies"! A reading of this chapter (translated and printed as the appendix to the present article) would seem to

---

84. Loria's concept is remarkably similar to the recapitulation theory of the biologists, *i.e.*, the human embryo recapitulates the evolutionary process of the race. The formulation of the concept in these words is borrowed from James C. Malin.

I must here express my admiration for the keen insight exercised by Malin in 1946 while speculating about Loria's influence upon Turner—the first time anyone had emphasized in print the significance of Turner's quotation from the Italian economist. Having nothing more to go on than this quotation, he was yet able to reconstruct the actual theory underlying Loria's system and to recognize List and Herder as forerunners of Loria. Loria cited these two, among others, as sources. See his *Analisi*, 2: 8 n. 2. Malin has also pointed out the great importance attached to these ideas by Turner. See James C. Malin, *Essays on Historiography* (Lawrence, 1946), 14-17.

Fulmer Mood's contribution to the discussion of this aspect should also be noted. In 1939 he pointed to List as a forerunner of Turner in employing the "stages of history" concept. See his "The Development of Frederick Jackson Turner as a Historical Thinker," Colonial Society of Massachusetts, *Transactions*, 34: 305-307 (Boston, 1943). An excellent discussion of List's system is found in Rabbeno, *American Commercial Policy*, 325-354.

85. *Early Writings*, 279. Note the fundamental contradiction in Turner's thought. American history could not have recapitulated universal history if its "peculiar features" dominated the country's "national life."

leave little question that Turner was greatly dependent upon the *Analisi* while writing both the "Problems" essay of 1892 and the "Frontier" essay of 1893.

In addition to the similarities in ideas and in phrasing pointed out above, numerous other instances of dependence might be cited. Thus, compare Loria's rebirth of mankind in America, and the brilliant illumination to be gained by crossing the continent from the New York factories to the Dakota fields (from east to west, note), with Turner's perennial rebirth of American life and his description of the process of evolution from *west to east*;[86] compare Loria's improvement upon Edward Gans (who had placed himself Janus-like upon the Capitoline hill of Rome to observe the transit of civilization) by taking the colonies as a vantage point, with Turner's stationing his observer at Cumberland Gap to "watch the procession of civilization";[87] Loria's transporting men from Elizabethan England to the virginal environment of America and the resultant social and economic metamorphosis, with Turner's confronting a European with the wilderness and the resultant social and economic metamorphosis;[88] and, finally, though by no means all, Loria's use of Ercalano and Pompeii, those "palimpsests of Nature," with Turner's of the same rare term of "palimpsest" in dealing with the eastern States as a page in history.[89]

Viewed in this light, a letter from Loria to Turner, dated at Padua on August 18, 1894, appears to take on considerable sig-

---

86. *Analisi*, 2: 10, 15; and *Early Writings*, 187, 198. The material cited from Loria is found in the appendix to this part of the book.

87. *Analisi*, 2: 15; and *Early Writings*, 199.

88. *Analisi*, 2: 9-10; and *Early Writings*, 188.

89. *Analisi*, 2: 8, with *Early Writings*, 285. An excellent illustration of other parallels that might be cited are Turner's use in the 1892 essay of the "law of rent" (*Early Writings*, 82). As Malin pointed out in his *Essays*, 19, that idea was dragged into the essay by the heels, and apparently Turner never used it again. However, taken in conjunction with Loria's emphasis on the law of rent, its appearance in 1892 becomes quite understandable. It would also appear to be a reasonable conclusion that if a full translation of Loria were available, parallels equally striking would be found in other places, in addition to the *Analisi*, 2: 8-15.

nificance.[90] In it, Loria expressed his cordial thanks to Turner for having sent him a copy of Orin Grant Libby's monograph, published in June 1894.[91] Indeed, Loria was a logical man to receive a copy because the data compiled by Libby may be said to have confirmed some of the Italian's deep-seated convictions.

A most important aspect of Loria's work was his description of "the economic foundations of politics." In treating this topic he described the political results stemming from the conflict between agriculture and industry (broadly defined) under certain conditions which were present in the early days of the American Republic. According to him, the economic conflict thus engendered provoked a corresponding political conflict. This explained how "the ruling class may come to be divided into an agrarian and an industrial party in countries where the population is sparse and where land rent does not exist."[92]

Although European parties were also established upon economic bases, a host of other considerations prevented purely economic ends being sought there. These considerations, however, were happily unknown to America and therefore

. . . the divergent revenue interests [rent and profit] can . . . be perfectly well safeguarded by purely economic laws. Consequently, not only the platforms, but also the ends and aims of the American political parties are essentially economic in character. It is a perfectly well-known fact that the Republican party of the United States, which upholds federalism and protection, is composed of the commercial and manufacturing classes; and that the free-trade and States-rights Democratic party recruits its ranks from the class of landed proprietors. The struggle between these two parties is thus essentially economic, since it corresponds exactly to the most important division of their revenues. The economic character of American political parties is, indeed, so marked that we see them change

---

90. A typewritten copy of this letter, probably made by Turner, is in the Ely Papers.

91. Orin Grant Libby, *The Geographical Distribution of the Vote of the Thirteen States on the Federal Constitution, 1787-8* (Bulletin of the University of Wisconsin, Economics, Political Science, and History Series, vol. 1, no. 1. Madison, Wis., 1894).

92. Loria, *Economic Foundations*, 154.

whenever social conditions or the interests of their members are altered in any way.[93]

Several pages later we find this interesting statement:

Whenever rents prevail in one part of a State and profits in another, the conflict that breaks out between the two assumes the character of a territorial struggle, and sectional politics thus arise as the corollary and natural product of the underlying economic sectionalism.[94]

Turner had still another reason for sending Libby's monograph to Loria for approval and comment. His own introduction to Libby's work made it clear that he was calling for a series of studies devoted to the investigation of economic sectionalism in the United States along the lines indicated by Loria, although the latter was not mentioned by name.[95]

The continuity of the relation between Turner and Loria is clearly revealed by an incident involving Turner and Selig Perlman. In the fall of 1909 Perlman took a course with Turner at Wisconsin. Upon learning that he read Italian, Turner asked him to translate a post card from Loria in that language. This note expressed sincere admiration and extravagant praise for an unnamed work by Turner which Loria had received from him.[96]

The essential point in citing these strong parallels between Loria and Turner is not at all to deal with the question of the latter's originality. If that question is deemed to be important in its own right, it is irrelevant here. Unquestionably, there were many other influences operating upon Turner, some of which

---

93. *Ibid.*, 155.

94. *Ibid.*, 167. See also the examples of sectional politics given on p. 168. None of them concern America, but this would make even more logical Turner's sending the monograph to Loria as an American illustration of his ideas.

95. Compare Turner's introduction in Libby, *The Geographical Distribution of the Vote*, 1-6, with part 3, "The Economic Foundations of Politics," in Loria's *Economic Foundations*, 117-354, *passim*. Note that this work was available in a French edition in 1893; the Italian original was published in 1886; and the *Analisi* of 1889 was written in this spirit.

96. Conversation of Fulmer Mood with Selig Perlman, Madison, Wis., June 2, 1950.

will be discussed in Part II of this book, and it would be an error to attribute the frontier thesis *solely* to Loria.[97] Nevertheless, it does appear to be a reasonable conclusion that all of Turner's prior reading and studying, and the tendencies evident in his very early work, were crystallized, illuminated, and "fixed" by acquaintance with the Italian's "landed property system of political economy."

If this conclusion is justified, it may be of some aid in eliminating a major obstacle to a satisfactory resolution of the present professional uncertainty concerning the validity of Turner's teachings, *i.e.*, the widespread difference of opinion over what the frontier thesis contained, and what it should be interpreted to mean. No simple question of semantics is here involved, as is obvious after reading the literature on the subject. George W. Pierson's account of the results of a questionnaire designed to get a clear expression of historical thinking about Turner is an excellent illustration of the difficulty inherent in the controversy.[98]

The Turner frontier hypothesis, as formulated in his essays of 1892 and 1893, contains at least six specific propositions whose meaning is now given a new degree of certainty:

1. The thesis *was* based on an elaborate and detailed system designed to analyze scientifically the structure of all human society.

2. American history was *literally* a record of historical evolution.

3. "Free land" literally meant *free land*, without price, unoccupied, accessible to all, and capable of cultivation by simple manual labor.

---

97. For example, Fulmer Mood has convincingly shown the influence of William F. Allen and Francis A. Walker upon Turner. See his "Development of Frederick Jackson Turner as a Historical Thinker," Colonial Society of Massachusetts, *Transactions*, 34: 295-303 (Boston, 1943), and "The Concept of the Frontier, 1871-1898," *Agricultural History*, 19: 24-30 (January 1945).

98. George W. Pierson, "American Historians and the Frontier Hypothesis in 1941," *Wisconsin Magazine of History*, 26: 36-60, 170-185 (September, December 1942).

4. The presence or absence of free land *was* the fundamental determining factor in society.

5. The passing of the frontier *literally* meant that the safety valve was closed.

6. The closing of the safety valve meant that a new epoch in American history was dawning.

Without laboring the obvious, it should be emphasized that these interpretations are restricted to Turner's original statement, because the later development and application of his ideas must be studied as a problem separate from the present one of inception. Loria's system of economics provides not only the philosophical and methodological background for Turner's formulation of his ideas on the significance of the frontier in American history, but Loria's system supplied the essential theoretical content of these six propositions. He who would understand Turner must first master Loria.

F.

Appendix to Part I:
Loria's Chapter on "The Historical Revelation of the Colonies"[99]

Anyone accustomed to viewing the history of mankind with a teleological prejudice would judge the unfolding of the early stages of the development of colonies under the very eyes of old Europe to be the result of a great and wise predestination. Such a person would maintain that Divine Providence had invented a way to compensate European civilization for those wide gaps in its economic history, which have been neglected by historians of all times, for it could be said that Providence has always called into being a new world, which, developing in

---

99. Chapter 2 of Loria, *Analisi*, 2: 8-15. George Banfi of the Italian department at Cornell University has kindly translated the chapter and read other pertinent portions of the volume.

full sight of the old one, reveals to the latter its own past. Just as Ercalano and Pompeii, those "palimpsests of Nature," have petrified an instant of the ancient era, preserving for us a dead period still full of life, in the same way the early stages of colonial development recreate in the vivacious colors of youth, an era which for us is long since past. The colonies really are, as [Sir William] Petty would say, a political animal from which social physiology is able to garner treasures; they are for economic science what the mountains are for geology, since if the latter make the primitive stratifications of the earth accessible to modern science, the colonies enable us to read in the book of the present, pages torn from social history. Moreover, if it is true, as Hegel puts it, that universal history could not have revealed itself as a system if it had not been for the Mediterranean, that meeting place of antiquity, then it is also true that social history could not be fully explained if the colonies did not reveal, in their accelerating progress, the synthesis which illuminates it.

What is the historical synthesis which is revealed to us by the colonies? Think of a group of men, living in the England of the time of Elizabeth, or James I, and imagine the network of economic relations that bind them. In front of them is developing a great manufacturing system, which has just come into flower, and there is also developing, the system of great landed estates, built upon the ruins of patriarchal agriculture. Wealth is concentrating in a few hands, a financial oligarchy is taking shape; production is increasing, but it is ever more unequally distributed. In London and Manchester both rich and poor multiply. The Gothic structure of the feudal institutions is crumbling, and bourgeois property, insatiable in its lust for conquest, is freed. It is the beginning of the modern economic system which brings in its train a long wake of sorrow, greatness, and infinite misery. And now suppose that a fairylike caprice suddenly transports these British people who, yesterday, in the cities of the United Kingdom, assumed those production relations which were based upon large-scale industry and the wages system, to a virgin region, say to Pennsylvania or Virginia. Strangely enough, those same production relations become definitely impossible in this new setting, and the maintenance of fixed character, habits, and ideas is completely unable to create in the colonies the economic institutions which existed in the motherland. The same men, transported from a region where all the land was occupied, to a new region where land is available to everyone, undergo a metamorphosis, without their own volition, of the economic relations which had hitherto bound them. In the new land, in which "there is nothing old except the trees of the virgin forest," a rebirth of mankind takes place, and the economic structure of primitive Europe is recreated. Moreover, all of human progress, worked out during two thousand years of development, is unable to prevent the reproduction of the social phenomena consonant to a reproduction of the primitive external surroundings. After it has assumed a social system reproducing the primitive economy, the colony proceeds at an accelerated pace to pass through the stages of economic evolution, approaching closer and closer to the conditions of its motherland. Finally, it attains that position, but not, however, without having passed through four stages, four eras, the same ones which the older Europeans had to undergo, during the course of several centuries, in order to go from the primitive condition to their present economic system.

Finally, in this accelerated metamorphosis of economic relations in the colonies, the decadence and death of each economic form is preceded by a metamorphosis in the conditions of landed property, or in the degree of productivity of the marginal land. However, it is not preceded by any noticeable metamorphosis in the intellectual, or more generally subjective, human conditions.

Such is the history of modern colonies. But a study of medieval and ancient colonies would show us the reproduction of the same phenomena; the colony, if medieval, beginning with a primitive economic form and going through three stages, or, if ancient, two stages, in the direction of the social conditions of its motherland. In fact, one notices in the ancient colonies a first stage in which either common or small property is predominant, and it is only in a later period that slavery is introduced. . . .[100]

But even if we limit ourselves to contemplating social evolution in modern colonies, we can readily grasp the revelation they bring to the science of history. If the colonies assume production relations opposite to those of the motherland despite the psychological identity of their inhabitants and those of the home country, if the men transposed into a virgin land themselves begin, as a result of necessity, social relations opposite to those to which they were subjected in the old land, at the very least this indicates that social phenomena, both in the old and new fatherland, are not exclusively the result of man, but are partly due to physiographical conditions. But then, when one sees that the economic relations assumed by the growing colonies present a profound identity with those assumed by primitive mankind, where the land situation was identical to that of the colonies, despite the fact that the social conditioning of the men was absolutely different, the most positive conclusion may be reached that the cause of social phenomena is not man but rather the natural environment. Thus, if we have only two possible factors to explain social phenomena, man and the earth; if with a set of man-made institutions common to both societies we can have completely different social conditions, and with identical landed conditions we necessarily have identical social conditions, we are forced to conclude that the moving force of the social process is land, and man is not the agent of this process but its spectator.

The importance of this result is easily seen. The theory of the economic development of colonies as summarized above destroys all philosophical systems which find intelligence, or its various manifestations, as the cause of the historical movement of mankind. How can we admit Comte and Buckle's theorem that social phenomena are the product of intellectual development, or the Hegelian concept that history is the evolving expression

---

100. An illustration of this point from ancient and medieval times is omitted from this translation. L. B.

of the idea; how can we admit [Ferdinand] Lassalle's aphorism
that the human spirit is the creator of history; when it is demonstrated that a new society, though fortified by the intellectual
and material heritage accumulated by a hundred previous gen-
erations, finds itself forced to assume the economic relations of
the primitive era, solely because it settles down in a free land, in
the same situation that primitive man found himself. Colonial
civilization, arising from natural physical conditions, and independent of the psychological conditioning of man, is contrary to
the concept of human civilization dependent upon the intellectual and moral development of society. It strengthens the concept
of a close dependence of social history upon nature, and the
concept of a great and mechanical synthesis of man and his environment.

If, in respect to these phases, research on colonial evolution
makes a great contribution to the science of history, it does not
bring less splendid light to the economic doctrines; for one law
is revealed by the entire history of the colonies, *i.e.*, landed property is not only a factor of the economic organism, but it is the
pedestal upon which the whole social system is built. To us,
citizens of Western Europe, inclined to attribute to the production system an exclusive influence in the modern economy
because of the wonders of industrial manufacturing, to us, such
a concept appears to be a reproduction in different terms of the
physiocratic prejudice. However, where the modern industrial
process is not yet dominant, or at least to date does not over-
shadow the economic importance of landed property, as in
Russia, or even more so in the colonies, in those places writers
employ a synthesis based more upon land, and therefore more
true to economic phenomena. It is not long since that a distinguished Russian publicist [Wassiltschikoff] pointed out with
good reason:

In all the profound speculations on the labor question, in all the
sterile devices invented to conciliate capital and labor (devices
which resemble a small beam joining two enormous walls), one for-
gets that under the larvae of the labor question, another essential
question is nestled, the land question, and that the very profound
cause of the social ills troubling Western Europe, lies in the harm-

ful effects upon the major part of the population of exclusion from landed property.

And a few years later, from the opposite shore of the Atlantic, an impartial observer [Henry George] noticed:

It is not in the relation between capital and labor that one has to look for the explanation of the differentiated development of our civilization. The basic cause of the inequality in the distribution of wealth is the inequality in landed property; for landed property is the fundamental phenomena which determines the social, political, economic condition of each nation.

Yes, in the modern age, as in the olden one, landed property is the dominating phenomenon of the entire economy; and in this respect, the present differs from the past only in the fact that the relations of landed property were then responsible for a bloody revolution while that is not true of our age; since in the olden times developments manifested themselves opposite to those noted by [Dietrich Hermann] Hegewisch that finances and taxes have provoked frequent revolutions in modern states, but this was not so in the ancient ones.

Such are the results that arise from research into the genesis and social development of modern colonies; this is the subject with which we propose to deal. Edward Gans, to observe the history of law, placed himself on the Capitoline hill and, glancing with eyes looking backward and forward simultaneously at both pre-Roman and post-Roman history, attempts to deduce from their contrast with Roman history, the hidden meaning of man's historical development. We put ourselves in the glorious setting of young liberty and, observing from it the economic development of the European world, we wish to abstract from a comparison of it with colonial development the profound and synthetic meaning of all social development. This research, let us admit, requires long and difficult work, but it is well worth the effort and repays it abundantly. From the New York factories and the Dakota fields comes a light, which projected over the medieval ruins, over the ruins of antiquity and of the primitive barbarian ages, enlightens them with a sudden splendor,

gives life to their fossil remains, interprets the mysterious char-
acters which they have written upon them, and removes their
secret from them, together with our own secret as well. America
offers the key to the historical enigma which Europe has sought
for centuries in vain, and the country that has no history reflects
and reveals luminously the mystery of universal history.

Part Two

THE HISTORICAL
BACKGROUND OF
TURNER'S FRONTIER ESSAY

◇◇◇

AT THIS LATE DATE in American historiography,[1] it may
be a commonplace to observe that many of the ideas usually
ascribed to Frederick Jackson Turner were "in the air" prior
to the presentation of his frontier essay in 1893. Numerous historians have previously indicated that the state of the public
domain, the westward expansion of the frontier, the safety-
valve theory, and similar topics commanded considerable atten-

---

1. A condensed version of this essay was presented at a session of the
American Historical Association in Chicago on Dec. 28, 1950, and is here
reprinted from *Agricultural History*, 25: 50-82 (April 1951).

tion in the closing decades of the nineteenth century.[2] But the interesting suggestion has also been made that, although the concept of the frontier was itself old, the particular manner in which it was applied after 1870 gave new significance to the old idea. Hence a somewhat detailed examination of the historical setting in which Turner operated may prove to be of interest.

The analysis here given is not designed to deal with the subject of Turner's originality. It is, however, concerned with the possibility that the frontier essay, in many ways, and to an unusual degree, was the direct product of its historical setting— and must, therefore, be evaluated in that light. The analysis explores that possibility, describes some of the sources from which Turner drew inspiration, and attempts thereby to clarify further the meaning of his concepts and terminology. In addition, it surveys the powerful forces at work tending both to produce the frontier thesis and to insure its rapid and widespread acceptance.

A.

Era of Communication Revolution

Frederick Jackson Turner was born at Portage, Wisconsin, on November 14, 1861, and some thirty-two years later, on

---

2. Herman Clarence Nixon, "The Precursors of Turner in the Interpretation of the American Frontier," *South Atlantic Quarterly*, 28: 83-89 (Jan. 1929); James C. Malin, "Space and History," *Agricultural History*, 18: 65-74 (Apr. 1944); Fulmer Mood, "The Concept of the Frontier, 1871-1898," *ibid.*, 19: 24-30 (Jan. 1945); Henry Nash Smith, *Virgin Land: The American West as Symbol and Myth* (Cambridge, Mass., 1950), *passim.* Smith's book delineates the historical development of "the notion that our society has been shaped by the pull of a vacant continent drawing population westward" from its eighteenth-century origins to Turner. In this respect, therefore, the book is invaluable, but I take exception to Smith's formulation which at least implies that Turner's contemporaries generally accepted "his contention that the frontier and the West had dominated American development. . . ." Mood, in the article cited above and in subsequent writings, has emphasized the distinction between the concept of the frontier per se, and the use Turner and others, before and after him, made of it in applying it to history.

July 12, 1893, he read his now famous essay entitled "The Significance of the Frontier in American History," before a session of the American Historical Association at the World's Columbian Exposition in Chicago. The span of time between these two dates roughly parallels a series of remarkable developments which may rightly be judged as unprecedented in all history. If we adopt the terminology of Robert G. Albion, a modern historian, and the chronology of David A. Wells, Turner's contemporary, the last third of the nineteenth century is aptly characterized as the era of the "Communication Revolution."[3]

The term "Revolution" is not an overstatement. The fundamental changes which took place in the transportation of commodities and in the transmission of information during that period merit no less an epithet. Wells depicted the process as it appeared to him in 1889 in this striking fashion:

The economic changes that have occurred during the last quarter of a century—or during the present generation of living men—have unquestionably been more important and varied than during any former corresponding period of the world's history. It would seem, indeed, as if the world, during all the years since the inception of civilization, has been working up on the line of equipment for industrial effort—inventing and perfecting tools and machinery, building workshops and factories, and devising instrumentalities for the easy

---

3. David A. Wells, *Recent Economic Changes* (New York, 1889), v-vi; Robert G. Albion, "The 'Communications Revolution,'" *American Historical Review*, 37: 718-720 (July 1932). For a brief but illuminating analysis of this development, see James C. Malin, *The Grassland of North America* (Lawrence, Kansas, 1947), 169-172. I have taken the liberty of dropping the "s" from "Communications."

Albion dated the Communication Revolution from the turnpike and canal era of the early nineteenth century. Malin has suggested that the term has more validity if applied to the latter decades of the century. He views the change from animal power to mechanically-powered communications, *i.e.*, steam and electricity, as of critical importance, particularly the developments after 1875.

The excellent analysis that Malin compressed into the four pages cited above may profitably be supplemented by his "Notes on the Literature of Populism," *Kansas Historical Quarterly*, 1: 160-164 (Feb. 1932), "The Background of the First Bills to Establish a Bureau of Markets, 1911-12," *Agricultural History*, 6: 107-129 (July 1932), and "Mobility and History," *ibid.*, 17: 177-191 (Oct. 1943).

intercommunication of persons and thoughts, and the cheap exchange of products and services; that this equipment having at last been made ready, the work of using it has, for the first time in our day and generation, fairly begun. . . . As an immediate consequence the world has never seen anything comparable to the results of the recent system of transportation by land and water. . . .[4]

In brief, Wells was describing the application to communications of mechanical power on such wide scale, and of such advanced technology, as to produce qualitatively different results than ever before. The vast improvements in railroad transport, ocean shipping, and underwater cable telegraphy might especially be singled out for attention. New inventions, new materials, and new methods brought about the efficient use of the compound marine engine in a steel ship, as well as greatly improved locomotives hauling huge loads on steel rails, and submarine cables secure enough to guarantee uninterrupted service. To these technological changes must be added the advantages gained in the consolidation and incorporation of railroad, steamship, and cable lines, and the resulting managerial efficiencies in their operation. Finally, the extension of these services to virtually all but the most remote corners of the world was an important step in the process of overcoming space and time barriers.[5]

If, in addition, we note similar developments in telephone, telegraph, and inland water transportation, and emphasize the impact of the completion of the Suez Canal in 1869, then the fundamental changes of the period are outlined, at least in skeletal form.[6] Of course, the first appearance, or discovery, of most

4. Wells, *Recent Economic Changes*, v.

5. *Ibid.*, 1-70; John H. Clapham, *An Economic History of Modern Britain* (London, 1932), 2: 67-75, 211-217; John G. B. Hutchins, *The American Maritime Industries and Public Policy, 1789-1914* (Cambridge, Mass., 1941), 397-516; Emory R. Johnson and others, *History of Domestic and Foreign Commerce of the United States* (Washington, 1915), 1: 296-300; Malin, *The Grassland of North America*, 169-172.

6. Both Wells and Clapham stressed the great importance of the Suez Canal in directly overcoming the economic barriers of distance and indirectly in stimulating improvements in transport facilities. See Wells, *Recent Economic Changes*, 29-36; and Clapham, *Economic History*, 2: 214-215.

of the innovations noted above antedates 1865. The crucial point is that only after that year, and more particularly after 1875, can these innovations be said to have registered their economic consequences decisively.[7] Thus, by the early eighties, with the international cable net essentially completed, the result, according to John H. Clapham, was that "The world, on the economist's projection, had shrunk into a single market."[8] The remaining years of the nineteenth century were to bind even tighter the global strands of commerce, and by 1900 international exchange of commodities and services took place on a scale virtually unimaginable fifty years earlier.

Underscoring the importance of the new global economy to contemporary observers was the far-reaching sweep of the industrial, financial, commercial, and agricultural changes accompanying its emergence. These changes produced widespread and complex disturbances and resulted in continually shifting locational patterns of industry and agriculture. In the process of adjusting successfully to the establishment of new economic equilibriums, tremendous pressures were placed upon entrepreneurs of all types. The strains and difficulties associated with meeting the new conditions are possibly best indicated by the title, "The Great Depression," that has been bestowed upon the period, 1873-1896, in the literature of economic history.[9] As one

---

7. Wells, *Recent Economic Changes*, 37-44; Clapham, *Economic History*, 2: 211-219; Joseph A. Schumpeter, *Business Cycles* (New York, 1939), 1: 323; Malin, *The Grassland of North America*, 170-171; P'ei-kang Chang, *Agriculture and Industrialization* (Cambridge, Mass., 1949), 98. During the 1870s, and particularly after 1874, rate wars were probably more important in slashing rates than technological improvements. See William Z. Ripley, *Railroads, Rates and Regulation* (New York, 1912), 21-24.

8. Clapham, *Economic History*, 2: 217.

9. *Ibid.*, 2: 279-285, 3: 1-40, 72-90 (London, 1938); Wells, *Recent Economic Changes*, 1-26, 70-113; Schumpeter, *Business Cycles*, 1: 333-341; H. L. Beales, "The 'Great Depression' in Industry and Trade," *Economic History Review* (London), 5(1): 65-67 (Oct. 1934); Hans Rosenberg, "Political and Social Consequences of the Great Depression of 1873-1896 in Central Europe," *ibid.*, 13(1-2): 58-59 (1943); Walter W. Rostow, *British Economy of the Nineteenth Century* (Oxford, 1948), 58-61.

Historians of the United States have not treated the period 1873-1896 as possessing the characteristics of a "Great Depression." Yet contemporary

careful student of the period, Hans Rosenberg, has said:

The Great Depression marked the decisive turning-point in the
nineteenth-century history of the relationship between the state and
the economy. The crash of 1873 was a death-blow to that kind of
state interventionism which had endeavoured to destroy mercantilist
hangovers and to build a new framework of economic life on the
'natural rationality' of the market mechanism. . . . From this time
onwards it tended to be the destiny of the state to function as the
supreme agent of economic co-ordination and integration on a
national scale. Not natural law but a 'New Deal' was to establish
order in the realm of economic society by forcing the government
to reassume old functions and usurp new ones.[10]

Lack of space precludes the discussion of other significant
economic, political, and social consequences resulting from, or
accompanying, the Communication Revolution.[11] But its impact
upon agriculture is central to an analysis of the historical setting in which Turner matured and warrants extended treatment
here.

American periodicals reflected the same concern as their British counterparts with the causes of the "trade depression," the "industrial depression,"
"economic disturbances," etc. An excellent example is the controversy
between David A. Wells and the editors of the *Commercial and Financial
Chronicle* over the causes of "The Economic Disturbances Since 1873."
Wells published a series of articles with that title in 1887 in the *Popular
Science Monthly*. There he emphasized overproduction as the primary
cause. The *Chronicle* bitterly attacked his point of view, arguing instead
that currency contraction was responsible. As might be expected, the
controversy was almost identical with the one raging in England at the
same time. See footnote 11. The discussion in the *Chronicle* began Dec.
12, 1887 and ended on Dec. 22, 1888. For specific citations, see "Economic
Disturbances Since 1873" in the indexes of volumes 47-49 of the *Chronicle*.

   10. Rosenberg, in *Economic History Review*, 13(1-2): 65-66.

   11. For a good discussion of both the contemporary and historical
literature on the subject, see Rostow's chapter, "Explanations of the Great
Depression," in his *British Economy*, 145-160, and also 58-61. Lack of space
prevents discussion of the impact of great social and political changes
such as the unification of Germany and Italy, and above all the Civil War
in the United States. In many ways these developments were a necessary
prelude to the unfolding of the Communication Revolution, and a well-
rounded study would need to examine them in some detail.

B.
Communication Revolution and Agricultural Change

Formerly agrarian crises were of a local character, limited to provincial or national markets relatively isolated by the undeveloped state of transportation. The revolution in ocean and rail transport ended that situation by bringing the markets of the world into closer contact at an acceleratingly rapid pace.[12] Falling rates and marked expansion of shipping facilities reshaped world agriculture. The long-term, cost-reducing effects of large-scale investment in railroads and shipping, plus the frenzied search for new markets to absorb the huge quantities of capital goods and capital available for export, opened up enormous tracts of virgin land in Argentina, Australia, Manitoba, and, above all, the Great American West.[13] Extensive application of horse-drawn agricultural machinery was of considerable importance in facilitating the exploitation of the fertile new regions, and, conversely, this development put very heavy pressure on the older areas to improve their methods of husbandry.

Science and invention played still other roles in enlarging

---

12. Wells, *Recent Economic Changes*, 34, 35, 37, 40, 43; Lord Ernle, *English Farming, Past and Present* (ed. 5, London, 1936), 377-384; Clapham, *Economic History*, 2: 213, 279-284, 3: 9-16, 72-90; Schumpeter, *Business Cycles*, 1: 323-324; Witt Bowden, Michael Karpovich, and Abbott Payson Usher, *An Economic History of Europe Since 1750* (New York, 1937), 581-594; and Shepard B. Clough, *France, A History of National Economics, 1789-1939* (New York, 1939), 214-225.

13. Wells, *Recent Economic Changes*, 88-90, 176; W. A. Coutts, *Agricultural Depression in the United States, Its Causes and Remedies* (Michigan Political Science Association, *Publications*, v. 2, no. 6, Apr. 1897), 62; Davis R. Dewey, *Financial History of the United States* (ed. 2, New York, 1903), 370; Clapham, *Economic History*, 2: 234-241, 3:32-40; Bowden, Karpovich, and Usher, *Economic History of Europe*, 629-640; Rostow, *British Economy*, 97-98.

the total food supply. The result, because of the particular conditions which determine agricultural production, was that even the rapid growth in population and the slow rise in mass per capita consuming power could not counterbalance the vastly enlarged stocks.[14] Almost inevitably, a disastrous decline in the price level of agricultural commodities set in between 1873 and 1896, a development that led to an upswing in the number of commissions to investigate the agricultural depression.[15]

It is not an overstatement, therefore, to assert that the Communication Revolution produced at least three unprecedented historical phenomena: an international agrarian market, an international agrarian depression, and, as a climax, international agrarian discontent. The interrelationships between these phenomena were clearly seen at the time, and, in 1896, C. F. Emerick of Columbia University presented an analysis of such enduring excellence as still to repay careful study. He opened his discussion with this arresting statement:

The closing years of the nineteenth century are witnessing the unusual spectacle of restless discontent on the part of the tiller of the soil. Nearly every civilized country has its agrarian problem in one form or another. . . . In view, therefore, of the traditional habit of

---

14. Coutts, *Agricultural Depression*, 17-18, 57, 95; C. F. Emerick, "An Analysis of Agricultural Discontent in the United States," *Political Science Quarterly*, 11: 436, 447, 621 (Sept., Dec. 1896); Schumpeter, *Business Cycles*, 1: 320.

By "particular conditions," I am referring to the "economic lag" in agriculture. The "inefficient producers" are not quickly driven out in periods of depression. On the contrary, both as nations and as individuals, they are forced to plant more acreage, produce greater quantities, and thereby aggravate the situation. This is the heart of the "overproduction" crisis which overtook agriculture from 1873 to 1896.

15. Wells, *Recent Economic Changes*, 114-191; Clapham, *Economic History*, 3: 72-83; Ernle, *English Farming*, 377-384.

The agricultural depression affected American farmers in varying degrees all during the Great Depression. But, generally speaking, they did not receive its full impact until the early 1890s. Prior to that, years of prosperity alternated with years of "hard times." Moreover, significant variations in regional economic patterns complicate the formulation of generalizations about farm prosperity or depression.

mind of rural populations, their present condition of unrest in nearly every civilized land is most extraordinary.[16]

Of all the varied factors that went into producing these conditions, one stands out pre-eminently—the post-Civil War extension of railroads into the American West, and the subsequent utilization of its enormous agricultural potential. Clapham thus evaluated the impact of the 110,000 miles of new railway construction in the United States between 1870 and 1890: "If a single national contribution towards the making of the new era had to be selected for its world-wide economic importance, it would probably be this."[17]

---

16. Emerick, in *Political Science Quarterly*, 11: 433-434. This long article by Emerick (11: 433-463, 601-639, 12: 93-127) is extremely valuable in placing American agricultural discontent in its proper world framework.

For various aspects of the subject, see J. Stephen Jeans, "American Railways and British Farmers," *Nineteenth Century*, 28: 392-409 (Sept. 1890); William E. Bear, "The Agricultural Problem," *Economic Journal* (London), 3: 391-407, 569-583 (Sept., Dec. 1893); Edward Porritt, "The Unrest of English Farmers," *Yale Review*, 2: 54-63 (May 1893); "Agricultural Distress on the Continent," *Spectator*, 72: 78-79 (Jan. 20, 1894); Albion W. Tourgee, "The Reversal of Malthus," *American Journal of Sociology*, 2: 13-24 (July 1896); and J. Laurence Laughlin, "Causes of Agricultural Unrest," *Atlantic Monthly*, 78: 577-585 (Nov. 1896).

The following quotation from "A Pessimistic View of Agriculture" reflects the mood of many contemporary observers: "Almost everywhere, certainly in England, France, Germany, Italy, Scandinavia, and the United States, the agriculturists, formerly so instinctively Conservative, are becoming fiercely discontented, declare that they gain less by civilisation than any section of the community, and are looking about for remedies of the most drastic character. . . . Outside a huge factory like Great Britain, the majority will always cultivate, because there is nothing else for them to do; if they cultivate they will produce; and if they produce, with the new and rapidly increasing facilities of communication, food will be cheap,—the very origin of the agricultural discontent." *Spectator*, 70: 247 (Feb. 25, 1893).

17. Clapham, *Economic History*, 2: 213. Pages 218-219 and 279-280 amplify the point. See also Wells, *Recent Economic Changes*, 89-90; Josiah Strong, *Our Country: Its Possible Future and Its Present Crisis* (New York, 1885), 7; William Trimble, "Historical Aspects of the Surplus Food Production of the United States, 1862-1902," American Historical Association, *Report, 1918*, 1: 223, 228, 236; Johnson and others, *History of Domestic and Foreign Commerce of the United States*, 1: 266, 296; Schum-

It did not take long research by skilled historians to reveal the significance of the opening of the Trans-Missouri West. The increased volume of the American agricultural surplus was of such magnitude in the markets of the world as to make recognition of its importance omnipresent.[18] As early as 1880, Ex-Governor Horatio Seymour of New York entitled his presidential address to the New York State Agricultural Society, "The Conflict Between American and European Agriculture."[19] He pointed to the sharp cuts in transportation rates and went on to say:

This fact, that North America with its vast extent of fertile vacant lands, thus almost touches Europe with its over-crowded population, is one which excites the most varied speculations with regard to the results which must follow, bearing upon all phases of civilization, politics and power. History tells of no event more striking or significant.

Among the future tendencies which Seymour discussed in his address were drastic changes in European systems of land tenure, increasing conflicts between industrial and landed capitalists, acceleration of the flow of rural population to the cities, and a steady rise in emigration to America. His keen perception was underscored in the years that immediately followed. European harvests were extremely bad, and American harvests extremely good. Accordingly, Continental and British markets were flooded with American wheat, corn, and meat to a degree hitherto unknown.[20] Hence, it is not surprising that the census of agriculture, published in 1883, contained an analysis similar to Seymour's. Similar, except that the tense differed; Seymour's

---

peter, *Business Cycles*, 1: 319; Bowden, Karpovich, and Usher, *Economic History of Europe*, 582.

18. See Trimble, in American Historical Association, *Report, 1918*, 1: 229-239, for a convenient survey. It is hardly an overstatement to say that it is difficult to read the newspapers and periodicals of the late nineteenth century without being impressed by the growing recognition of American competition.

19. New York State Agricultural Society, *Transactions*, 1877-1882, 33: 113-129 (Albany, 1884). The quotation is from p. 115.

20. U. S. Department of Agriculture, *Report, 1883*, 326.

predictions for the future were now described as accomplished facts.[21]

Another publication of the same year, 1883, is of key importance in depicting the contemporary recognition given to the growing American agricultural surplus. Special attention was given the subject by J. R. Dodge, statistician of the United States Department of Agriculture, in his report for that year.[22] In a section entitled "American Competition with European Agriculture," he reviewed the disastrous effects of this competition upon European farmers and drew attention to the anxiety among individuals and governments as to whether this state of affairs would continue. He noted that a British investigating commission had been sent to the United States for first-hand information, and according to Dodge, "The city and country press of those [European] countries has teemed with discussions of the situation, and writers on national and political economy have treated the subject at length in pamphlets and serials."

Believing that this material would be of interest to readers of this report, Dodge included translations of pertinent excerpts from French, German, and Austrian sources. Nearly all observers stressed the grave consequences for old-world agriculture resulting from the favorable conditions under which the new regions were being opened. The importance attached to American competition may perhaps best be indicated by quoting the views of Alexander Peez, then a member of the Austrian Reichsrath.

In the sixteenth century American competition ruined the mining industries of Europe, changed the direction of the world's commerce, brought about by the increased amount of precious metals a revolution in prices, transformed the social conditions, and prepared the terrible civil war of the seventeenth century—the thirty years' war. May the competition of America in the nineteenth cen-

---

21. William H. Brewer, "The Cereals," U. S. Census Office, 10th Census, 1880, *Report on the Productions of Agriculture* (Washington, 1883), 9.

22. U. S. Department of Agriculture, *Report, 1883*, 251-423. For the general discussion of American competition, see pp. 326-329. The first quotation below is from p. 327. The paragraph by Peez is on p. 342.

tury lead to more happy results. No doubt it is the greatest economic event of modern times.

The disastrous consequences of the ever-increasing flood of grain and meat pouring out of the West were by no means felt in Europe alone. Eastern farmers experienced its depressing effects by the seventies, and after 1882 the pressure intensified sharply. Two sets of statistics are illuminating in this connection. American exports of wheat totaled roughly 39 million bushels in 1871, 57 million in 1876, 122 million in 1881, 154 million in 1886, and rose to the startling amount of 226 million in 1891. The next few years were to see somewhat of a slackening, but, notwithstanding, in 1895, the highly respectable total of 126 million bushels was exported. During the same years, New York farm prices of wheat declined, almost uninterruptedly, from $1.51 per bushel in 1871 to 65 cents in 1895.[23]

C.
American Public Domain

Although the depressing impact of Western competition upon both Eastern and European agriculture attracted wide attention in the eighties, this impact apparently had little effect in diminishing the tributes paid by Americans to the land system, the Homestead Act, and the glories of the public domain. On the contrary, a good deal of ill-concealed satisfaction was taken by those who commented upon the resulting ruin of European agriculture. If anything, this ruin served only to further in-

---

23. U. S. Department of Agriculture, *Yearbook, 1896*, 562, diagram 2; Samuel E. Ronk, "Prices Received by Producers in New York State, 1841-1933" (unpublished Ph.D. thesis, Cornell University, 1934), 120-121.

Elsewhere, I have dealt with the impact of western competition upon New York farmers, 1873-1896. In many respects the results were similar to the effect upon European agriculture. Some indication of this may be seen in the fact that the New York Farmers' Alliance was formed as early as March 1877, principally to devise means of coping with Western competition. See Lee Benson, *Merchants, Farmers, & Railroads* (Cambridge, Mass., 1955), 80-114.

crease admiration for the West and to reinforce the veneration in which the American land system was held.[24] The impressive national statistics chalked up as settlement rolled westward were hailed throughout the country as matters for pride and rejoicing. Indeed, so widespread were these sentiments that not until 1890 did a leading agricultural journal, the *Country Gentleman*, angrily call attention to the great folly of Eastern farmers joining "the general congratulations over our wonderful national growth!" It held that this "insane passion for 'development'" was ruining Eastern agriculture, and it berated that region's farmers for cheering on their own destruction.[25] Unfortunately, it is difficult to determine even the approximate degree to which these fundamental agricultural developments served to focus attention upon the West. Certainly, other factors contributed to the process, but these developments deserve to be assigned considerable importance.

24. Before Turner's 1893 essay was delivered, and for some time thereafter, Francis Amasa Walker was probably the most important single influence shaping the frontier concept and preaching the grandeur of the American march to the Pacific. In numerous articles, speeches, and publications, Walker, who exercised considerable influence upon American scholars in the late nineteenth century, called attention to the importance of land in American development. In an article on "American Agriculture," *Princeton Review*, 9: 249-264 (1882), Walker, with keen delight, sarcastically commented upon the contempt displayed by European writers for American farming practices in "the light of present day," *i.e.*, the ruinous impact of the American agricultural surplus. The article is conveniently reprinted in the two-volume collection of his works, edited by Davis R. Dewey, *Discussions in Economics and Statistics* (New York, 1899), 2: 159-175. This article, and several others, are well worth reading to appreciate in full James C. Malin's comment that many of the ideas associated with Turner were "in the air." In this connection, see also Worthington C. Ford, "Public Lands of the United States," in John J. Lalor, ed., *Cyclopaedia of Political Science, Political Economy, and of the Political History of the United States* (Chicago, 1884), 2: 460-479; and A. R. Spofford, "Homestead and Exemption Laws," *ibid.*, 2: 462-464 (1883). See Mood, in *Agricultural History*, 19: 24-30, for an excellent exposition of Walker's influence in shaping the frontier concept.

25. *Country Gentleman*, 55: 822 (Oct. 16, 1890). The dating of this paper's campaign against the land system as beginning in 1890 was attested to by its editor, Gilbert M. Tucker. See his vitriolic address, "The Irrigation Schemes of the West," New York State Agricultural Society, *Transactions, 1899*, 413.

Along with enthusiastic tributes paid to the westward movement, indeed, almost as a necessary corollary, increasing anxiety developed about the state of the public domain. If, as was asserted, America owed her great good fortune, at least in part, to the safety valve of the public domain, clearly, strenuous efforts had to be made to keep the valve open. Thus, in the seventies and eighties, the land question grew in importance. The problems of land grants, forfeitures, Indian policy, restrictions against alien landholding, the single tax, the report of the Public Lands Commission in 1880, the compilation by Thomas Donaldson in 1883 of his *Public Domain*, the activities of the General Land Office—all these contributed at various times to the agitation.[26] The movement reached such a pitch that, by the middle eighties, few prominent periodicals in the country failed to carry articles on the subject of land monopolization.[27]

Seen against this background of intense worldwide concern in the extension of agricultural settlement westward and the accelerating momentum of land reform, the growing attention given by contemporary scholars to the role played by land in shaping American history appears understandable. It should be stressed here that many American scholars were then taking graduate work abroad and thus were strongly influenced by European thinking upon the subject. Moreover, this influence was reinforced by the close interest in European developments generally characterizing American intellectuals at the time. Hence, their ideas about American agricultural competition and the historical impact of American "free land" were shaped in good measure by European thought. And, it is safe to say, the erroneous European notions of American "free land," as embodied, for example, in the works of Adam Smith, John Stuart

---

26. Paul Wallace Gates, "The Homestead Law in an Incongruous Land System," *American Historical Review*, 41: 677, 681 (July 1936); David Maldwyn Ellis, "The Forfeiture of Railroad Land Grants, 1867-1894," *Mississippi Valley Historical Review*, 33: 29-36 (June 1946); Roy M. Robbins, *Our Landed Heritage* (Princeton, 1942), 270-279.

27. *Ibid.*, 273; Shosuke Sato, *History of the Land Question in the United States* (Baltimore, 1886), i-ii.

Mill, Karl Marx, etc., were based more on speculative crystal gazing, enthusiastic pamphlets, and superficial travel accounts than upon careful research.[28] These errors were crystallized and given wide currency when the flood of wheat, corn, and meat from the "free" or "cheap" lands hit European agriculture. It would thus appear that the Communication Revolution and the Great Depression of 1873-1896 need to be considered in analyzing the role contemporary scholars assigned to land in the social process.

At Johns Hopkins University, Herbert Baxter Adams had begun discussing the effect of land upon the development of the United States and its institutions at least as early as 1880, and his seminar continued to take up various aspects for some time thereafter.[29] In 1885, the Reverend Josiah Strong published his widely circulated, pseudo-scholarly tract, *Our Country*. It treated, among other subjects, the importance of the West, the continuous expansion to the Pacific, the effect upon American life of vast quantities of unoccupied public lands, and the possible consequences of their exhaustion.[30] Finally, the appearance in 1888 of James Bryce's *American Commonwealth* stressed in more

---

28. Adam Smith, *The Wealth of Nations* (Modern Library ed., New York, 1937), 359, 392-393; John Stuart Mill, *Principles of Political Economy* (Boston, 1848), 1: 415; Karl Marx, *Capital*, tr. from the third German ed. by Samuel Moore and Edward Aveling (Chicago, 1926), 1: 838-848. The explicit term, "free land," does not occur in these writings, but the germ is there. Smith, for example, on p. 393, asserted that "land [uncultivated] . . . is in North America to be had almost for nothing, or at a price much below the value of the natural produce. . . ."
   The fanciful notions about "free land" subscribed to by leading European thinkers is well exemplified in the work of Achille Loria, an outstanding Italian economist and sociologist. He represents the quintessence of the European tendency to discuss American history in terms of "free" or "cheap" land. See Part I of this book. European influences upon American scholars are treated in Merle Curti, *The Growth of American Thought* (New York, 1943), 580-593.

29. Fulmer Mood, "The Development of Frederick Jackson Turner as a Historical Thinker," Colonial Society of Massachusetts, *Transactions*, 34: 321-322 (Boston, 1943).

30. Strong, *Our Country*, ch. 2-3, 11-12.

sober fashion the significance of many topics previously touched upon by Strong.[31]

Nonetheless, scholarly interest in the land question even in the eighties need not be exaggerated. The important monograph by Shosuke Sato, *History of the Land Question in the United States,* is revealing in this respect. He began his work with a brief but penetrating outline of the fundamental problems in American history needing study in connection with the public domain. It is significant that, as late as 1886, he found it necessary to add: "The importance of the public domain, however, seems to have been rarely and but recently emphasized by the student of American history."[32] As this pioneering monograph was included in the Johns Hopkins University *Studies,* it is doubtful that Herbert Baxter Adams, the editor of the series, would have allowed the statement to stand uncorrected if he had thought it merely an instance of a student "puffing" the importance of his own work.[33]

Possibly one of the more important reasons for scholarly neglect of the public domain, despite concern over land monopolization, was, to use Lord Bryce's phrase, that the "time of trial," when the country's lands would be exhausted, still appeared comfortably distant. Hence, no sense of immediate crisis developed. Estimates made in the middle and late eighties by men who placed considerable importance upon the existence of large areas of vacant land, including Josiah Strong, Shosuke Sato,

---

31. James Bryce, *The American Commonwealth* (London, 1888), v. 3, particularly ch. 114-116.

32. Sato, *History of the Land Question,* 7. Sato's monograph may be an excellent example of how the Communication Revolution focused interest upon American land and the public domain. The work "was undertaken in pursuance of special instructions from the Japanese Government to investigate certain questions of agrarian and economic interest in the United States." *Ibid.,* i.

33. Adams was certainly in an excellent position to know if Sato was right because his seminar was examining the land question intensively. Sato's list, although by no means identical with those in Turner's problems essay of 1892 and his frontier essay of 1893, is similar enough to be suggestive.

and James Bryce, dated the exhaustion as no earlier than 1900.[34] Indeed, Richmond Mayo-Smith, in his book, *Emigration and Immigration*, published in 1890, although arguing strongly for restriction of immigration, conceded that abundant land existed to provide opportunities for immigrants. In order to meet this argument for unrestricted immigration, he maintained that the large majority of the immigrants now refused to go to the land and preferred instead to settle in compact urban colonies.[35]

Three basic conclusions have been suggested in the foregoing pages. First, one direct result of the Communication Revolution was to focus attention upon the importance of the American West and to contribute to a growth of interest in questions relating to the public domain. Second, despite this interest, at least as late as 1890, the date of exhaustion of the arable public lands was generally believed to be years away. Finally, there-fore, the calamitous effects assumed to follow upon the heels of that event appeared far off—a distant prospect which did not lend a sense of urgency to the subject or engender widespread

---

34. Strong, *Our Country*, 155-156; Sato, *History of the Land Question*, 7-8; Bryce, *American Commonwealth*, 3: 661-662.

Strong used the phrase "before the end of the century," but writing in 1885, he predicted exhaustion in "fifteen or twenty years." Incidentally, in the revised edition of 1891, he apparently saw no need of changing his dating. To support his position, Strong quoted the following statement made in 1883 by Robert Giffen, president of the London Statistical Society: "'Whatever way we may look at the matter, then, it seems certain that, in twenty-five years' time, and probably before that date, the limita-tion of area in the United States will be felt. There will be no longer vast tracts of virgin land for the settler. The whole available area will be peopled agriculturally, as the Eastern States are now peopled.'"

It is true that in 1887 Albert Bushnell Hart maintained that the public domain was actually exhausted. See his "The Disposition of Our Public Lands," *Quarterly Journal of Economics*, 1: 169-183, 250-254 (Jan. 1887). However, his views were based on the most erroneous statistics, obviously bore little relation to reality, and apparently were not taken seriously by many contemporary observers.

In the present essay, "land exhaustion" refers only to the alleged dis-appearance of unoccupied arable land. It is not employed here in the sense of "soil exhaustion."

35. Richmond Mayo-Smith, *Emigration and Immigration* (New York, 1890), 115-118.

and fervent discussion among American scholars or the public at large.

This situation was to change rapidly as the fundamental tendencies inherent in the Communication Revolution worked themselves out. "The 'Heartbreaking' Nineties," as the decade has been called, were strongly marked by economic depression and social unrest. In those years, a note of desperate urgency *was* lent to topics heretofore discussed in more academic and leisurely terms. The forces tending to intensify the agricultural depression were particularly responsible for charging the atmosphere. As a result, the impact of the West upon American life received increasing attention, and the exhaustion of the public domain became a "burning issue of the day."[36]

D.
C. Wood Davis, Neo-Malthusian

During the early nineties, few questions of public policy were debated without both sides dragging in, usually by main force, some reference to the state of the public domain. Only a strong catalytic agent was needed to precipitate such a climate of opinion given the basic economic and social setting. And as history frequently has it, the requisite catalyst soon appeared in the person of C. Wood Davis of Sedgewick County, Kansas. Davis, a transplanted Yankee, later to become famous through the Middle West as "Cotton Wood" Davis, merits much more attention than it is possible to give here. Born in Massachusetts in 1832, he was at one time auditor of the Michigan Central

---

36. It should be noted that in 1890 the farm population constituted 46.7 per cent of the total population, making it by far the largest single group in the country. This figure is from an unpublished memorandum by K. L. Robinson of the National Bureau of Economic Research. I am indebted to F. F. Hill of Cornell University for seeing a copy.

For an excellent picture of the strains and tensions of the period, see the first chapter of Part 3, "The 'Heartbreaking' Nineties," in Joseph A. Dorfman, *The Economic Mind in American Civilization* (New York, 1949), 3: 215-237.

Railroad and later traffic manager of the Kansas Pacific. Resigning from the latter road in the late sixties, he engaged in varied business interests, one of which, a large tract in Sedgewick County, was first acquired in 1870, and thereafter farmed on a considerable scale.[37]

Sometime early in 1889, disturbed, as he candidly admitted, by the increasingly depressed state of agriculture which affected him personally, and alarmed by the political restlessness accompanying it, Davis began a serious study to discover the causes of the farmer's unsatisfactory condition. Self-confessedly beginning his investigation in that year, and impressed with the doctrines of Thomas Robert Malthus—doctrines, incidentally, which were then enjoying a strong revival of interest—he emerged in 1890 as a full-fledged Malthusian. Now he professed to be convinced that the depression was "wholly due to that land hunger and homemaking instinct so strong in all branches of the Aryan race." Production had temporarily outrun population because of "a rapidly increasing, restless, energetic population, and a practically unlimited area of fertile land, free as the air we breathe." As a result, "The excessive development of the West has seemed to negative the Malthusian theory," but the abnormal condition of overproduction was fast approaching its natural end. With population rapidly increasing and the arable land virtually exhausted, "The farmer is assured high prices at an early day and for all the future." Thus, probably before the end of the century, "both the memory and doctrine of Malthus will be fully rehabilitated."[38]

---

37. William Elsey Connelley, ed., *A Standard History of Kansas and Kansans* (Chicago, 1918), 3: 1236-1237; *Country Gentleman*, 55: 496 (June 19, 1890).

38. C. Wood Davis, in *Country Gentleman*, 55: 383-384, 621 (May 15, Aug. 7, 1890). See also *ibid.*, 56: 453, 473 (June 4, 1891). Among other glad tidings, Davis assured farmers that "not later than 1895 every acre of good farm land in the United States will sell readily for one hundred golden dollars." *Ibid.*, 56: 24 (Jan. 8, 1891).

The revival of Malthus is discussed by Edward Atkinson, "Must Humanity Starve at Last?" *Forum*, 5: 603-612 (Aug. 1888); H. S. Pomeroy, "The Malthusian Idea," *Andover Review*, 15: 173-189 (Feb. 1891); E. B.

Obviously, the key point in Davis' thesis was that little arable land now remained which could be used for food production, with particular stress being laid upon the virtual exhaustion of the public domain. To the neo-Malthusian Davis, more than to any other individual, must go the credit, or the blame, for having first implanted the notion that 1890 marked the exhaustion of the public lands. To establish this rather original assertion, he compiled elaborate series of statistics, made impressively extravagant assumptions, and stated his polemics in high-powered prose worthy of a modern advertising copy-writer.[39] His fecund pen turned out a steady stream of articles for the *Forum*, the *Arena*, the *Country Gentleman*,[40] and leading dailies, articles

Andrews, "Are There Too Many of Us?" *North American Review*, 155: 596-607 (Nov. 1892).

39. A typical set of Davis' calculations follows: "There seems to be abundant data showing that the arable lands of the United States are so far exhausted that the cultivated area cannot be increased more than 4 per cent in the next 5 years; 7 per cent in 10 years, and 16 per cent in 30 years, while population will increase 12½ per cent in 5 years, 24 per cent in 10 years and 60 per cent in 30 years. . . ." *Country Gentleman*, 55: 796 (Oct. 9, 1890).

As for the public domain: ". . . there is not (outside a few limited Indian reservations, of which the Indians will retain all the best lands) a single quarter section of the public domain worth farming; while, on the contrary, there are many thousands of quarter sections which have been abandoned after those settling upon them have been starved out." *Ibid.*, 796.

Some of his assumptions were: very little land suitable for agriculture existed in Canada; no new methods of farming would be introduced in the sub-humid areas; only a very small area was suitable for irrigation; and finally, taking the country as a whole, there would be little if any improvement in agricultural methods.

40. C. Wood Davis, "Why the Farmer Is Not Prosperous," "When the Farmer Will be Prosperous," "The Exhaustion of the Arable Lands," "The Probabilities of Agriculture," *Forum*, 9: 231-242, 348-360, 461-475, 10: 291-305 (Apr., May, June, Nov. 1890). These four articles contain much repetition; see especially 9: 241, 348, 359-360, 469-474, and 10: 291, 295. See also C. Wood Davis, "The Wheat Supply of Europe and America," *Arena*, 3: 641-657 (May 1891).

Davis' letters and articles frequently appeared in the *Country Gentleman* during the early nineties. The volume for 1891 contains 17 separate items by Davis on pages 23-24, 85-86, 105-106, 125-126, 145-146, 164, 205-206, 229, 252, 418, 453, 473, 493, 513, 532-533, 553, 655, 751-752, 895, 913,

which were freely quoted from in numerous other periodicals and newspapers.[41] First appearing on a major scale in 1890, his writings soon attracted national attention, even if they were greeted with much less than complete acceptance. But attacks upon his position admirably served to advertise it. During the years, 1890 to 1892, for example, the pages of the *Country Gentleman* frequently formed an ink-stained battleground fought over by him, his supporters, and his critics.[42]

932, and 971-972. The volume for 1890 includes 21 separate Davis offerings. The *Country Gentleman*, in puffing Davis' important article in the *Forum* for June 1890, made this statement: "For many years he has been a frequent contributor to the best class of daily papers, and has more recently taken a prominent place in the monthlies and *Country Gentleman*." *Ibid.*, 55: 496 (June 19, 1890). The New York *Sun* was one of the leading dailies in which Davis' articles appeared.

41. *Husbandman* (Elmira, N. Y.), July 22, 1891, p. 4; *Review of Reviews* (Amer. ed.), 3: 499 (June 1891); Erastus Wiman, "The Farmer on Top," *North American Review*, 153: 17 (July 1891). Wiman credited Davis' calculations with "forming the basis of much of the discussion now going forward on this most important topic of the food supply and the farmer's position. . . ."

Even when not specifically cited by name, Davis' views inspired comments and predictions by various publicists. For a case in point, see the editorial of the *Poughkeepsie* (N.Y.) *Eagle*, reprinted in the *Country Gentleman*, 57: 286 (Apr. 14, 1892).

42. Many of Davis' letters bear witness to the cool reception given him. A typical example follows: "The writer [Davis] having stated that wheat would bring a good price after the coming harvest, and in all probability *never again be cheap*, and such statements being questioned by many a 'doubting Thomas,' it is well to examine the basis of such belief. . . ." *Ibid.*, 55: 423 (May 22, 1890).

Confident of the exhaustion of the arable lands, Davis firmly advised farmers to hold back their wheat for "assured" higher prices. Despite his predictions, wheat continued to drop, and disappointed farmers' tempers rose. C. L. H. of Minnesota put it in this sarcastic vein: "That Two-Dollar Wheat of which we used to catch such beautiful glimpses through the charming pen-pictures of Mr. C. Wood Davis, seems as far off as ever." *Ibid.*, 57: 270 (Apr. 7, 1892). Eventually Davis attempted to reply, in his words, to the "army of critics." *Ibid.*, 57: 663 (Sept. 10, 1892).

If Davis had so desired he could have taken much pride in the eminent position held by many of the men who ridiculed his ideas. Thus, Prince Kropotkin, without mentioning Davis by name, but clearly intending him as the target, began an article: "Few books have exercised so pernicious an influence upon the general development of economic thought as

The innate appeal of Davis' oversimplified analysis is attested
to by the frequency with which variations of it were employed
in the controversies of the period. At a time when social protest
was beginning to cause uneasy stirrings in conservative breasts,
one reason is readily apparent for the rapid response to his optimistic panacea. Since prosperity was just around the corner,
why agitate? If, as he asserted, overproduction was the only
cause of agricultural distress, the depression being "originated,
supported and prolonged solely and naturally by the farmer,
and by him alone," it was quite logical for Davis to denounce
the "visionary schemes" of the Southern Farmers' Alliance.[43]

Malthus's 'Essay on the Principles of Population'. . . ." *Forum*, 9: 614 (Aug.
1890). Davis took on the Prince in the November 1890 *Forum* article
cited above.

J. R. Dodge, the statistician of the U. S. Department of Agriculture, was
outraged by Davis' statistics. In fact he was so outraged that he included
11 pages on "The Permanency of Agricultural Production" to refute
"Some modern disciples of Malthus" in the U. S. Department of Agriculture, Report of the Statistician, n. s., *Report 83*, Apr. 1891. For the
row this kicked up, see the *Country Gentleman*, 56: 358, 378, 453, 473
(Apr. 30, May 7, June 4, 11, 1891). Thus began a decade of bitter controversy between Davis and the Department of Agriculture in general
and Dodge in particular. At the end of the century, Davis was still at it.
See his "Wheat: Crookes *vs.* Atkinson, Dodge, *Et Al*," *Forum*, 27: 101-
113 (Mar. 1899).

Davis had important supporters as well as critics. In August 1890, Senator Anthony Higgins of Delaware delivered a speech in the United
States Senate, calling special attention to the articles by Davis in the
Country Gentleman and the *Forum*. *Country Gentleman*, 56:258 (Mar.
26, 1891).

43. Davis, in *Country Gentleman*, 55: 383-384 (May 15, 1890). He
urged: "Do not let us longer try to shift the responsibility to other shoul-
ders, as it is neither manly nor right to do so. . . ." For his denunciation
of the Southern Alliance, see *ibid.*, 55: 937 (Nov. 27, 1890).

Interestingly enough, despite his avowals of sole responsibility for the
depression resting upon the farmers, Davis not only campaigned bitterly
against transactions in grain "futures" as "the worst evil the farmer has
to contend with," but strongly supported the nationalization of railroads.
Ibid., 56: 751-752 (Sept. 17, 1891). See also Connelley, *A Standard History
of Kansas and Kansans*, 3: 1237; and C. Wood Davis, "Should the Nation
Own the Railways," *Arena*, 4: 152-159, 273-292 (July, Aug. 1891). A close
reading of his literary productions makes it clear that Davis was a firm
believer in the maxim, "Never let your left hand know what your right
is doing."

Thus, the *Country Gentleman* enthusiastically accepted the essence of Davis' thesis, gave it considerable prominence week after week, but shaped his conclusions to fit more closely the needs of its Eastern constituency.

E.
The Public Domain in Politics

The *Country Gentleman* recognized, however, as Davis did not, that his funeral oration over the public domain was premature. In a long editorial on October 16, 1890, entitled "No More 'Development' Wanted," the magazine proposed a more beneficial kind of agitation.

There is one subject which, in considering the present agricultural interests of the country, has escaped the attention to which it seems eminently entitled—we refer to the attitude of the general government as regards the farther distribution of its public lands. There is a strong and deep feeling—which only needs more general discussion and greater concentration of effort to be rendered effective —that it is now quite time for the entire stoppage of the selling and giving away of the national territory for farming purposes—for the repeal of all "homestead" and "pre-emption" laws of whatever name or nature, leaving the government to retain in its own possession, until changing times shall seem to indicate the wisdom of another change of management, every tillable acre not already alienated.

According to the *Country Gentleman*, such repeal would restore prosperity; therefore, it continued:

Here is practical work for our granges, alliances, leagues, wheels and similar associations of farmers. Let them give a wide berth to party politicians and to the preachers of new doctrines in finance and social order, and unite in one demand of the powers that be— *no further alienation of the public territory for the purposes of agriculture or any of the arts related thereto.*[44]

To this theme, the *Country Gentleman* returned incessantly

44. *Country Gentleman,* 55: 822 (Oct. 16, 1890).

over the years, and its position was widely echoed in the East.[45] In fact, it was able to note with satisfaction that even the *Orange Judd Farmer*, published in Chicago and slanted to Midwestern farmers, gave voice to similar sentiments.[46]

Other than conservative forces were able to utilize Davis' polemics. Indeed, a most engaging quality of his universal specific was its dual character. With delightful, but probably unconscious, irony, the representatives of the Southern Farmers' Alliance, violently denounced by him, ignored his optimistic forecasts, but found it convenient to employ the exhausted-domain theme in urging their own legislative program. For example, at the Cincinnati convention of May 1891, Senator William A. Peffer, the Kansas Populist, argued that since the safety valve of the West was now being closed, it became imperative for the Populist demands to be enacted if American farmers were to retain a stake in the land.[47]

---

45. Ten years later the magazine was still at it. See footnote 25 above. Convenient expressions of these sentiments by the president of the New York State Agricultural Society, the secretary-treasurer of the Connecticut Board of Agriculture, the Massachusetts Agricultural College Club, the New York *Tribune*, etc., are found in *ibid.*, 55: 1020-1021 (Dec. 25, 1890), 56: 10, 70-71, 165 (Jan. 1, 22, Feb. 26, 1891). Numerous other citations might be given from Eastern agricultural journals, city dailies, and local weeklies.
   One of the basic reasons for Eastern farmers rejecting the Populist movement was opposition to Western demands regarding the public domain. See the well-studied-out address of President James Wood in the New York State Agricultural Society, *Transactions, 1889*, 20-41.

46. *Country Gentleman*, 56: 278 (Apr. 2, 1891).

47. Elizabeth N. Barr, "The Populist Uprising," in Connelley, *A Standard History of Kansas and Kansans*, 2: 1159. Hamlin Garland made a similar point the same year. See Smith, *Virgin Land*, 247. For still another version, see Chester McArthur Destler, "Agricultural Readjustment and Agrarian Unrest in Illinois, 1880-1896," *Agricultural History*, 21: 104-116 (Apr. 1947).
   Significantly, Peffer's speech was made on May 19, just after the publication of Davis' *Arena* article. As the *Arena* was strongly sympathetic to the Alliance movement, it seems probable that Peffer read the magazine regularly. That the argument of the exhausted West was new to Peffer may be judged from his "The Farmers' Defensive Movement" in the *Forum*, 8: 464-473 (Dec. 1889). It would have been completely logical for Peffer to have made the point there, but no trace of it appears.

Peffer's version by no means exhausted the possible comments upon the theme by hard-pressed farmers. In the East, where Davis' arguments had been strongly utilized by conservative forces opposing agrarian movements, representatives of farm organizations, such as the Grange and the Farmers' League, angrily denounced roseate predictions of population fast out-running production as "buncombe." Although in full agreement that the alienation of the public domain should cease, they maintained that the optimistic pronouncements concerning land exhaustion were concocted for sinister purposes and would only result in preventing farmers from taking political action designed to meet their real needs. Such recognition in no way inhibited expression of sectional antagonism toward Western competition. As depression increasingly settled down upon Eastern agriculture, bitter speeches were made and strong resolutions passed, castigating various aspects of the land system at meetings of the Grange, the Farmers' League, the farmers' institutes, and agricultural societies. Eastern periodicals and newspapers cooperated by giving wide publicity to the sectional antagonism. One result of the East-West clash was to heighten interest in the public domain and various proposals pertaining to its disposition.[48]

The point of citing these varied pronouncements upon the public domain is not at all to examine their validity. Rather it is to illustrate the manner in which the exhausted-lands leitmotif became intertwined with discussion of agricultural depression and discontent. To round out this aspect, the views of another Kansan, J. Willis Gleed, merit brief summary. His views were expressed in the same magazine, the *Forum*, and at about the same time, March 1890, as the articles by Davis which first at-

---

48. *Husbandman* (Elmira, N. Y.), July 22, 1891, p. 4, Feb. 3, 1892, p. 1, Mar. 30, 1892, p. 1, June 1, 1892, p. 3; *Country Gentleman* 55: 957, 963, 1006 (Dec. 4, 18, 1890), 60: 370 (May 9, 1895); New York *Tribune*, Dec. 15, 1890; Dundee (N.Y.) *Observer*, Jan. 7, 1891; Otsego *Farmer* (Oneonta, N.Y.), Jan. 23, 1891; Association for Improving the Condition of the Poor, *A.I.C.P. Notes*, Dec. 1896, 27; New York State Grange, *Journal of Proceedings, 1891*, 109.

tracted national attention.[49] In addition to being professor of real estate at the University of Kansas, he operated with his brother, Charles S. Gleed, one of the leading law firms in the State.[50] It appears that among their clients were a number of land mortgage companies,[51] companies hard hit by the depression, and fast losing the confidence of the investing public. It comes as no shock, therefore, that Gleed, avowedly desirous of reassuring Eastern investors in Western mortgages, seized upon exhaustion of the public domain as an iron-clad guarantee of present and future loans. A rise in land values, he maintained, would inevitably follow. Such a rise, of course, was the best possible guarantee of the stability of mortgage companies; wise investors would act accordingly.[52]

It follows most logically that if the exhaustion or closure of the arable public domain was to be the blessing Davis and others foresaw, proposals to delay the process "unnaturally" would rouse their bitter opposition. Hence, attempts to open Indian reservations to white settlement were severely censured; but undoubtedly their choicest epithets were reserved for proponents of arid-land reclamation. Here the school of thought represented by Davis came into head-on collision with the group led by Major John W. Powell.[53]

---

49. James Willis Gleed, "Western Mortgages," *Forum*, 9: 93-105 (March 1890). I do not know whether Gleed was acquainted with Davis but such a relationship would not be surprising under the circumstances.

50. *Ibid.*, 11: 479 (June 1891); Connelley, *A Standard History of Kansas and Kansans*, 5: 2315.

51. It is not certain that Gleed actually represented these companies in 1890, but in 1895 his firm was handling at least 125 cases for land mortgage companies. Letter of J. Willis Gleed to A. C. Mitchell, Dec. 24, 1895, in the J. B. Watkins Collection at the University of Kansas. I am indebted to Allan G. Bogue of the University of Western Ontario for this information. Gleed wrote another article on "Western Lands and Mortgages," *Forum*, 11: 468-471 (June 1891). Certainly both articles reflect far more than casual interest and knowledge of the affairs of mortgage companies.

52. Gleed, in the *Forum*, 9: 100-101.

53. An editorial in the *Country Gentleman*, 55: 882 (Nov. 6, 1890), put it this way: "If the attention of the members of these bodies [farm organizations] can be called off from chimerical and useless projects, and united upon the one simple plan of demanding of their representatives in

Powell, since 1878, had been urging the importance of irrigating the arid lands, and in the late eighties he was appointed to direct the irrigation surveys authorized by Congress.[54] In the spring of 1890, at almost the exact moment when Davis' articles in the *Forum* concerning land exhaustion were published, Powell wrote two important articles for the *Century Magazine*,[55] urging the reclamation of 120,000,000 acres. It is important to note that Powell admitted ample land existed for agriculture in the United States without reclamation. His arguments in favor of irrigation were not based upon the exhaustion of the public domain, or of the arable lands, but rather that the arid lands in the West constituted the best lands. Further, the proud men of the West, gathered to exploit its vast natural resources, were "too enterprising and too industrous to beg bread from the farms of the East."

Nonetheless, the exhausted-land theme was too irresistible an argument to be overlooked for long. By 1891 it was being worked to the hilt by Westerners favoring irrigation. Land Office Commissioner Thomas H. Carter, former Republican national chairman and later Senator from Montana, pointed in his report to the dreadful spectacle of "homeseeking citizens . . . exhausting each other's strength and substance in a fierce struggle to obtain title" in the Oklahoma rush, and elsewhere, as positive proof of the urgent need for reclamation.[56]

Congress, not only action for stopping the alienation of our public lands in general, but also active and determined opposition to the *Powell irrigation inequity, in particular* [italics added], the greatest calamity that has threatened our agriculture for many years may easily be averted." An interesting letter by Davis contains an "expose" of the Union Pacific's leading role in the irrigation movement. *Ibid.,* 56: 418 (May 21, 1891).

54. Walter Prescott Webb, *The Great Plains* (New York, 1931), 354-356.

55. J. W. Powell, "The Irrigable Lands of the Arid Region," and "The Non-Irrigable Lands of the Arid Region," *Century Magazine,* 39: 766-776, 915-922 (Mar., Apr. 1890); see especially p. 766-768. For similar views, see Nelson A. Miles, "Our Unwatered Empire," *North American Review,* 150: 370-381 (Mar. 1890).

56. U. S. General Land Office, *Annual Report, 1891,* 51. Opponents of the "Arid Land-Plot," recognizing the potency of the argument, concentrated their fire upon it. Here is a sample: "One of the strongest

That Oklahoma "proved" the existence of land exhaustion was a cardinal tenet of faith among strangely diverse groups. For example, Davis, fervently opposed to irrigation, and the land commissioner, Carter, enthusiastically championing it, could both use Oklahoma to clinch their arguments simply by ringing the different changes possible upon the theme.[57] Such ambivalent use of Oklahoma was widespread and suggests the ease with which the exhaustion theme could be used to establish almost any point. The Oklahoma rush, the excitement over the Cherokee Outlet, the frenzied scenes as various Indian and military reservations were thrown open to settlement—all these were invariably cited by groups anxious for one reason or another to prove land exhaustion.

Despite the wide publicity stemming from the battle over irrigation[58]—and the publicity resulting from its use in numerous other controversies—we have it on the best authority that few people had swallowed the exhausted-land propaganda by early 1891. Davis admitted as much in this revealing statement:

It is as remarkable as true that, with very rare exceptions, even the most advanced of Americans, as well as Europeans, have thus far failed to compass the situation and cannot conceive it as possible that the time—as measured by national life—is very near when Amer-

---

arguments used by the grabbers, or at least the one given the most prominence, is that there is an overwhelming thirst for homes on the public lands, and that the general government owes it to the dear people to at once take steps to render the arid region fit for cultivation. The rush for the vacant lands in Oklahoma is cited in proof of this, and buckets of tears are shed over the alleged sufferings endured 'in the wild scramble for a few acres of God's earth,' and the spectacle of 'men and women fighting with desperate energy for a small piece of land.' " Then followed a blistering attack upon the "alleged sufferings" and mendacity of "home-seekers" who really wanted to secure title and sell out; the land-exhaustion argument was "moonshine." Letter by C. C., San Francisco, in *Country Gentleman*, 56: 911-912 (Nov. 12, 1891).

57. One wing of the anti-irrigation movement denounced the Oklahoma argument as "moonshine." See footnote 56. But Davis' entire thesis rested on proving exhaustion. Exhaustion, according to him, was quite fortunate and the only way agricultural prosperity could be assured. Carter also argued exhaustion, but in his version it was a calamity making irrigation mandatory.

58. Webb, *The Great Plains*, 356-358.

ica will cease to press upon the markets of the world an enormous surplus of food-stuffs.[59]

A further illustration of how unconvinced American public opinion was of the existence of a land shortage may be gleaned from an article published in July 1891. The following quotation takes on considerable significance because its author, Erastus Wiman, an ardent supporter of Davis, was attempting to prove that a land shortage *did exist*.

That a "land-hunger" should at this early date in the history of the country exist, and be unappeased, would seem impossible on a continent where land areas were supposed to be illimitable, and whose soil was supposed to be inexhaustible. That no lands are available is a conclusion so unexpected and so extraordinary that it is no wonder people doubt the truth of such a statement.[60]

Not for long were Americans to be left in this blissful state of ignorance. Powerful reinforcements were on the way to aid Davis and Wiman in establishing the truth of their revelation. An analysis of these forces requires consideration of the "new immigration," a topic of ever-increasing importance in the late eighties and thereafter. Again lack of space precludes detailed discussion, but it may be stated that this development involved fundamentally important problems and formed an important strand in the contemporary American social fabric.[61]

---

59. Davis, in *Country Gentleman*, 56: 125 (Feb. 12, 1891). In the *Arena*, 3: 651 (May 1891), Davis said that "to the many who entertain the idea that the new States and Territories are capable of a vast agricultural development it will be a revelation to learn that in all the wide expanse of the public domain there is but a small bit of land, here and there, that can be profitably brought under cultivation."

60. Erastus Wiman, "The Farmer on Top," *North American Review*, 153: 14 (July 1891). Here is another thesis in which the exhausted-land theme was stock in trade. Wiman, a former Canadian, was the most prominent figure in the movement for either annexation of Canada or commercial union and unrestricted reciprocity. His article was clearly inspired by reading Davis in the May 1891 *Arena*. For a very interesting description of Wiman's activities, see Sir Charles Tupper, "The Wiman Conspiracy Unmasked," *North American Review*, 152: 549-556 (May 1891).

61. Among the problems involved in the immigration question were agricultural discontent, labor unrest, growing social protest movements in general, sharp political splits between native and foreign-born citizens,

F.

"New Immigration," Land Exhaustion, Christian Imperialism

It may even be possible to select a specific date and argue that the presidential address of Francis A. Walker before the American Economic Association on December 26, 1890, marked the beginning of a new phase of the immigration question. It is necessary here to stress the prestige and influence exercised by General Walker, and to emphasize also that the American Economic Association was one of the most important American scholarly groups then in existence. Walker, in company with numerous leading intellectuals, had been increasingly alarmed by the influx of "alien breeds" into the United States, and his address was a clarion call to the association to consider the matter.

. . . the prospect before the nation is a gloomy one. The subject deserves, demands, instant and full consideration. The Economic Association can do no better service to the country than by taking it up for earnest, candid, searching investigation, and by bringing the question sharply and forcibly, in all its bearings, before the American people.[62]

---

and of major importance—the deep-rooted fear and contempt of the new ethnic groups.

See Carl Wittke, *We Who Built America* (New York, 1939), 407-408, 498-514; John Higham, "European Immigration in American Patriotic Thought" (unpublished Ph.D. thesis, University of Wisconsin, 1949), 1-95; Edward N. Saveth, *American Historians and European Immigrants, 1875-1925* (New York, 1948), *passim;* Edwin Mims, Jr., *American History and Immigration* (Bronxville, N. Y., 1950), 13-56.

62. Francis A. Walker, "The Tide of Economic Thought," American Economic Association, *Publications*, 6(1-2): 37 (1891). See also Dorfman, *The Economic Mind in American Civilization*, 3: 101-102, 205-211. Frank W. Taussig in 1897 called Walker "unquestionably the most prominent and the best known of American writers" in the economic field. Jeannette P. Nichols, "Walker, Francis Amasa . . . ," *Dictionary of American Biography*, 19: 342-344 (New York, 1936).

The address was most opportune. Less than three months later, the lynching of eleven Italians in New Orleans on March 11, 1891, raised the immigration agitation to a fever pitch and sounded "like an alarm-bell, rousing every one to the danger."[63] Influential adherents of immigration restriction were quick to take advantage of the incident and set up a chorus of demands to shut the gates.[64]

At this strategic moment, the issue of the *Arena* for May, 1891, appeared, with Davis' piece, "The Wheat Supply of Europe and America," which was an elaboration of his previous findings that the arable land, public and private, was virtually exhausted. The article was presented with great fanfare, B. O. Flower, the editor, proudly proclaiming that "almost a year was required by Mr. Davis to secure from Europe, Asia, Australia, South and North America the official data employed in this essay. It is probably the most complete and exhaustive examination of the wheat problem that has ever appeared in any review."[65]

Given the potent possibilities of the land-exhaustion argument, the exponents of agricultural prosperity and immigration restriction joined hands, as might be expected, in a very short time. The marriage may be said to have been first consummated effectively in the editorial pages of the July, 1891, issue of the *Review of Reviews*, a leading advocate of restriction.[66] Two

63. John Hawks Noble, "The Present State of the Immigration Question," *Political Science Quarterly*, 7: 232 (June 1892).

64. A good illustration of the impact of the New Orleans massacre is the turn about in the editorial policy of the *Nation*. On Feb. 5, 1891, it deprecated the fears of "alarmists" and maintained present laws were sufficient. On Apr. 16, 1891, one month after the lynching, it demanded a restrictive English-speaking test for immigrants. By Apr. 30, 1891, an editorial was able to comment upon the rather widespread response to its proposal by the American press. See the *Nation*, 52: 108, 312, 354-355.

65. "Notes and Announcements," *Arena*, 3: xxviii (May 1891).

66. This precise dating is based on a study of the literature on immigration during Jan. 1, 1882-Jan. 1, 1892. The first *effective* linkage between immigration restriction and imminent land exhaustion appears to have been made in the *Review of Reviews* (Amer. ed.), 3: 571-572 (July 1891). It is significant that the June issue of the *Review* contained a summary of Davis' article with the introductory note: "Leading place in the May *Arena* is given to a paper of Mr. C. Wood Davis on 'The Wheat Supply

weighty reasons were given for the recent revulsion of American feeling toward immigration. One was the change in the character of the immigrants; the other was stated thus: "The free homestead area in the United States is practically exhausted, and the westward agricultural migration has been carried already beyond the safe limits of the rain-belt, with the inevitable result of disappointment, local distress, and occasional abandonment of drouth-afflicted lands."

Davis' article would probably have attracted considerable attention in any event, but from this time on the subject of land exhaustion became an inseparable part of the immigration question. The assertion may be made in this positive fashion because both sides in the controversy over restriction agreed on that, if nothing else. Thus, Edward Atkinson, strongly in favor of

---

of Europe and America.' " *Ibid.*, 3: 499 (June 1891). These circumstances, and the close similarity in the wording used by the *Review* to Davis' phraseology, make plausible the speculation that the latter was the direct source of inspiration for the merger between immigration restriction and land exhaustion.

It is true that in 1887 Worthington C. Ford used much the same argument in calling for some degree of control over immigration. See his "Regulating Immigration," *Epoch*, 1: 229-230 (Apr. 15, 1887). Other slight anticipations of the linkage can be found before July 1891. See Hjalmar H. Boyesen, "Dangers of Unrestricted Immigration," *Forum*, 3: 534-535 (July 1887); "The American Field for Emigration," *Chambers' Journal* (Edinburgh), s. 5, 6: 820-823 (Dec. 28, 1889); and Henry Cabot Lodge, "The Restriction of Immigration," *North American Review*, 152: 31 (Jan. 1891).

Nonetheless, the crucial point is that until land entries fell off sharply, as they did in the nineties because of the severe agricultural depression, the land-exhaustion argument could not have been taken seriously. At least there is no evidence that it was used prior to July 1891 by Richmond Mayo-Smith, Francis A. Walker, or Albert Shaw—three influential adherents of immigration restriction. As noted in footnote 35, Mayo-Smith conceded in 1890 that abundant land existed for settlement. Walker did not use the exhausted-land theme in his article on "Immigration and Degradation" in the *Forum* 11: 634-644 (Aug. 1891), although it might well have been employed there effectively. Finally, as late as June 1891, the *Review*, edited by Shaw, deplored the stimulus to immigration stemming from "free gifts of our public lands." To check the resulting "influx," a stiff literacy test was editorially demanded. *Ibid.*, 3: 443. Shaw's abrupt flip-flop between June and July indicates a very rapid conversion to the exhaustion theme.

continued immigration, argued that there was "Incalculable Room for Immigrants":

The argument upon which the proposition for taxation or exclusion is based seems to be mainly that our free land has been disposed of by the Government, and that we have no longer any land to give away. That may be admitted. What has it to do with the question? The disposal of land by original owners, either the government, the state, or private persons, has no necessary connection with the occupancy and productive use of land.[67]

General Walker, strongly opposed to a policy of unrestricted immigration, in August, 1892, conceded that the shortage-of-land argument was the chief consideration in moving the public mind and went on:

A generation or less ago, a vast extent of free public lands offered to every new-comer a home and a farm simply for the seeking. . . . If not here, then there, lands of excellent quality and easy of cultivation lay open to his choice. Such a resort to the soil, so open, so free, hardly allowed a labor problem to exist. To-day, the tracts of public land worth taking up under the homestead and preëmption acts are few and far between. . . . Reluctant as we may be to recognize it, a labor-problem is at last upon us. No longer can a *continent of free virgin lands* [italics added] avert from us the social struggle which the old world has known so long and so painfully.[68]

To indicate that this powerful line of argument continued to prevail, General Walker, in another article, published in June 1896, made the same point.[69]

Henceforth, Davis had the big guns of the contemporary intellectual world loudly proclaiming with him the exhaustion of the public domain. The immigration question, according to Senator Henry Cabot Lodge in September, 1891, was "receiving every day more and more of the public attention, and those who are taking it up, and who are coming to feel that it is the gravest

---

67. Edward Atkinson, "Incalculable Room for Immigrants," *Forum*, 13: 361-362 (May 1892).

68. Francis A. Walker, "Immigration," *Yale Review*, 1: 129-130 (Aug. 1892).

69. Francis A. Walker, "Restriction of Immigration," *Atlantic Monthly*, 78: 826 (June 1896).

subject before the American people, are the most earnest and thoughtful men in the community."[70]

Among these "thoughtful men," besides, of course, the Senator, were General Walker, Richmond Mayo-Smith, John Fiske, Richard T. Ely, Albert Shaw, Nathaniel S. Shaler, and a considerable number of leading academicians.[71] By May 31, 1894, mingled feelings of anger and fear had so stirred wide sections of the American intellectual and social elite that the Immigration Restriction League was organized, appropriately enough,at Boston.[72] One set of literary statistics mirrored the growth of interest in the immigration question which gave rise to the league. Under the two titles of "Immigrants" and "Immigration," *Poole's*

---

70. Henry Cabot Lodge, "The Political Issues of 1892," *Forum*, 12: 104 (Sept. 1891).

71. James Phinney Munroe, *A Life of Francis Amasa Walker* (New York, 1923), 300, states that, from the late eighties to his death in 1897, bimetallism and immigration "overshadowed, for him, all other economic immediate problems." The bibliography compiled by Munroe attests to the frequency with which Walker addressed himself to immigration. His writings reveal a strong, if not fanatical, belief in the necessity for restriction.

Richmond Mayo-Smith's *Emigration and Immigration* (New York, 1890) was a widely read and most influential book on the subject. He contributed numerous articles in similar vein to the *Political Science Quarterly* and was a vice president of the Immigration Restriction League. Other vice presidents were Nathaniel S. Shaler and Senator Lodge, with John Fiske occupying the presidency. Letterhead of the Immigration Restriction League, in the collection of its publications at Cornell University.

Albert Shaw was editor of the *Review of Reviews*, and its violent editorials on the subject leave no doubt about his position.

Richard T. Ely's second seminar at the University of Wisconsin in September 1892 was given over to discussion of immigration restriction. Subsequent meetings attested to his deep interest and strong feelings on the subject. See his Economic Seminary Minutes, 1892-93, p. 3, 51-56, in the Ely Collection, State Historical Society of Wisconsin.

For an enlightening discussion of the views of historians generally, see Saveth, *American Historians and European Immigrants*, 200-201, and *passim*.

72. Immigration Restriction League, Boston, *Annual Report of the Executive Committee*, Jan. 14, 1895. The report boasted of 531 members in 14 states. The Cornell University Library has a complete collection of the League's publications.

Index to Periodical Literature from 1882 to 1887 lists 10 articles, from 1887 to 1892, 43, and from 1892 to 1896, 68.[73]

In discussing the impact of the restriction movement upon American intellectuals, the *Review of Reviews* should be singled out for special attention. Founded in England in 1890 and edited by W. T. Stead, it aspired to the lofty ambition of creating what it pleased to call a Civic Church—a civic church which would attain an inspirational role in the English-speaking world equivalent to that exercised by the Catholic Church in its prime over the intelligence of Christendom. The *Review*—which was to serve as the bible of the new church—explicitly stated its creed in the first issue: "We believe in God, in England, and in Humanity! The English-speaking race is one of the chief of God's chosen agents for executing coming improvements in the lot of mankind."[74] Understandably enough, with the publication of a separate American edition, the creed was deftly reworded to avoid irritating Yankee sensibilities. The *Review* now believed "in God, in Humanity, and in the English-speaking race. . . ."[75]

Holding to such dogmas, it is not surprising that the first American issue, appearing in April 1891, just after the New Orleans lynching, immediately expressed concern with the immigration problem.[76] Soon the *Review* was frenetically up in arms against the spoliation of the native "pedigree-stock by . . . the refuse of the murder-breeds of Southern Europe."[77] Characterized by the magazine in one of its more restrained moments as "people of alien races and strange languages,"[78] these immi-

---

73. *Poole's Index to Periodical Literature* (rev. ed., New York, 1938), *Supplements*, 1: 215, 2: 208-209, 3: 275. Not only did the number of articles grow but they were increasingly opposed to immigration.

74. "To All English-Speaking Folk," *Review of Reviews* (London), 1: 15-20 (Jan. 1890). The quotation is from p. 17. For the *Review's* Biblical aspirations, see p. 20.

75. *Ibid.*, 3: 3 (Jan. 1891). This reprinting of the address, "To All English-Speaking Folk," was prompted by the announcement of a forthcoming American edition.

76. *Review of Reviews* (Amer. ed.), 3: 228 (Apr. 1891).

77. *Ibid.*, 3: 331 (May 1891).

78. *Ibid.*, 3: 443 (June 1891).

grants were viewed as a grave menace to the success of the English-speaking people's divine mission. During the early nineties, it was a comparatively rare issue that appeared without some space being given to the immigration question. Under the editorship of Albert Shaw, an early Johns Hopkins Ph.D., the *Review* rapidly attained a place of considerable influence in American thought.[79] As a result, the restriction movement was assured a consistent organ for its preachments, and, moreover, one that circulated widely among scholars.

Among the eminent contributors to the *Review* was the Reverend Josiah Strong, secretary of the North American Evangelical Alliance, and widely renowned after 1885 as author of the religious tract, *Our Country*.[80] Strong's close affinity to the *Review* was only natural. As early as 1882, eight years before the magazine appeared, he had vigorously been preaching a doctrine which may appropriately be called Anglo-Saxon Christian Imperialism—a doctrine similar in many respects to that of the *Review*, and quite possibly its direct inspiration.[81] Accord-

---

79. On the occasion of its first anniversary the American edition claimed a circulation of 70,000. It could also boast, and apparently with some degree of accuracy, that it was the "generally expressed opinion of experienced observers. . . . that the quick rise of this *Review* to a place of influence and consideration has been without precedent in the history of American periodicals." *Ibid.*, 5: 263 (Apr. 1892). Herbert Baxter Adams heartily endorsed the *Review*. *Ibid.* (London), Mar. 1891. So also did Richard T. Ely. Shaw to Ely, Nov. 23, 1892, in the Ely Collection.

Shaw was the first elected member of the American Historical Association. He was active in the American Economic Association and president of the American Political Science Association in 1906. His obituary in the *American Historical Review*, 53: 220-221 (Oct. 1947) contains this glowing tribute: "In 1890 he turned . . . to the career that made him a recorder of current history month by month, the editorship of the American *Review of Reviews*. For forty-six years his name and that of this important impartial chronicle were synonymous. The *Review of Reviews* was a periodical of great significance in its day and of great usefulness to the historian of the period. It set a high standard of fairness and of unemotional rationality. . . . Dr. Shaw wrote many studies and received many honors; but his monument and his memorial are the American *Review of Reviews* at the turn of the century."

80. Strong's next book was based in part upon articles written for the *Review*. See his *New Era* (New York, 1893), v.

81. Strong, *Our Country*, 159. Here he pointed out that his views were

ing to him, the "Anglo-Saxon race," because of its peculiar attributes, was divinely commissioned to spread Christianity throughout the world, and thus bring about the Kingdom of God on earth.[82] As has been noted above, Strong laid great emphasis upon the coming exhaustion of the public lands. In his scheme of things, the chief importance of exhaustion lay in the fact that:

. . . God, with infinite wisdom and skill, is training the Anglo-Saxon race for an hour sure to come in the world's future. Heretofore there has always been . . . a comparatively unoccupied land westward, into which the crowded countries of the East have poured their surplus populations. But the widening waves of migration . . . meet to-day on our Pacific coast. There are no more new worlds. The unoccupied arable lands of the earth are limited, and will soon be taken. The time is coming when the pressure of population on the means of subsistence will be felt here as it is now felt in Europe and Asia. Then will the world enter upon a new stage of its history —*the final competition of races, for which the Anglo-Saxon is being schooled.* . . . Then this race of unequalled energy, with all the majesty of numbers and the might of wealth behind it . . . having developed peculiarly aggressive traits calculated to impress its institutions upon mankind, will spread itself over the earth.[83]

Now, it logically follows that since the United States was to be the center from which the expansion took place, the wellspring of its strength must be kept pure and undiluted. As Strong put it in his *New Era* in 1893, this need only emphasized "the importance to mankind and to the coming Kingdom of guarding against the deterioration of the Anglo-Saxon stock in the United States by immigration."[84] In such fashion, divine blessing was invoked for the restriction movement, and an important addition made to its armory of argument.

---

expressed in a public lecture three years before the appearance of John Fiske's article on "Manifest Destiny" in *Harper's Magazine* for March 1885, containing "some of the same ideas." For a statement on the Anglo-Saxon's mission, quite similar in tone and language to Josiah Strong's, see the *Review of Reviews*, 1: 15-16 (Jan. 1890).

82. Strong, *Our Country*, 160-161.

83. *Ibid.*, 174-175.

84. Strong, *New Era*, 80. See also his *Our Country*, 40-43, for an earlier warning on the immigration danger.

Here also was a most important contribution, direct and indirect, to what James C. Malin has called the "closed-space" doctrines characteristic of the period: direct, in Strong's emphasis upon the importance of land exhaustion as the key impulse setting in motion his tidal wave of Anglo-Saxon Christian Imperialism; indirect, in that Strong strengthened the immigration restriction movement which used land exhaustion as stock in trade.

The article on Strong in the *Dictionary of American Biography* gives some indication of his influence:

The book [*Our Country*] created a sensation. It was translated into foreign languages, Oriental as well as European, and reissued in new and revised editions in America. It made Strong a national figure, brought him repeated requests for lectures and speeches, and was the occasion of his appointment as secretary of the American Evangelical Alliance.[85]

That Strong's doctrines also reached into high places is amply suggested by the copy of *Our Country* that Andrew D. White presented to the Cornell University Library. It bears the comment by White, dated April 3, 1887, "an exceedingly valuable and interesting little book."[86]

---

85. John Haynes Holmes, "Strong, Josiah . . . ," *Dictionary of American Biography*, 18: 150 (New York, 1936).

The 1891 edition of *Our Country* boasted of 148,000 copies in circulation and claimed also that a large part of the book had been reprinted by newspapers in the "East, West, South and Canada," not to omit London and Glasgow. By 1893, the title page of the *New Era* listed *Our Country* as "In its 160th Thousand."

86. Strong was of considerable importance in the intellectual history of the period. Many of the ideas, for example, expressed by James Bryce in his famous *American Commonwealth* upon the importance of the West, the role of the public lands as a safety valve, the uniqueness of American experience, etc., are substantially found in Strong's 1885 book.

James C. Malin has called attention to the possibility that Strong may have influenced Turner's views on these subjects. See *Agricultural History*, 18: 68 n. 7 (Apr. 1944). Following his lead, a speculative but not implausible chain of reasoning suggests that Andrew D. White was a factor in impressing Bryce with Strong's assumptions. Among the acknowledgments listed in the preface to the *American Commonwealth*, 1: x, is the "Hon. Andrew D. White." It is unlikely that Turner failed to read Bryce. Therefore, even if Turner had not read one of the 148,000 copies

G.

Turner, Loria, and the Climate of Opinion

A considerable number of other variations upon the well-worn theme developed here might be given, but little reason appears to further belabor the issue.[87] During the last quarter of the nineteenth century, the fundamental economic and social forces set in motion by the Communication Revolution, or accompanying its spread, resulted in marked attention being given by Americans to the public domain and to ideas of closed space. Striking changes in economics, politics, and social organization were taking place, and even greater ones appeared in the offing. Whether from honest conviction or merely from convenience in debate, considerable numbers of influential men pointed to the state of the public domain as a major factor in these changes. In the early nineties, the climate of intellectual opinion was

---

of *Our Country* published by 1891 he may have been affected indirectly through Bryce. This particular chain of reasoning may be wholly untenable, but in scanning the literature of the period one can not fail to be impressed with the many and varied imprints of Strong's influence.

Strong's emphasis on the crucial importance of the West appears to have derived from the fact that *Our Country* was written avowedly to gain financial support for home missionary work in the West. See ch. 14, "Money and the Kingdom," *Our Country*, 180-222. In his 1893 book, the *New Era*, covering much the same ground, his emphasis on the importance of the West is missing.

87. Among others, the campaigns for better farming, conservation, land reform, opening up Indian reservations, and banning alien landholding used land exhaustion as a salient argument. In this essay I have only been able to suggest the intricate interweavings between the various strands of the theme. Further research would seem to be called for if the impact of these pressure groups upon American public opinion is to be properly evaluated. Nonetheless, I incline to the belief that in the nineties, and for considerable time thereafter, the American people in general thought alarmist accounts of the demise of the arable land very much exaggerated. Thus, C. Wood Davis was greeted with numerous invitations to come out and see for himself that there was "plenty of land out West," and Canadians ridiculed the "hoary nonsense" of his "Malthusian ideas," pointing to the immense Canadian prairies awaiting cultivation.

definitely affected by their argument, though it may seriously be doubted that the American people as a whole subscribed to its validity.

However, the essential question that remains to be discussed is not the general extent to which public opinion was affected, but the specific extent to which the contemporary historical setting affected Frederick Jackson Turner's thinking about American history. Possibly the best way to introduce this question is to quote from an article written by C. Wood Davis in June, 1891.[88] Entitled "Some Impending Changes," it began:

> When we reflect that the prime factor in the unexampled prosperity of the United States, and our comparative freedom from many of the social and economic problems long confronting Europe, has been the existence of an almost unlimited area of fertile land to which the unemployed could freely resort; that, practically, such lands are now fully occupied, and that such occupancy has occasioned a sudden halt in the westward movement of population at the line found to be the extreme western limit of profitable agriculture, it may be well to inquire what changes are likely to result from the exhaustion of the tillable portion of the public domain.

After pointing to "the eagerness with which worthless tracts [Indian reservations] are contended for, by myriads of the landless," as complete proof of exhaustion, Davis noted:

> Heretofore, when the invention of a labor-saving device threw numbers of men out of employment, a portion, especially of the more thrifty, resorted to the public domain from which they proceeded to carve a farm, or bought the farms of others contemplating removal to the public lands, or in other cases, found employment in one of the many channels constantly being opened for labor in the improvement of the new States.

All this was now to be changed, and new opportunities no longer existed for laborer, capitalist, or railway projector. Of course, farmers and landowners were to achieve earthly paradise, and this is the justification for referring to Davis' optimistic agrarian panacea. Ultimately, however, the "unendurable

---

88. *Country Gentleman*, 56: 493, 513 (June 18, 25, 1891).

distress" of the growing army of unemployed proletarians would cause "social disturbances of grave significance." Malthus' pessimism, which did so much to enshroud political economy with its reputation as "the gloomy science," was essentially shared by his disciple in 1891, "in the absence of the safety-valve heretofore existing in the public domain." The dire results foreseen by Davis may be summed up in his prediction that with the safety valve gone, American uniqueness would disappear, the country would revert to much the same caste system as in Western Europe, and a great standing army would have to be created rather "than to support in pot-house idleness such elements as follow the lead of Johann Most."

Whether or not Turner read this analysis is not particularly crucial. No attempt is being made here to establish a direct Davis-Turner chain of reasoning. What is significant is that the ideas embodied in Davis' article did not represent an isolated and obscure episode in the intellectual history of the early nineties. On the contrary, they were a not uncommon version of a topic entering deep into the roots of contemporary American thought, a topic which in many guises was coming to engage the attention of ordinary and extraordinary citizens alike, in short, a topic that Turner as a literate man simply *had* to be familiar with—independent of any personal and immediate knowledge of C. Wood Davis of Sedgewick County, Kansas.

This contention appears to be eminently reasonable merely on the face of it, but more direct evidence can also be brought to bear upon the issue. For one thing, in 1888 the State Historical Society of Wisconsin, along with the University of Wisconsin Department of History, initiated a project to study organized immigration into Wisconsin. Reuben G. Thwaites, the corresponding secretary of the society, was most enthusiastic about the project, describing it as of "the utmost importance and significance."[89] And in an address before the historical society on January 28, 1891, Herbert Baxter Adams called the

---

89. Wisconsin State Historical Society, *Proceedings,* 36: 47 (Madison, 1889), and 37: 57-63 (1890).

study, "One of the most hopeful signs of the times in Wisconsin" and one that promised to yield "sociological results of profound interest not only to the State but to the whole country."[90]

Turner's historical essays written between 1891 and 1893 definitely reflect this interest in immigration, and they also reflect his concern with many of the contemporary themes discussed above. The effect of immigration upon America, the impact of America upon Europe, the influence of free land and the possible results of its exhaustion, and the breakdown of American commercial isolation, all were pointed to as demanding historical investigation.[91] Indeed, in 1891, Turner was so disturbed by scholarly inattention to immigration that he gloomily observed: "The story of the peopling of America has not yet been written. We do not understand ourselves."[92]

Particularly noteworthy in Turner's treatment is the striking similarity revealed in tone and emphasis of observations made upon the same themes by many of his contemporaries. Again no direct links between Turner and specific individuals will be attempted. Nonetheless, read in conjunction with the writings of David A. Wells, Horatio Seymour, Francis A. Walker, Josiah Strong, James Bryce, Shosuke Sato, C. Wood Davis, and Richmond Mayo-Smith (and a host of others might be appropriately named), little doubt remains, at least in my mind, that young Turner's early essays were permeated with polemical ideas *directly* stemming from his intellectual milieu.[93]

---

90. *Ibid.*, 38: 93-94 (1891).

91. *The Early Writings of Frederick Jackson Turner* (Madison, 1938), 60, 61-62, 63-64, 73-74, 78, 82, 83, 188, 229.

92. *Ibid.*, 64. One of the earliest dissertations done under his direction dealt with the migration of Germans to Wisconsin.

93. Cited above in footnotes 3, 19, 24, 30, 31, 34, 35, 86, and 88. The similarity with Richmond Mayo-Smith is not explicit as cited above. But the following quotation received considerable attention at the time. In essence it appeared on p. 418 of his 3-part article, "Control of Immigration," in the *Political Science Quarterly*, 3: 46-77, 197-225, 409-424 (Mar., June, Sept. 1888), but the version here given comes from his 1890 *Emigration and Immigration*, 56-57.

"It is scarcely possible to exaggerate the influence of the plentiful supply of land on the social history of this country. . . .

"Few people realize how this abundance of land has simplified all

Indeed, given Turner's philosophy of history at the time, it would have been almost impossible for any other development to have occurred. In 1891, in his essay on "The Significance of History," Turner stressed the dictum that *"Each age writes the history of the past anew with reference to the conditions uppermost in its own time."*[94]

That this dictum should be interpreted as evidence of Turner's "present-mindedness" appears to be strikingly confirmed by an undergraduate thesis written under his direction in 1894. Entitled, "The Effect of the Settlement of the Public Domain on Immigration,"[95] it was, in reality, a brief but earnest plea for restriction, based upon lessons supposedly drawn from history. Turnerian in spirit and in underlying assumptions, the thesis may be summarized as follows:

Macaulay emphasized the importance to America of large areas

---

social problems for us in this country. We have laughed at the fear of over-population,—that nightmare of the countries of Europe. There has always been room for the restless and energetic. When a man failed in the East he could go to the West. When trade became unprofitable, a man could take to agriculture. Our public land has been our great safety-valve, relieving the pressure of economic stress and failure. This enormous expansion has been due very largely to it."

Mayo-Smith's formulation clearly did not go unnoticed by scholars in the period. See the article by Davis R. Dewey, "Public Land of the United States," in R. H. Inglis Palgrave, ed., *Dictionary of Political Economy* (London, 1896), 2: 553-554.

94. Turner, *The Early Writings* . . . , 52.

95. Court Wayland Lamoreux's thesis submitted for the degree of bachelor of letters in the civic historical course, University of Wisconsin, 1894. Opposite the title page is the notation, "Approved: Frederick J. Turner, Professor of Am. Hist." I am indebted to Fulmer Mood of the University of Texas for his kindness in calling the thesis to my attention.

Lamoreux's thesis shows that a fair amount of work went into its composition, but it might really be called an oversized term paper. Almost every one of its 31 pages is stamped with unmistakable signs of Turner's influence. As such, the thesis offers an interesting sample of the interpretations placed upon Turner's teachings in 1894 by his students.

In this connection, it is interesting to note that Turner's frontier essay is not cited in the bibliography. Instead, the thesis gives the strong impression that it was based in large measure upon lecture notes taken in Turner's classes. For Turner's emphasis on the functional role of history, see *The Early Writings* . . . , 58-67.

of vacant land, and the resulting dangers to our institutions when the supply was exhausted. We are now at that stage, and must therefore re-examine the desirability of immigration. In the past immigration was a benefit. Sturdy yeomen coming in search of freedom were able to go to the public lands and carve out homes. The mighty West distributed and Americanized our foreign element, and acted as a safety valve for the restless and discontented.

Now our arable public land is practically gone. As a result, population is piling up in urban areas, particularly alien population, because immigrants no longer go to the West. *All writers* look with alarm at the swarming of Southern Europeans thronging to the cities. There, the new type of immigrant coming to our shores is extremely difficult to assimilate and presents a grave threat to our institutions. With the passing of the frontier we are entering upon a new era. If immigration does not stop of its own accord, we must adopt restrictive measures or we face the serious danger of losing our American nationality.

Of particular interest to us are the sources used by Court Wayland Lamoreux, the author of the thesis. Most of the writers discussed in the present article were drawn upon, and Lamoreux cited many of the works footnoted above. He freely employed the arguments, and indeed the phraseology, of Josiah Strong, Francis A. Walker, C. Wood Davis, Richmond Mayo-Smith, John W. Powell, and others—sometimes with due acknowledgment but more often not. The essential "present-mindedness" of Lamoreux's study is clearly revealed by its bibliography. Not a single reference antedated 1883, and the bulk of the references consisted of magazine articles written in the early nineties. Accordingly, the thesis reflects not only Turnerian inspiration, but the arguments of writers favoring immigration restriction, arid-land reclamation, Christian imperialism, agricultural prosperity, etc.

The fact that Turner "approved" the completed thesis does not, of course, constitute explicit evidence that he inspired, or endorsed, its sentiments. However, the circumstances strongly suggest that this was the case. In the first place, it was a logical topic for him to have assigned or approved—a topic flowing directly out of both his interest in immigration and the ideas expressed in his frontier essay of 1893. A close reading of

Lamoreux's thesis makes it obvious that the student was simply presenting material which confirmed his teacher's precepts— material in harmony with the frontier concept at every point. Moreover, the deductions drawn from this material were most logical, *if* the assumptions made by Turner in his essay were correct. Finally, and of considerable importance, the thesis is a clear application of the direct functional approach to history then subscribed to by Turner. The settlement of the public domain was being studied to prove the necessity for immigration restriction—the earnest redundancy with which the thesis urged such restriction brooks no other interpretation. Here, with a vengeance, was history being written "with reference to the conditions uppermost in its own time."

Additional support for this line of reasoning can be mustered. It is known that Turner was influenced by Francis A. Walker,[96] and written evidence exists that he read the *Review of Reviews*.[97] Both Walker and the *Review* were in the forefront of the immigration restriction battle and constantly used the land exhaustion argument. Moreover, their arguments favoring restriction were vigorously championed on the Wisconsin campus by Richard T. Ely, then Turner's colleague, friend, and former teacher. Upon coming to Wisconsin to head the newly created School of Economics, Political Science, and History—and Turner was largely instrumental in bringing him there—Ely took up the immigration question in his second formal seminar on September 28, 1892. Subsequent meetings discussed the topic in considerable detail, and Ely continually urged the need for restriction.[98]

---

96. Mood, in Colonial Society of Massachusetts, *Transactions*, 34: 295-303, 305-308, and in *Agricultural History*, 19: 24-30.

97. Turner to Ely, Mar. 14, 1892, in the Ely Collection, State Historical Society of Wisconsin.

98. Fortunately, Ely kept detailed notes on his seminars. See his Economic Seminary Notes, 1892-93, in the Ely Collection.

Ely's strong influence upon the intellectual life of the period is treated in Sidney Fine, "Richard T. Ely, Forerunner of Progressivism, 1880-1901," *Mississippi Valley Historical Review*, 37: 599-624 (Mar. 1951).

In reading the contemporary literature it is difficult to avoid the impression that most intellectuals operated in a fairly tight-knit orbit of ideas. One is continually struck by the repetition of core ideas in strik-

At a time when immigration commanded widespread interest, it is unlikely that he failed to discuss the topic with his colleague. Therefore, little doubt remains that before Turner wrote his frontier essay he was at least exposed to the contemporary arguments centering around the importance of the public domain. And the available evidence suggests that Turner essentially shared the opinions of Ely and Walker.

In this connection, it appears significant that one of the first scholars to voice approval of the frontier thesis was John Fiske, the first president of the Immigration Restriction League.[99] As the thesis written in 1894 by Turner's student shows, two separate but related arguments could be drawn from his teachings to support the restriction crusade. One, the exhaustion of the public domain, was in no sense original with Turner, having been used for that purpose since July, 1891. And, strictly speaking, neither was the argument which revolved around the beneficent qualities of the frontier. Richmond Mayo-Smith, at least as early as March 1888,[100] stated in print that immigrants no longer underwent the cleansing conditions of "frontier life." The frontier had enabled America to "digest almost anything sent to us," and purified even "the depraved dregs of European civilization." Furthermore, in earlier times, the difficulties of emigrating to America, resulted, according to him, in a kind of Darwinian "process of natural selection." Now, an undesirable class of foreigners was being aided, indeed encouraged, to emigrate. They congregated in large cities rather than going to the West, and were not being attracted "by the abundance of free land, but by the growth of the factory system, which gives it [this immigration] an entirely different character."

---

ingly similar phraseology. Indeed, a relatively small group of men seem to have set the intellectual tone of the era, and Ely was one of the elite.

99. "Turner's Autobiographical Letter," *Wisconsin Magazine of History*, 19: 96 (Sept. 1935).

100. Richmond Mayo-Smith, "Control of Immigration," *Political Science Quarterly*, 3: 46-77, 197-225, 409-424 (Mar., June, Sept. 1888). The four phrases here quoted are from p. 68, 413, 76, and 56 respectively. Mayo-Smith did not name Darwin, but he was clearly thinking along the lines suggested by the English scientist. See p. 61-62, 76-77. For his discussion of undesirable immigrants, see p. 61-77.

Prior to Turner's 1893 essay, it does not appear that the immigration restriction literature gave any prominence to the lessening impact of the frontier, although the congestion in the cities was frequently pointed to as refuting the need for immigrant labor in the West. But in September, 1894, Richmond Mayo-Smith, then a vice president of the Immigration Restriction League, returned to the theme.[101] By this time, he was even more forcibly impressed with the inherent possibilities of invoking the potent magic of the "frontier." Using language and examples that are quite reminiscent of Turner—so reminiscent in fact as to suggest strongly that he had read the frontier essay in the interim—Mayo-Smith paid tribute to the physical environment as an assimilating force and maintained:

The most powerful influence of this sort is, to my mind, what may be termed the 'frontier life,' which has been the peculiar factor in the development of this country. From the beginning the settlers have been obliged to carry on a persistent struggle with nature and with savage foes. . . . They developed a spirit of self-reliance, a

---

101. Richmond Mayo-Smith, "Assimilation of Nationalities in the United States," *Political Science Quarterly*, 9: 426-444, 649-670 (Sept., Dec. 1894). The quotation is from p. 439-441.

The close parallels between the two men suggest an interesting possibility. In view of the considerable prestige enjoyed by the *Political Science Quarterly* at the time, it is not difficult to believe that Turner read Mayo-Smith's articles in 1888. If he had, the latter might be said to have helped pave the way for the frontier essay, and in turn Mayo-Smith might well have been impressed with Turner's development of the frontier theme in 1893. One slight, but possibly significant, straw in the wind is the fact that in 1888 Mayo-Smith used the terms frontier and frontier life several times, and without quotation marks. However, in 1894, after Turner's essay was read and published, he wrote it this way, "frontier life." The introduction of quotation marks, along with definite similarities in language, and choice of examples, to Turner, would seem to give some basis for the speculation raised here.

In a letter dated Feb. 10, 1894, now in the Turner Collection, Houghton Library, Harvard University, Theodore Roosevelt wrote to Turner: "I have been greatly interested in your pamphlet, 'On the Frontier.' It comes at the right time for me, for I intend to make use of it in writing the third volume of my 'Winning of the West,' of course making full acknowledgement. I think you have struck some first class ideas, and have put into definite shape *a good deal of thought which has been floating around rather loosely* [italics added].

capacity for self-government, which are the most prominent characteristics of the American people. . . . Many of the immigrants have been subjected to this influence with precisely the same results as were felt by the original colonists. . . . [But] The frontier life is largely a thing of the past. The best land has been taken up. . . . In this respect the physical environment, as an assimilating power, is a diminishing force.

Increasingly thereafter, adherents of restriction struck these notes. Immigrants no longer underwent the purifying baptism of frontier life, and the public domain was gone; hence, the "new immigrants" settling in congested cities could not be assimilated, and constituted a grave menace to American institutions.[102]

Possibly one illustration will further demonstrate the neatness with which the frontier thesis fitted into the temper of the times and the ease with which its doctrines could become powerful ammunition in contemporary ideological warfare. With the Populist movement gathering strength as the debtor South and West tended to merge forces against the creditor Northeast, its opponents repeatedly charged that a "new sectionalism" was being fostered which threatened to sever national ties.[103] In the campaign year of 1896, after Bryan's nomination by the Democrats, the situation appeared to assume serious proportions, and excitement ran high.

Earlier in the year, Walter Hines Page, then editor of the *Atlantic Monthly*, had succeeded in getting Turner to promise him an article based upon the frontier essay. An alert editor, Page, after the Democratic convention, asked Turner to send his copy in time for September publication, urging that Bryan's nomination made the article "immensely more timely." Although reluctant as ever to be rushed into print, Turner finally yielded, admitting that "timeliness [is] everything."[104] Thus, the opening

102. Cyrus C. Adams, "Where Do the Immigrants Go?" *Chautauquan*, 23: 555 (Aug. 1896); John Chetwood, Jr., *Immigration Fallacies* (Boston, 1896), 15-16; Henry Pratt Fairchild, *Immigration* (New York, 1913), 373; Roy L. Garis, *Immigration Restriction* (New York, 1927), 204.

103. See, for example, Henry Litchfield West, "Two Republics or One?" *North American Review*, 162: 509-511 (Apr. 1896); William V. Allen, "Western Feeling Towards the East," *ibid.*, 162: 590 (May 1896).

104. Page to Turner, May 29, July 14, 24, Aug. 6, 1896, in the Turner Collection at Harvard.

paragraph of "The Problem of the West" reveals the extent to which Turner's early essays were often shaped by "present-mindedness."

> The problem of the West is nothing less than the problem of American development. A glance at the map of the United States reveals the truth. To write of a "Western sectionalism," bounded on the east by the Alleghanies is, in itself, to proclaim the writer a provincial. What is the West? What has it been in American life? To have the answers to these questions, is to understand the most significant features of the United States of to-day.[105]

H.
Resolving the "Frontier Issue"

In the previous essay, I pointed to the marked influence exercised upon Turner by the free-land system of Achille Loria, an Italian economist and sociologist enjoying considerable vogue

---

105. Frederick J. Turner, "The Problem of the West," *Atlantic Monthly*, 78: 289 (Sept. 1896). On p. 291 Turner referred to "an eminent Eastern man of letters," who had warned against the danger of the West. A handwritten note, inserted later by Turner on the printed copy of the article now in the Turner Collection at Harvard and eventually incorporated in the footnotes of his *Frontier* volume, indicates that he was referring to Charles Eliot Norton's article, "Some Aspects of Civilization in America," *Forum*, 20: 641-651 (Feb. 1896). Norton's article included a savage attack on the "ignorant and barbaric multitudes" of the frontier. "It is not only the ignorance of the foreign immigrant which is a danger to the commonwealth, but that also of the native-born who are on the outskirts or outside the pale of civilization." Could a redder flag have been dangled before Turner more calculated to arouse his Western patriotism?

One of the more important factors in the rapid acceptance of the frontier thesis appears to have been the neat way in which Turner's essay fitted into the contemporary political excitement. Thus Page wrote to Turner on Aug. 22, 1896: "The newspapers here are at once taking up your article for discussion—very favorably." Turner replied on Aug. 30 that he was sending Page a copy of an editorial in the Chicago *Tribune* "giving a western version of my Atlantic paper." The copy of this article in the Turner Collection at Harvard bears his handwritten comment: "See reviews, letters & editorials on this article in my folder on *Frontier in Am History* in Vilá docts FJT." Unfortunately, I have been unable to locate this folder.

in the early 1890's.[106] Loria's system represents the logical outcome of the manner in which European scholars treated "free
land." But the Italian's influence upon Turner must be understood against the background of the intellectual environment
in which the young Wisconsinite matured. In the light of the
homespun development of the "free-land" argument for polemical purposes, it would appear as if Turner's reading of Loria
in 1892 came as a stunning confirmation of all that he had been
groping for and all that he thought he saw around him. It
may, therefore, not be far off the mark to contend that the doctrines contained in Turner's early essays are attributable to three
specific factors: his acquaintance with Loria's free-land theory
of history; the pronounced impact upon him of the contemporary
setting; and his own particular development, owing to prior
training and deep-felt emotional attachment to the West.[107]

In 1945, Fulmer Mood leveled sharp criticism at the failure
of historians to end the professional uncertainty regarding the
validity of Turner's teachings. His plea was for historians to
"concentrate on the main professional obligation of the times,
namely the resolving of the frontier issue."[108] Surely, no one
will deny that the ideas contained in Turner's frontier essay
constitute, even yet, the most seminal thesis in American historiography. Just as surely, if the conclusions advanced in this
essay have merit, Mood was correct, and we must subject the
frontier thesis to a thorough and most searching re-evaluation.[109]

---

106. In that essay, the assertion is made that Turner's frontier hypothesis as formulated in his early essays contained six specific propositions.
The validity of that assertion can best be judged if the essay on Loria is
read along with the present one.

107. The best account of Turner's development is Mood's article in
the Colonial Society of Massachusetts, *Transactions*, 34: 283-352. See also
"Turner's Autobiographical Letter," *Wisconsin Magazine of History*, 19:
91-103 (Sept. 1935).

108. Mood, in *Agricultural History*, 19: 30.

109. To the best of my knowledge, there has never been a detailed
statement of the changing role that land has played as a factor of production in the economics of American agriculture from colonial days until
recent times. In fact, even the impact of "free land" upon American society has never been closely examined.

If the historical literature which describes in glowing terms the beneficent effects of "free land" is closely examined, it becomes obvious that the authors are simply making generalized assertions upon the subject, or depending upon other authors' generalizations. And yet, in view of the polemical setting in which "free land" worked itself into American historical literature, any generalizations upon the subject need to be treated with the gravest caution.

Another dubious generalization holds that the overwhelming, and relatively rapid, acceptance of Turner's thesis proves he was right—or at any rate, that he reflected the inner thinking of the American people. If the American people—as distinct from American historians—ever did come to accept the "closed-space" argument, and again no one has ever really investigated this subject, then it should be recognized that large doses of high-flown oratory and purple prose were necessary to produce such conviction.

One of the most promising signs that generalizations concerning "free land" are at last being subjected to systematic investigation appears in Thomas Le Duc, "The Disposal of the Public Domain on the Trans-Mississippi Plains: Some Opportunities for Investigation," *Agricultural History*, 24: 199-204 (Oct. 1950).

Part Three

$\mathcal{A}$ CRITIQUE OF BEARD
AND HIS CRITICS

Chapter One

BEARD'S MAIN HYPOTHESIS

◇◇

THE FIRST SENTENCE of *An Economic Interpretation of the Constitution of the United States* launched an attack upon the "three schools of interpretation that have dominated American historical research and generalization."[1] To stimulate historians to re-examine the American past, Charles A. Beard wrote a critique that was tactful, generous, incisive—and, in the end, devastating.[2] But, when he ventured into uncharted areas

---

1. All citations refer to the edition published in 1935 by the Macmillan Company (New York), which, except for a new introduction, is identical with the one published in 1913. It will be cited below as: Charles A. Beard, *Economic Interpretation*.

2. *Ibid.,* 1-4, 7-10.

and proposed an alternative interpretation, he became ambiguous and confusing. Why? To answer that question, our critique begins with an examination of the dualism in Beard's thought.[3]

A.

The Dualism in Beard's Thought

American historians, Beard argued, ought not "to reject without examination any new hypothesis, such as the theory of economic determinism," merely because of its origin in social antagonism or because of the "prevalence of many mere preconceptions bolstered with a show of learning. . . ."[4] He observed that "almost the only work in economic interpretation which has been done in the United States seems to have been inspired at the University of Wisconsin by Professor Turner," and he explicitly indicated that his own study would test the theory of history which was summarized and effectively brought to the attention of American scholars by Edwin R. A. Seligman of Columbia University:

Although the hypothesis that economic elements are the chief factors in the development of political institutions has thus been used in one or two serious works, and has been more or less discussed as a philosophic theory,[2] it has not been applied to the study of American history at large—certainly not with that infinite de-

---

3. In a stimulating essay, Richard Hofstadter has called attention to the "undercurrent of ambiguity in Beard's book." First published in 1950, the essay, "Charles Beard and the Constitution," has conveniently been reprinted in Howard K. Beale, ed., *Charles A. Beard: An Appraisal* (Lexington, Ky., 1954), 75-92. In contrast, Forrest McDonald maintains that Beard's book presented a "tightly and skillfully woven system of ideas." See his, *We The People: The Economic Origins of the Constitution* (Chicago, 1958), 6.

Students in all disciplines face the delicate problem of developing an attitude appropriate to the process of absorbing the contributions of predecessors while trying to advance beyond them. I hope that the tone of this essay reflects my great respect for Beard's contribution to American historiography.

4. Beard, *Economic Interpretation*, 4-6.

tailed analysis which it requires. . . . The theory of economic determinism has not been tried out in American history, and until it is tried out, it cannot be found wanting. Footnote 2 reads: "See Seligman, *The Economic Interpretation of History*."[5]

Impressed by his colleague's book, Beard, then at Columbia, complimented it highly:

The theory of the economic interpretation of history as stated by Professor Seligman seems as nearly axiomatic as any proposition in social science can be: "The existence of man depends upon his ability to sustain himself; the economic life is therefore the fundamental condition of all life. Since human life, however, is the life of man in society, individual existence moves within the framework of the social structure and is modified by it. What the conditions of maintenance are to the individual, the similar relations of production and consumption are to the community. To economic causes, therefore, must be traced in the last instance those transformations in the structure of society which themselves *condition the relations of social classes* [italics added] and the various manifestations of social life."[6]

We can suggest the ambiguity and confusion in Beard's argument by posing these questions: How could Beard have hailed Seligman's statement of the theory, titled his own book *An Economic Interpretation* . . . , and then called upon American historians to test "the theory of *economic determinism* [italics added]? How could he have used "economic interpretation" and "economic determinism" interchangeably throughout the first chapter which stated the book's objective and set its tone?

I. SELIGMAN AND THE ECONOMIC INTERPRETATION OF HISTORY; LORIA AND ECONOMIC DETERMINISM

In his introduction, Seligman noted that the "economic interpretation" of history differed significantly from "economic determinism." Moreover, in a chapter entitled "Freedom and Necessity," he elaborated on their differences and attempted to

---

5. *Ibid.*, 6-7.
6. *Ibid.*, 15, n. 1.

answer criticisms that "the theory of economic interpretation is a fatalistic theory, opposed to the doctrine of free will and overlooking the importance of great men in history; . . . [and] that it rests on the assumption of 'historical laws' the very existence of which is open to question. . . ." He then summarized his argument:

It is, therefore, an obviously incorrect statement of the problem to assert that the theory of economic interpretation, or the theory of social environment of which it is a part, is incompatible with the doctrine of free will. If by determinism we erroneously mean moral fatalism, determinism is not involved at all. *To call the general doctrine "economic determinism" as is occasionally done in France, is therefore essentially erroneous* [italics added]. The theory of social environment in no way implies fatalism. Social arrangements are human arrangements, and human beings are, in the sense indicated, free to form decisions and to make social choices; but they will invariably be guided in their decisions by the sum of ideas and impressions which have been transmitted to them through inheritance and environment. . . . To the extent, then, that the theory of economic interpretation is simply a part of the general doctrine of social environment, the contention that it necessarily leads to an unreasoning fatalism is baseless. Men are the product of history, but history is made by men.

In his chapter, "Freedom and Necessity," Seligman warned readers against the fallacy of iron laws of history; later he warned them against "Exaggerations of the Theory." "We must distinguish here," he observed, "as in every other domain of human inquiry, between the use and the abuse of a principle."[7] His choice of examples can perhaps be attributed to his role in having brought Achille Loria's work to the attention of American scholars. Since Loria's work had remarkable impact upon them after 1890,[8] Seligman may have felt obliged to single out

---

7. Edwin R. A. Seligman, *The Economic Interpretation of History* (New York, 1902), 3-4, 98-99, 135-145. The most illuminating and suggestive discussion that I have found of the differences between "economic determinism" and what Seligman called "economic interpretation," is an article by Sidney Hook, "Materialism," in Edwin R. A. Seligman, ed., *Encyclopedia of the Social Sciences* (New York, 1942), 10: 209-220.

8. See Part One of the present book.

his rigidly determinist version of the "general theory of economic interpretation" as an example of harmful exaggeration:

It is indeed a fact that some of the enthusiastic advocates of economic interpretation have claimed too much, or have advanced explanations which are, for the present at least, not susceptible of proof. Thus the most brilliant of the Italian economists—Achille Loria—has published a number of books in which he has attempted to interpret a vast mass of historical phenomena from the economic point of view. Many of his statements are correct, and have been successfully defended against the attacks of his critics; but some of his explanations are obviously unsatisfactory. *Above all he has laid too much stress upon the influence of land in modern society* [italics added] and has thus, in some cases, injured rather than aided the general theory of economic interpretation, of which only the particular application—even if an admirably suggestive one—is original with him.[9]

Summarized briefly, Loria's theory claimed that the presence or absence of "free land" determined the course of all human history.[10] As we have seen in the first essay, his "landed theory of profit" assumed the existence of an "inevitable antagonism between capitalistic profits and land rent," and provided the theoretical foundations for Turner's "frontier thesis" and the Wisconsin studies in "economic interpretation,"[11] upon which Beard depended so heavily. According to Loria, the reader will recall, this theory accounted for all American political conflicts:

. . . not only the platforms, but also the ends and aims of the American political parties are essentially economic in character. It is a perfectly well-known fact that the Republican party of the United States, which upholds federalism and protection, is composed of the commercial and manufacturing classes; and that the free-trade and States-rights Democratic party recruits its ranks from the class of landed proprietors. The struggle between these two parties in thus essentially economic, since it corresponds exactly to the most important division of their revenues. The economic character of

---

9. Seligman, *Economic Interpretation of History*, 135-136, 149-150, n. 1.

10. Achille Loria, "The Landed Theory of Profit," *Quarterly Journal of Economics*, 6: 108-109 (October 1891).

11. See Part One of the present book.

American political parties is, indeed, so marked that we see them change whenever social conditions or the interests of their members are altered in any way.[12]

This statement by Loria illustrates the two main versions of economic determinism. The cruder version asserts that egoism invariably controls human behavior; the less crude version steers clear of egoism, only to crack up on fatalism. Remarkably anti-historical in concept, it postulates essentially invariant relationships between economic and non-economic phenomena. Once the magic formula that explains all human behavior and all social relationships has been found (Loria's "free land" formula is the perfect example), application to specific times, places, and problems becomes a routine research exercise. The anti-historical nature of economic determinism is apparent in Loria's paraphrase of Hegel: "America offers the key to the historical enigma which Europe has sought for centuries in vain, and the country that has no history reflects and reveals luminously the mystery of universal history."[13] Little wonder that Seligman singled out Loria for critical attention in his chapter defending the theory of economic interpretation . . . [against] absurd exaggerations."

And yet, despite Seligman's warning against exaggerations of the Lorian type in particular and against fatalistic theories of history in general, and despite Beard's characterization of Seligman's statement "as [being as] nearly axiomatic as any proposition in social science can be," Beard continued to use "economic interpretation" and "economic determinism" interchangeably. Moreover, his periodic emphasis upon *economic* conflicts between agrarians and non-agrarians strongly indicates that he was influenced by Loria, both directly and indirectly via Turner's "frontier" version of the "free land" theory of history.[14] Thus, Beard's ideas did not derive from a consistent

---

12. Achille Loria, *The Economic Foundations of Society*, trans. Lindley M. Keasbey (London, 1899), 155.

13. Quoted above pp. 39-40.

14. The evidence that Beard was familiar with Loria's work is discussed in n. 25 below.

general theory; they derived from contradictory concepts, some taken from "economic determinism" and some from "economic interpretation." Inevitably, as a result of this unresolved dualism, his treatment of the Constitution was ambiguous and confusing.

B.
Madison and the Theory of Economic Determinism

The strand of economic determinism in Beard's thought dominated his treatment of Madison's *Federalist* No. 10. Avowedly trying to win a fair hearing for a theory regarded as suspect because of its associations with European radicalism, he claimed in his first chapter that "our own Madison had formulated it, after the most wide-reaching researches in history and politics." To support his claim, he quoted Madison's now famous passages which asserted that protection of the "diversity in the faculties of men, from which the rights of property originate . . . is the first object of government"; "The most common and durable source of [political] factions has been the various and unequal distribution of property"; "The regulation of these various and interfering [property] interests forms the principal task of modern legislation, and involves the spirit of party and faction in the necessary and ordinary operations of the government." In Q.E.D. fashion, Beard then concluded:

Here we have a masterly statement of the theory of economic determinism in politics. . . . Those who are inclined to repudiate the hypothesis of economic determinism as a European importation must, therefore, revise their views, on learning that one of the earliest, and certainly one of the clearest, statements of it came from a profound student of politics who sat in the Convention that framed our fundamental law.[15]

_____

15. Beard, *Economic Interpretation*, 13-16.

Beard's footnote to that paragraph illustrates the dualism in his thought, for it was there that he hailed Seligman's statement of the economic interpretation of history as "nearly axiomatic." That is, Beard quoted Madison in the text and Seligman in the note as though they were expounding the same theory of history. Actually, they differed radically. Madison sketched an essentially fatalistic theory of politics which conceived of social conflict as rooted in the "diversity in the faculties of men," the egoistic "self-love" unalterably "sown in the nature of man," and the "propensity of mankind to fall into mutual animosities"; Seligman presented a theory of man in society which tried to deal with all aspects of human behavior and which stressed the historically evolving "relations of social classes," as conditioned by "transformations in the structure of society."[16]

Probably because he did not recognize the radical differences between Madison and Seligman, Beard selected quotations that exaggerated their differences. As Robert E. Brown has recently emphasized, Beard omitted a section from Madison that identified non-economic sources of political conflict and that claimed, "So strong is this propensity of mankind to fall into mutual animosities, that where no substantial occasion presents itself, the most frivolous and fanciful distinctions have been sufficient to kindle their unfriendly passions and excite their most violent conflicts." Unlike Professor Brown who implies that Beard's omission of the section was designed "to make Madison an 'economic determinist,'" I believe that, at most, Beard's omission should be attributed to intellectual confusion.[17]

Madison did identify some non-economic sources of political conflict, but his theory essentially rested upon fatalistic, static assumptions of unchanging egoistic behavior and uneven distribution of "faculties." In his view, men belonging to different interest groups act politically in strict accord with calculations of cash benefits. He cited various examples of "clashing inter-

16. Compare Madison in Charles Beard, ed., *The Enduring Federalist* (Garden City, N. Y., 1948), 68-75, with Seligman, *Economic Interpretation of History*, 1-4, *passim*.

17. Robert E. Brown, *Charles Beard and the Constitution* (Princeton, N. J., 1956), 27-32, 92, 195; Beard, ed., *Enduring Federalist*, 70.

ests" likely to produce factions which could be *controlled* only by a well-designed, strong government. Of them, perhaps the following one best illustrates his idea of the relations between self-interest and political action:

The apportionment of taxes on the various descriptions of property is an act which seems to require the most exact impartiality; yet there is, perhaps, no legislative act in which greater opportunity and temptation are given to a predominant party to trample on the rules of justice. Every shilling with which they overburden the inferior number, is a shilling saved to their own pockets.[18]

Perhaps Beard was not justified in omitting the section in *Federalist* No. 10 which identified non-economic sources of political faction, but he was justified in stating that Madison advanced an economic determinist theory of politics. His omission is revealing, however, and it helps us to understand both his general intellectual outlook and his specific equation of Madison with Seligman. Since Beard could not have been expected to quote a seven-page article in full, his inclusions and exclusions indicate the relative importance he attached to the various arguments presented in *Federalist* No. 10. This deduction is particularly convincing when we consider his general intellectual outlook during the 1910's.

1. THE "PROGRESSIVE" VIEW OF "REALITY"

What we now know about Beard's sympathies, associations, and activities before 1913, supports Richard Hofstadter's observation that Beard could hardly have failed "to absorb the style of thought of the Populist-Progressive-muckraking era. . . ." At bottom, Hofstadter observed, reality had three characteristics for Progressive thinkers: "It was rough and sordid; it was hidden, neglected, and, so to speak, off-stage; and it was essentially a stream of external and material events, of which psychic events were a kind of pale reflex."[19]

---

18. Quoted in *Ibid.*, 70-71.
19. Richard Hofstadter, in Beale, ed., *Charles Beard*, 77-87. See the other essays in that volume for confirmation of Hofstadter's analysis, particularly in Howard K. Beale's discussion of, "Charles Beard: Historian."

If we agree that Beard accepted this view of reality, and if we recognize that Loria's theory of "free land" inspired the "work in economic interpretation" at Wisconsin, we can better understand how Beard came to equate Madison's views with Seligman's. Strongly influenced by his own general intellectual outlook and his own specific attitudes towards contemporary conflicts, Beard could have concluded that both men had uncovered the "reality" underlying all politics and had shown him how to go beyond the "vague abstractions [which now] dominate most of the thinking that is done in the field of law."[20] Put another way, a Progressive-minded historian, hot on the elusive trail of past reality, could have read his own preconceptions into Seligman's book. For, in his "final estimate," Seligman claimed that the theory of economic interpretation had done much for economics, but

. . . it has done even more for history. *It has taught us to search below the surface* [italics added]. . . . It is for this reason that history is nowadays at once far more fascinating and immeasurably more complicated than was formerly the case. History now seeks to gauge the influence of factors some of which turn out to be exceedingly elusive. It attempts to introduce into the past the outlines of a social science whose very principles have not yet been adequately and permanently elaborated.[21]

Viewed through Progressive eyes, the economic interpretation of history might well have appeared to be a "philosophical theory" that demolished meaningless abstractions and tautologies and that helped scholars discover in past reality what contemporary "inside-dopesters" were discovering in present reality:[22] namely, that ideas were a direct reflex of interests, and that allegedly impartial appeals to "justice," or to abstract

---

For a perceptive analysis from which I partially dissent, see Douglass Adair, "The Tenth Federalist Revisited," *William and Mary Quarterly*, 3rd ser., 8: 48-67 (January, 1951).

20. Beard, *Economic Interpretation*, p. 8. His first chapter abounds with phrases such as "the abstract stuff known as justice," "vague abstractions," "adherence to abstract terms," "law is not an abstract thing," and suggests the extent of his commitment to the view that the demolition of "abstractions" was necessary to the reconstruction of "reality."

21. Seligman, *Economic Interpretation of History*, 163-164.

constitutional "principles," or to the "advancement of general welfare," merely threw a cloak of rationalizations over naked economic conflicts.[23]

We find support for this reconstruction of Beard's thought in the omission from his first chapter of Madison's section on the non-economic sources of political faction. We need not rely upon selective inclusions and exclusions, however. More precise evidence is found in his later analysis and assessment of *The Federalist* as a whole. Conceding that the articles contained "much discussion of the details of the new frame-work of government, to which even some friends of reform took exceptions," Beard dismissed the details as unimportant and the discussions as glosses upon the basic argument. As he read them, "Madison and Hamilton both knew that these [details] were incidental matters when compared with the sound basis upon which the superstructure rested." His assessments of relative importance were unequivocal and single-minded:

. . . every fundamental appeal in it [*The Federalist*] is to some material and substantial interest . . . [various examples are given]. But above all, it is to the owners of personalty [i.e., non-landed property] anxious to find a foil against the attacks of levelling democracy, that the authors of *The Federalist* address their most cogent arguments in favor of ratification.[24]

From our previous observations about Beard's attitudes, it does not seem surprising that he should have seen the passages on property conflicts and interest groups as the inside story of the movement for the Constitution—the hard, material reality underlying the various arguments presented in all eighty-five *Federalist* articles.

For present purposes, it does not matter whether Beard correctly assessed either the contents of *The Federalist* or the convictions of its authors. Only two conclusions need be advanced here: 1) Contrary to Professor Brown's analysis, Beard did not

22. The "inside-dopester" term is borrowed from David Riesman; in my opinion, it is a neat description of the Progressive mind in action.

23. See the quotation from Beard on pp. 110-111 below, and his *Economic Interpretation*, 7-18.

24. *Ibid.*, 153-154, and 152-188.

ignore or conceal the non-economic arguments; he *dismissed* them as incidental and uninfluential. 2) He would not have presented such an economic determinist assessment of *The Federalist*, had he fully grasped Seligman's exposition of the economic interpretation of history. And, certainly, he would not then have cited Seligman's book as though it presented views similar to Madison's "masterly statement of the theory of economic determinism in politics."

I do not pretend to know exactly why Beard assessed *The Federalist* as he did, or why he did not fully understand Seligman's book. Nevertheless, it seems reasonable to believe that at least five factors affected what he saw in these works:

1. He had absorbed the Progressive style of thought, which severely discounted non-economic factors in explaining men's motives and actions.

2. He was predisposed to a theory of economic determinism by the contemporary American scene and the prevailing intellectual climate of opinion.

3. He was psychologically prepared to regard *Federalist* No. 10, in which Madison advanced an economic determinist theory of politics, as revealing the inner quality—"The true inwardness," as he put it, of the Fathers' thought.

4. Convinced that previous schools of American historiography were inadequate, and eager to replace them with a more "realistic" one, he believed that the Lorian theory of "free land" had thrown new light upon American development and that it derived from the Marxian theory of history that Seligman outlined, analyzed, and praised.[25]

---

25. After pointing to precursors, Seligman made Marx the real founder of the theory. But he drew a sharp distinction between Marx's theory of history which he praised highly, and his "scientific socialism" which he regarded as defective. *Economic Interpretation of History*, 16-56, *passim*. In the 1913 edition, Beard cited a number of European scholars who had contributed to the theory of history which he advocated testing, but avoided mentioning either Marx or Loria. In 1935, however, he conceded that "at the time this volume was written, I was, in common with all students who professed even a modest competence in modern history, conversant with the theories and writings of Marx." *Economic Interpretation*, xii-xiii. Apart from other considerations, Seligman's prominent role

5. For polemical purposes, as well as for the satisfaction of his own psychological needs, he wanted to find an early American statement of that theory and was, therefore, prepared to see Marx while reading Madison—and vice versa.

C.

The Strand of Economic Interpretation in Beard's Thought

Beard was not a straight-out economic determinist, but evidently he used the terms "economic determinism" and "economic interpretation" without fully grasping what either meant. Otherwise, he would not have confused Madison with Selig-

---

in bringing Loria to the attention of American scholars after 1890 makes it difficult for me to believe that Beard was not also acquainted with the Italian scholar's theories and writings in 1913. Compare, Beard, *The Economic Bases of Politics* (New York, 1922), with Part 3, "The Economic Foundations of Politics," in Loria, *Economic Foundations*. It seems significant that, trying to account for "how Turner happened to come upon his conception," Beard speculated that Loria was one of the "sources" from whom "Turner caught the glimpse which served as a guide to his work." Charles A. Beard, "Turner's 'The Frontier in American History,'" in Malcolm Cowley and Bernard Smith, eds., *Books That Changed Our Minds* (New York, 1940), 67-68.

Six months after I wrote the first draft of the present essay in California, I found documentary evidence in New York to support the earlier deduction that Beard was "acquainted with the Italian scholar's theories and writings in 1913." While charging out the Columbia University Library's copy of Loria, *The Economic Foundations of Society*, I happened to notice that the old-style charge card had been retained in the back flap. Unfortunately, the first entry was dated March 8, 1948, indicating that it was not the original card. However, by one of those "accidents" that transform routine historical research into an exciting adventure, the original charge card had been preserved in the French edition of Loria's book. It shows the initials, "CAB," next to the entry dated "7 Dec. 04"—appropriately enough, the volume was given to Columbia by "Prof. Seligman." That "CAB" stood for Charles Austin Beard seems reasonably certain. Among other things, the Columbia University *Catalogue and General Announcement, 1904-1905,* lists no other faculty member with those initials; Beard's name appears on p. 11.

man. Had Beard appreciated the differences between their theories, he would not have titled his book *An Economic Interpretation of the Constitution of the United States,* and then announced that he was going to test "the theory of economic determinism." And, had he believed that political actions were strictly determined by cash calculations, he would not have written this introduction to his inquiry into "The Economic Interests of the Members of the [Constitutional] Convention":

The purpose of such an inquiry is not, of course, to show that the Constitution was made for the personal benefit of the members of the Convention. Far from it. Neither is it of any moment to discover how many hundred thousand dollars accrued to them as a result of the foundation of the new government. The only point here considered is: Did they *represent distinct groups* [italics added] whose economic interests they understood and felt in concrete, definite form through their own personal experience with identical property rights, or were they working merely under the guidance of abstract principles of political science?[26]

After examining the individual property holdings and economic positions of the Convention delegates, he ended the chapter on this note:

It cannot be said, therefore, that the members of the Convention were "disinterested." On the contrary, we are forced to accept the profoundly significant conclusion that they knew through their personal experiences in economic affairs the precise results which the new government that they were setting up was designed to attain. As a group of doctrinaires, like the Frankfort assembly of 1848, they would have failed miserably; but as practical men they were able to build the new government upon the only foundations which could be stable: fundamental economic interests.[27]

While writing those passages, the strand of economic interpretation seems to have dominated Beard's thought. Though he overstated his case, (e.g., "precise results," "identical property rights") he clearly was praising the Founding Fathers as wise realists; he was not depicting them as egoists working solely or primarily for their own benefit. If those passages represented

---

26. Beard, *Economic Interpretation,* 73.
27. *Ibid.,* 151.

a position consistently adopted throughout the book, it could be argued that, in identifying the delegates' interests, he hoped to find a clue to their thinking and to demonstrate that their ideas did not spring from the nowhere of abstraction into the here of the United States, 1787. Beard could then be interpreted to have said that, as non-doctrinaires in touch with reality, the delegates' understanding of abstract principles of political science was informed by personal experience. As a result, they were able to build that "well-constructed Union," which Madison regarded as necessary to preserve Liberty and simultaneously to control the harmful effects of faction.

But the two passages that I have quoted did not stand alone. They are inconsistent with other passages. For example, two pages before Beard wrote that the Convention delegates were not doctrinaires, he wrote that "The overwhelming majority of members, at least five-sixths, were immediately, directly, and personally interested in the outcome of their labors at Philadelphia, and were to a greater or lesser extent economic beneficiaries from the adoption of the Constitution." He struck the same note of economic determinism in his final conclusions. "The members of the Philadelphia Convention which drafted the Constitution were, with a few exceptions, immediately, directly, and personally interested in, and derived economic advantages from the establishment of the new system."[28] Most significantly, as we shall see, he weighted his research design heavily in favor of documenting a direct, perceived relationship between economic interests and political ideas.

We must therefore agree with Professor Brown that Beard was inconsistent in his treatment of the Fathers' motives, as well as in his treatment of other problems which we shall take up later. No doubt, as Brown says, Beard "should have been more consistent."[29] Since he was not, however, his inconsistency must logically become the starting point of any instructive critique. For, if Beard's hypotheses are inconsistent, to demonstrate that *some* are in error, does not discredit them *all*.

28. *Ibid.*, 149, 324.
29. Brown, *Charles Beard*, 73.

D.
Beard's Questions and Hypotheses

Now that we have identified the dualism in Beard's thought, we can more easily identify his main hypothesis. A long extract from his first chapter helps us to do so:

It will be admitted without controversy that the Constitution was the creation of a certain number of men, and it was opposed by a certain number of men. Now, if it were possible to have an economic biography of all those connected with its framing and adoption —perhaps about 160,000 men altogether—the materials for scientific analysis and classification would be available. Such an economic biography would include a list of the real and personal property owned by all of these men and their families: lands and houses, with incumbrances, money at interest, slaves, capital invested in shipping and manufacturing, and in state and continental securities.

Suppose it could be shown from the classification of the men who supported and opposed the Constitution that there was no line of property division at all; that is, that men owning substantially the same amounts of the same kinds of property were equally divided on the matter of adoption or rejection—it would then become apparent that the Constitution had no ascertainable relation to economic groups or classes, but was the product of some abstract causes remote from the chief business of life—gaining a livelihood.

Suppose, on the other hand, that substantially all of the merchants, money lenders, security holders, manufacturers, shippers, capitalists, and financiers and their professional associates [all grouped by Beard under the heading, "personalty"] are to be found on one side in support of the Constitution and that substantially all or the major portion of the opposition came from the non-slaveholding farmers and the debtors—would it not be pretty conclusively demonstrated that our fundamental law was not the product of an abstraction known as "the whole people," but of a group of economic interests which must have expected beneficial results from its adoption? Obviously all the facts here desired cannot be discovered, but the data presented in the following chapters bear out the latter hypothesis, and thus a reasonable presumption in favor of the theory is created.

Of course, it may be shown (and perhaps can be shown) that the farmers and debtors who opposed the Constitution were, in fact, benefited by the general improvement which resulted from its adoption. It may likewise be shown, to take an extreme case, that the English nation derived immense advantages from the Norman Conquest and the orderly administrative processes which were introduced, as it undoubtedly did; nevertheless it does not follow that the vague thing known as "the advancement of general welfare" or some abstraction known as "justice" was the immediate, guiding purpose of the leaders in either of these great historic changes. The point is, that the direct, impelling motive in both cases was the economic advantages which the beneficiaries expected would accrue to themselves first, from their action. Further than this, economic interpretation cannot go. It may be that some larger world-process is working through each series of historical events; but ultimate causes lie beyond our horizon.[30]

This complex statement illustrates the confusion, ambiguity, and inconsistency in Beard's book. It illustrates also one of his major contributions to American historiography; while attempting to test a general theory of history, he *effectively* raised a set of significant questions and tried to answer them concretely in relation to a specific set of relevant historical events.

Restated in general terms, the extract from Beard shows that he raised questions about the *relationships* between men's membership in certain classes or groups and their ideas on a particular issue. It shows also that he raised questions about the *processes* by which men translate their ideas into action. For him, inquiry began with recognition of two sets of facts: first, that the system of government initiated by the Constitution replaced the system under the Articles of Confederation; second, that while some men favored the "great political transformation of 1787-89," others opposed it. From these elementary facts, he derived six sets of questions:

How did opinion on the Constitution divide, i.e., who favored it, who opposed it, who remained undecided, who remained indifferent? Did men holding similar opinions on the

---

30. Beard, *Economic Interpretation*, 16-18. Those pages sketched his design of proof and his method, as well as the hypothesis about the Constitution which he deduced from the theory of economic determinism.

issue tend to have some other attribute, or set of attributes, in common? Why did men hold certain opinions? What different roles did different men play in the sequence of events climaxed by the adoption of the Constitution? How did it come about that different men played such different roles? What changes did the Constitution bring about in the American system of government?[31]

I. CLEARING THE WAY FOR NEW HYPOTHESES

Beard designed his first hypothesis to clear the way for him to answer the questions he had raised. Those questions, he argued, had previously been either ignored or answered erroneously. Sharply critical of the constitutional histories by George

---

31. Two quotations are enough to suggest Beard's approach to the questions involved in studying the Constitution:

> In the adoption of the Constitution, says James Wilson, we have the gratifying spectacle of "a whole people exercising its first and greatest power—performing an act of sovereignty original and unlimited." Without questioning the statement that for juristic purposes the Constitution may be viewed as an expression of the will of the whole people, a historical view of the matter requires an analysis of "the people" into its constituent elements. In other words, how many of "the people" favored the adoption of the Constitution, and how many opposed it?

The economic determinist strand in Beard's thought is evident in the following formula for studying group divisions of opinion:

> As in natural science no organism is pretended to be understood as long as its merely superficial aspects are described, so in history no movement by a mass of people can be correctly comprehended until that mass is resolved into its component parts. To apply this concept to the problem before us: no mathematically exact conclusion can be reached concerning the material interests reflected in the Constitution until "the people" who favored its adoption and "the people" who opposed it are individualized and studied as economic beings dependent upon definite modes and processes of gaining a livelihood. A really fine analytical treatment of this problem would, therefore, require a study of the natural history of the (approximately) 160,000 men involved in the formation and adoption of the Constitution; but for the present we must rely on rougher generalizations, drawn from incomplete sources.

Ibid., 239, 253. On pp. 217-218, the movement is described as the "great political transformation."

Bancroft and G. T. Curtis, he was also critical of "the juristic theory of the origin and nature of the Constitution [which] is marked by the same lack of analysis of determining forces which characterized older historical writing in general . . . [he cites examples from George Bancroft and Chief Justice Marshall]. In the juristic view, the Constitution is not only the work of the whole people, but it also bears in it no traces of the party conflict from which it emerged."[32]

By rejecting the legal abstraction that the Constitution was "the work of the whole people," Beard was logically required to determine the actual division of opinion on the issue. Directed towards that problem, his next hypothesis asserted that the divisions were not random; men holding similar opinions on the issue also shared some other attributes or set of attributes. Implicit in the original text, the hypothesis was made more explicit in his introduction to the 1935 edition.

In the introduction to that edition, Beard conceded that older historians, such as Hildreth and Marshall, had recognized that the divisions of opinion were not random but were related to clashing economic interests. His concession, it deserves note, substantially modified his comments of 1913 about Marshall's other-worldly, juristic view of the Constitution. But, he went on to argue, "during the closing years of the nineteenth century this *realistic* [italics added] view of the Constitution had been largely submerged in abstract discussions of states' rights and national sovereignty and in formal, logical, and discriminative analyses of judicial opinions. It was admitted, of course, that there had been a bitter conflict over the formation and adoption of the Constitution; but the struggle was usually explained, if explained at all, by reference to the fact that some men cherished states' rights and others favored central government."[33]

Beard asserted that, two decades after the publication of his study, one of his critics had resurrected the tautology that he

32. *Ibid.*, 10-12.
33. *Ibid.*, vi-vii.

had originally set out to destroy. The "view . . . expressed recently by Professor Theodore Clark Smith" simply reasserted the view prevailing at "the time I began my inquiries. . . ." Moralistic and value-laden, it begged the question and substituted epithets for analysis and explanation. Convinced in 1913 that the struggle over the Constitution could not be satisfactorily explained "as a contest between sections ending in a victory of straight-thinking national-minded men over narrower and more local opponents," Beard saw no reason in 1935 to change his thinking. He again rejected the hypothesis that "makes the conflict over the Constitution purely psychological in character . . . [and] assumes that straight-thinking and national-mindedness are entities, particularities, or forces, apparently independent of all earthly considerations coming under the head of 'economic.' "[34]

Although Beard stated his position more explicitly in 1935, by 1913, he had already rejected the view that the "whole people" created the Constitution and that men could be differentiated only by their opinions on the issue. To fill the resulting intellectual void, he advanced several vaguely-formulated hypotheses to explain "How some men got to be 'national-minded' and 'straight-thinking,' and others became narrow and local in their ideas. . . ." In effect, these hypotheses provide answers to the first three questions posed on pages 111-112. The first set dealt with the numerical divisions of opinion (including no opinion); the second with the group membership of men holding different opinions; the third with the content of opinion (such as, the motives for holding it, the intensity with which it is held, knowledge of issue, propensity for action).

2. NUMERICAL DIVISIONS OF OPINION

In his first positive hypothesis, Beard asserted that approximately 160,000 of the country's adult white males took part in

---

34. *Ibid.,* ix-x.

the creation of the Constitution.[35] In related, but vague hypotheses, he asserted that, of the men who did not take part, a considerable proportion . . . [were] debarred from participating in the elections of delegates to the ratifying state conventions by the prevailing property qualifications on the suffrage," and that "Far more were disfranchised through apathy and lack of understanding of the significance of politics."[36] Thus, Beard identified three types of men who did not participate: 1) the legally "disfranchised" who had no opportunity to decide whether they wanted to vote; 2) the "franchised" who may have known something about the issue but remained indifferent to the result; and 3) the "franchised" who lacked information about the issue and did not understand what it involved and how it affected them.

Beard presented other hypotheses about the numerical divisions of opinion; these referred to men who played some active role in the contest over the Constitution. In the country as a whole, voters divided approximately five to three in favor of ratification (about 100,000 Federalists to about 60,000 Antifederalists).[37] That hypothesis is clear, but his hypotheses about the divisions of opinion in the individual states are vague, unsystematic, and incomplete.

3. DIVISIONS OF OPINION AMONG GROUPS

Despite his casual references throughout the book to groups differentiated by ethnic, religious, social, and political attributes, Beard, in his second set of hypotheses, identified men only in economic terms. Unfortunately, even with attention restricted to economic attributes, he did not develop a system of classification that would have permitted him to arrange men in economic categories that were logically distinct and included all "classes and social groups" in the United States during the 1780's. But an observation that applies to his book generally

35. *Ibid.,* 249-250.
36. *Ibid.,* 240-242.
37. *Ibid.,* 243-251, 253-291.

applies specifically to his contribution here: He recognized that a problem existed and set to work upon it—always the two most difficult phases of any intellectual enterprise:

> The importance of a survey of the distribution of property in 1787 for economic as well as political history is so evident that it is strange that no attempt has been made to undertake it on a large scale. Not even a beginning has been made. It is, therefore, necessary for us to rely for the present upon the general statements of historians who have written more or less at length about the period under consideration. . . .[38]

Like all pioneers forced to work on tough problems with poor tools, Beard did not get far. Apart from the effect of the unresolved dualism in his thought, his book suffered from his rudimentary system of classification, the low-grade quality of the data he extracted from secondary sources to fill its categories, and his inability to apply the system rigorously. A balanced appraisal of Beard's work, however, must recognize that many of the shortcomings in his book reflected the very shortcomings in American historiography which he delineated. Scholars can advance beyond their predecessors; they cannot escape them.

As the long extract from Beard's first chapter indicates (pp. 110-111 above), his system of economic classification established two main categories: the *amount* of property, and the *kind* of property. In dealing with the first one, he was especially ambiguous and inconsistent. Apparently, he differentiated primarily between holders of "large" amounts of property and holders of "small" amounts, disregarding the possibility that some large holders may have owed debts, and some small holders may have owned their property, free and clear. Beard grouped together all large holders and differentiated them from all small holders. If I have understood him correctly, he intended the term "debtors" to refer only to men who, at most, held relatively small amounts of property. Indications exist that he also intended to differentiate among large and small property holders by geographic section, and by residence in rural or urban area.

---

38. *Ibid.,* 19.

Less ambiguous about the kinds of property, Beard described them as "personalty" and "realty," or, in more traditional terms, "capital as opposed to land." In turn, he divided these groupings into a considerable number of others which partially overlapped still others that belong under the heading, "amount of property." For example, at times he seemed to use "small farmer" and "debtor" as synonyms; at other times, he used them to identify men who belonged to separate economic groups.

It is significant that Beard's categories, "personalty" and "realty," did not correspond to the "various and interfering interests" that Madison described as forming "the most common and durable source[s] of [political] factions."[39] They did correspond almost exactly, however, to the groups that Loria identified when he discussed "the bipartition of revenue and sovereignty." More specifically, Beard could have derived his categories from Loria's notion that the American party system expressed "the inevitable antagonism between capitalistic profits and rent."[40]

For our purposes, it is not particularly important whether Loria inspired Beard's categories. What is important is that Madison did not inspire them. The system of classification Beard used did not follow Madison's description of the "interests" that "divide . . . [nations] into different classes, actuated by different sentiments and views." And, had Beard followed Madison, he would have given less emphasis to conflicts between "groups of personal property interests" and "groups of real property holders."[41]

Accurate restatement of Beard's claims about the division of opinion among economic groups is difficult for two main reasons:

1) He did not apply his system of classification rigorously. If he had, he would have been forced to deal with an unwieldy number of distinct groups. But he did not try to do so. Among

---

39. *Ibid.,* 19-51, 63, *passim;* Beard, ed., *Enduring Federalist,* 70.
40. Loria, *Economic Foundations,* 153-155.
41. Beard, *Economic Interpretation,* 26, 31.

other groups that appear in his book only fleetingly—and confusingly—are: seaboard small farmers, northern large landowners outside of New York, speculators in eastern lands, small holders of "personalty" (e.g., mechanics, shopkeepers), and urban "working-men." Moreover, some of the terms he used make it hard to decide to whom he was referring, e.g., "money lenders," "capitalists," "financiers."

2) Beard apparently did not have his claims clearly in mind. Thus, it is hard to tell what political position he assigned to some of the economic groups he identified (either in the country at large or in specific states), or what proportion of each group he assigned to the three main positions (Federalist, Antifederalist, voluntary non-voter).

Nevertheless, although it is difficult to restate Beard's claims accurately, it is not impossible. The statements that follow are necessarily somewhat arbitrary and vague, but they present his hypotheses with reasonable accuracy.

Of the country's adult free white males, about 75 per cent did not take part in the political conflict over the Constitution. About one-third of the 75 per cent lacked sufficient property to meet the requirements for suffrage in the several states.[42] Most of the men who met the requirements but who failed to vote were small farmers and rural artisans, particularly ones who lived in interior areas with poor access to polling places and with poor sources of information. Apparently, Beard thought that many voluntary non-voters might also be found among other groups. But his comments are too fragmentary to permit specific estimates. He evidently thought, however, that the most active participants were well-to-do men who lived in seaboard cities, large towns, "or the more thickly populated areas," especially holders of public securities and men interested in "commercial regulations advantageous to personalty operations in shipping and manufacturing and in western land speculations."[43]

Of the eligible voters who effectively expressed their opin-

---

42. This estimate is discussed below on pp. 176-177.
43. Beard, *Economic Interpretation*, 27, 50-51, 64, 251-252.

ions on the Constitution, Beard claimed, the following groups gave overwhelming majorities to the Federalists: holders of state and national securities, money lenders, financiers, capitalists seeking outlets for investment (including speculators in western lands), merchants, shippers, manufacturers, professional associates and dependents of all the above groups of "personalty interests," franchised mechanics and "working-men" in the seaboard cities and large towns, slaveholders who "combined a wide range of personalty operations with their planting," and, to a somewhat lesser extent, planters not engaged in such operations. If we take into account observations made two years later in his *Economic Origins of Jeffersonian Democracy*, we can infer also that Beard believed seaboard small farmers gave some support to the Federalists. Finally, although he admittedly could not explain their behavior, he noted that the small farmers of the Shenandoah Valley in Virginia almost unanimously supported the Federalists.[44]

Beard claimed that *small-scale* rural and urban debtors, i.e., relatively poor men who found it difficult to repay their debts, gave overwhelming majorities to the Antifederalists. Although small debtor-farmers who lived in the interior and did not own slaves gave particularly strong support to the Antifederalists, small farmers in general gave them substantial majorities. Moreover, in the South, "powerful and popular men who have speculated deeply in British confiscated property . . ." gave the Antifederalists considerable support. Finally, the landed proprietors of the Hudson Valley voted en masse for them.[45]

4. A "MEMORANDUM OF CORRECTION" AND ITS IMPLICATIONS

Beard's ambiguous statements have forced me to use imprecise terms in restating his claims, but they at least suggest the relative strength of the two parties among the economic groups he identified. One thing is fairly clear. Despite vague indications

---

44. *Ibid.*, 29-51, 282-283, 290-292; Charles A. Beard, *Economic Origins of Jeffersonian Democracy* (New York, 1915), 2-3.

45. *Ibid.*, 2-3; Beard, *Economic Interpretation*, 27-29, 127-129, 283, 291.

that some divisions existed within these groups, his descriptions in 1913 and 1915 both suggested that, in most cases, "substantially all" the members of a group held the same opinion on the Constitution. But his introduction in 1935 contained a brief "memorandum of correction" that modified his claims about "class-solidarity" and had far-reaching implications for many of his hypotheses and for his book as a whole:

> Page 29 [of his text] may be taken to imply that the "landed aristocracy" of New York was *solidly* opposed to the Constitution, leaving no room for exceptions. Seldom, if ever, is there total class-solidarity in historical conflicts, and Doctor Thomas C. Cochran is entirely right in objecting to the implied generalization [in a monograph published in 1932]. He properly calls attention to the fact that "while the 'Manor Lords' feared land taxes they also held public securities to an extent which made many of them favorable to the establishment of adequate [federal] revenue. Thus while the strength of the Anti-Federalists rested on the landed classes, the most powerful of these landlords were often found in the opposition ranks." Hence, although his interpretation is economic, it corrects a generalization too sweeping in character, and should be properly noted.[46]

Beard apparently failed to recognize the implications of his memorandum of correction. If he was mistaken in his original assumptions and the landed proprietors of New York were members simultaneously of "realty" and "personalty" groups, might not other men also have had diversified, "conflicting" interests? If the landed proprietors failed to display "total class-solidarity," might not divisions of opinion also exist in other groups? For example, might not members of the same economic group agree on objectives but disagree on methods for attaining them? Or, might not members of the same group have conflicting interests, e.g., farmers in different areas competing for the same markets, merchants in different areas competing for the same trade? According to the assumptions of an *economic determinist* interpretation, wouldn't they, therefore, hold opposite opinions on the Constitution?

Other implications of Beard's "memorandum" could be

---

46. *Ibid.,* xv.

developed, but they would only belabor the point that Dr. Cochran's correction revealed the serious inadequacies of Beard's system of classification, demonstrated that the American economy during the late-eighteenth century was less specialized than Beard had assumed, and emphasized that men belonged simultaneously to a number of different groups with conflicting "interests." Thus, developed to its logical conclusions, Beard's memorandum actually required him to revise drastically his original assumptions, hypotheses, design of proof, and method of analysis.

5. CONTENT OF OPINION

Although Beard would have been required to revise his book drastically had he recognized the implications of his memorandum, he would not have been required to abandon his economic determinist hypotheses about the content of opinion. That is, he would have had to change his system for classifying men, and he probably would have had to revise his claims about the numerical divisions among various groups. But, after making those changes, he could still have offered his version of "an economic interpretation" of the Constitution. As he observed, nothing in the memorandum logically required him to alter the original argument that ideas were a direct reflex of interests, and that the same motives influenced Federalists and Antifederalists alike. That is, they adopted positions on the Constitution that they believed were best calculated to serve their economic interests; their differences in opinion stemmed directly from their membership in different economic interest groups. And their different interests were responsible also for differences in the intensity of their convictions, their knowledge of the issue, and their propensity for action.

Whatever Beard's original or subsequent *conception* of his study may have been, not even his most sympathetic reader can reasonably deny that his *hypotheses* about the motives of Federalists and Antifederalists were essentially economic determinist in character. True, some of his formulations were ambiguous and, taken in isolation, need not be interpreted as economic determinist. For example, his design of proof assumed that, if certain divisions of opinion were found to have existed, "it would then become apparent that the Constitution had no ascertainable relation to economic groups or classes, but was the product of some abstract causes remote from the chief business of life—gaining a livelihood." If certain other divisions were found, it would then be "pretty conclusively demonstrated that our fundamental law was not the product of an abstraction known as 'the whole people,' but of a group of economic interests which must have expected beneficial results from its adoption."

In certain contexts, the phrases, "ascertainable relation" and "beneficial results," might seem consonant with Seligman's statement of the economic interpretation of history. But Beard emphatically denied that the "immediate, guiding purpose" of the leaders who brought about the great historic change in American government was that "vague thing known as 'the advancement of general welfare' or some abstraction known as 'justice.' . . . The point is, that the direct, impelling motive . . . was the economic advantages which the beneficiaries expected would accrue to themselves first, from their action." Even if we strain logic and argue that this statement does not rule out other motives, its economic determinist character is unmistakable. And we can hardly contend that Beard's hypothesis applied only to leaders, for he did not distinguish between their motives and those of their followers.

Although Beard heavily stressed conflicts between members of groups that he termed "personalty" and "realty," he explicitly noted that economic groups with different interests—in some cases, even antagonistic interests—shared the same political position and formed working alliances to achieve their separate objectives. Thus, he noted the different interests and motives of holders of public securities, merchants, manufacturers, western land speculators, southern planters, urban mechanics and workingmen, and the "professional classes" attached to "personalty"—all groups which he placed in the Federalist coalition.

Instead of claiming that every Federalist group had the same bundle of interests and motives, Beard claimed that they shared a common characteristic: The Constitution offered each group at least one advantage that overbalanced any of its possible disadvantages to them. One example makes the point:

The third group of landed proprietors were the slaveholders of the South. It seems curious at first glance that the representatives of the southern states which sold raw materials and wanted competition in shipping were willing to join in a union that subjected them to commercial regulations devised immediately in behalf of northern interests. An examination of the records shows that they were aware of this apparent incongruity, but that there were *overbalancing compensations* [italics added] to be secured in a strong federal government . . . [for one thing, many Southerners "combined a wide range of personalty operations with their planting."].

The Southern planter was also as much concerned in maintaining order against slave revolts as the creditor in Massachusetts was concerned in putting down Shay's "desperate debtors." And the possibilities of such servile insurrections were by no means remote. Every slave owner must have felt more secure in 1789 when he knew that the governor of his state could call in the strong arm of the federal administration in case a domestic disturbance got beyond the local police and militia. The North might make discriminatory commercial regulations, but they could be regarded as a sort of insurance against conflagrations that might bring ruin in their train. It was obviously better to ship products under adverse legislation than to have no products to ship.[47]

Like the Federalists, the Antifederalists were members of groups that had different interests but shared a common characteristic; they would benefit from the defeat of the Constitution. Specifically, Beard asserted that, although their interests differed, small debtor-farmers and New York "Manor Lords" both opposed the Constitution.

In short, Beard depicted the conflict over the Constitution as a conflict between *two rival coalitions*, not between *two rival groups*.

---

47. *Ibid.*, 29-30.

6. TRANSLATING IDEAS INTO REALITY

As the hypotheses outlined above suggest, Beard was pre-occupied with the problem of how men get their ideas, specifically with the relationships between ideas and interests. But his most interesting and significant hypotheses deal with the way men translate their ideas into reality; concretely, they deal with the roles played by different men and groups in the sequence of events that led to the framing and adoption of the Constitution.

Beard had a keen sense of the political process. An interested observer of, and participant in, contemporary politics, he knew that a system of government based formally and firmly upon majority rule and the "will of the people" did not always guarantee effective rule of the majority or effective expression of the "people's will"—particularly in a heterogeneous society occupying a vast, diversified territory. As we shall see later, he did not confuse the formalities of the law with the realities of politics.[48]

Beard recognized that in the 1780's men exercised unequal power in the political process, but he was too preoccupied with the relationships between ideas and interests to give sufficient attention to the actual workings of the machinery of opinion-making and decision-making. For example, although he sketched the different roles of men in the movement for the Constitution, he drew only the crudest distinctions between Federalist leaders and Federalist and Antifederalist masses; Antifederalist leaders he barely mentioned by name.

Apparently, the strand of economic determinism in Beard's thought prevented him from seeing that his interpretation of the Constitution logically required a detailed description of the different roles men played in the sequence of events and a detailed explanation of how they came to play them. Nevertheless, a number of vaguely-stated claims bearing on those topics

---

48. See, for example, his scattered comments in *ibid.*, 50-51, 64-72, 154-156, 251-252.

are scattered throughout the book and can be assembled and reformulated with reasonable fidelity. But, to minimize repetition, hereafter, we will not attempt to maintain the analytic distinction between the roles men played in events and the factors responsible for their playing them. And, for our purposes, Beard's claims about the Constitution's impact upon the American political system require only brief notice.

   a. A "Peaceable" Revolution. Following the lead provided in 1891 by John W. Burgess, his teacher and colleague, Beard treated the sequence of events, climaxed by the adoption of the Constitution, as a great political revolution—non-violent but a genuine political revolution. Burgess, it is worth noting, can hardly be characterized as a Progressive-minded scholar. His personal frame of reference, as well as his general intellectual outlook, differed radically from those of his erstwhile pupil. To my knowledge, no one has ever suggested that he believed in a "conspiracy" theory of history—a charge levelled at Beard by Professor Brown (and other critics). Actually, Burgess was the leading American exponent of the "Teutonic" theory of political science, against which Beard rebelled so strenuously that he overstated and distorted his own ideas.[49]

   In Burgess' view, a fundamentally illegal process, a "peaceable" revolution, transformed the system of government under the Articles of Confederation into the system based upon the Constitution.[50] He did not condemn the revolutionary leaders as unpatriotic conspirators, he praised them for creating a strong central State. Finding themselves unable to remedy the Confederation's grave deficiencies by legal means, they devised and executed a series of brilliant maneuvers which brought the "natural leaders of the American people" into convention at Philadelphia, in May, 1787. There they deliberated:

---

49. See Max Lerner's illuminating analysis of Beard's reaction to Burgess in Beale, ed., *Charles Beard*, 26-34. For the view that Beard presented a "conspiracy theory of the Constitution," see Brown, *Charles Beard*, 56, 61, 138, 141, 143, 169, 176.

50. John W. Burgess, *Political Science and Comparative Constitutional Law* (Boston, 1891), 1: 98-108. The quotations below are from pp. 104-105 and 106.

. . . upon the whole question of the American state. They closed the doors upon the idle curiosity and the crude criticism of the multitude, adopted the rule of the majority in their acts, and proceeded to reorganize the American state and frame for it an entirely new central government. . . . It certainly was not understood by the Confederate Congress, or by the legislatures of the commonwealths, or by the public generally, that they were to undertake any such problem. It was generally supposed that they were there for the purpose simply of improving the machinery of the Confederate government and increasing somewhat its powers. There was, also, but one legal way for them to proceed in reorganizing the American state as the original basis of the constitution which they were about to propose, viz; they must send the plan therefor, *as a preliminary proposition*, to the Confederate Congress, procure its adoption by that body and its recommendation by that body to the legislatures of the commonwealths, and finally secure its approval by the legislature of every commonwealth. The new sovereignty, thus legally established, might then be legally and constitutionally appealed to for the adoption of any plan of government which the convention might choose to propose. The convention did not, however, proceed in any such manner. What they actually did, stripped of all fiction and verbiage, was to assume constituent powers, ordain a constitution of government and of liberty, and demand the *plébiscite* thereon, over the heads of all existing legally organized powers. Had Julius or Napoleon committed these acts they would have been pronounced coup d'état [sic]. Looked at from the side of the people exercising the *plébiscite*, we term the movement revolution.

After a brief discussion of the "fiction and verbiage" in which the "convention clothed its acts and assumptions," Burgess concluded:

Of course the mass of the people were not at all able to analyze the real character of this procedure. It is probable that many of the members of the convention itself did not fully comprehend just what they were doing. Not many of them had had sufficient education as publicists to be able to generalize the scientific import of their acts.

Exposure to Burgess' ideas both hurt and helped Beard. Undoubtedly, his book suffers from his over-reaction to the "Teutonic theory," but it also owes much to Burgess' analysis that the Constitution was the product of revolution.[51] Beard acknowledged his indebtedness. "The revolutionary nature of the work of the Philadelphia Convention is correctly characterized by Professor John W. Burgess when he states that had such acts been performed by Julius or Napoleon, they would have been pronounced *coups d'état*." In support of Burgess' views, he observed that Madison (and others) invoked "the right of revolution" to justify the Convention delegates' "revolutionary departure from their instructions." But, he did not confine himself to filling in the brief outline of his teacher; he went beyond it by posing a series of questions about the roles played by different men in the revolutionary sequence of events.[52]

b. How Did the "Peaceable" Revolution Come About? Characterizing the Constitutional movement as a revolution, Burgess did not try to explain its success—except, perhaps, in his reference to "the natural leaders of the American people." Beard, in effect, asked how those men became the "natural leaders."

More precisely, he directed attention to some questions implicit in these problems: Why were certain men able to translate their ideas into reality? Why were some men able to exert greater influence upon the processes of opinion-making and decision-making than the men who opposed them? His answers were inconsistent, ambiguous, and incomplete. But, read in context, they represent a brilliant historiographic contribution and have not yet been adequately examined and exploited.

Restated and rearranged, Beard's observations divide the

---

51. Recollection that nineteenth and twentieth century "strong men" and dictators have frequently used popular referendums to ratify illegal seizures of power should give pause to historians tempted to dismiss Burgess' analysis as pointless and his analogies as misleading. Since well-organized minorities can act with greater speed and efficiency than unorganized majorities, referendums in crisis situations—or in situations characterized by an air of crisis—do not necessarily reflect majority opinion in countries that observe the forms of popular sovereignty. Historians who dismiss Burgess' analysis must demonstrate that the plebiscite demanded "over the heads of all existing legally organized powers" actually implemented the "will of the people," they cannot assume it.

52. Beard, *Economic Interpretation*, 218, and 52-63, 217-238.

sequence of events into six stages which are analytically distinct and chronologically consecutive. The first stage was already under way before the Revolution against England ended. It covered the period from January, 1781, through the summer of 1786, and was characterized by more or less unorganized agitation for radical changes in the system of government under the Articles of Confederation. The second stage began with the Annapolis Commercial Convention (September 1786), at which Madison and Hamilton played leading roles, and was the period of organized agitation and organized preliminaries to the Constitutional Convention. The third stage covered the Convention, which met in May and adjourned in September, 1787. The fourth stage began with Congress transmitting the proposed Constitution to the several states, and ended with the state legislatures establishing the procedures for holding ratifying conventions. At this point, the several stages overlap chronologically. Several states completed the entire cycle before others completed the fourth stage. Briefly, the fifth stage covered the election of delegates to ratifying conventions; the sixth, the ratifying process within each state.

Although I believe Beard's analysis has been accurately reconstructed here, I do not suggest that he presented it in this form, or that he systematically examined developments during any one of the stages. He gave more attention to some stages than others, but nowhere did he attempt to provide a systematic, explicit, and precise description of the sequence of events ending with the adoption of the Constitution. The first sentence of his preface warned readers: "The following pages are frankly fragmentary." Occasionally he slipped and treated hypotheses as though they had been convincingly demonstrated when they had not even been clearly formulated. But time and again he emphasized that his primary purpose was to raise questions and that, for his tentative answers, he was forced to rely upon data from inadequate secondary sources.[53]

Following Seligman's lead, Beard assumed that in the 1780's

---

53. *Ibid.*, xix, 19, 74, 243, 253-254.

the structure of American society encouraged and permitted men to play greatly different roles in the political process. This was true, to some extent, because unequal legal status gave men unequal power to influence events, but to a much greater extent they differed because of extra-legal factors. Those factors included differences in the amount and kind of property, occupation, extra-legal social status, education, personal qualities, physical location, control of communication media, and the relative ease of traveling swiftly from one place to another when moved by interest or inclination. Thus, either because of their legal status, or their position in the social structure, men not only were likely to want to play different roles in events, they were permitted to do so by their possession of greatly different powers.

To repeat an earlier observation, Beard was handicapped by his "Progressive-minded" view of "reality" when he dealt with the relationships between ideas and interests. Superficially "tough-minded," that view of reality actually is unrealistic and naive. To do nothing more than simply identify the economic interests or class positions of men leaves us a long way from having solved the problems of how men get their ideas and why they act. As Seligman observed in criticizing Loria's "extremist" views, no claim "can be countenanced" that holds "all social life is nothing but a reflex of the economic life."[54] But, when Beard dealt with the actual workings of the political process, his Progressivism helped him to penetrate below the surface of formal political institutions and to discover some useful things about the nature and exercise of political power in a Lockean liberal society. Put differently, it made him a more perceptive analyst of the objective realities of power than of the subjective processes that influence the ideas of men and their propensities for action.[55]

---

54. Seligman, *Economic Interpretation of History*, 149-150, n. 1.

55. See Beard, *Economic Interpretation*, 154-155, for an example of his applying observations derived from "tariff hearings in Washington" to the decision-making process in general.

Having identified the dualism in Beard's thought and the two types of problems with which he dealt, we can now begin the statement of his main hypothesis in general terms.

As a result of the Revolution against Great Britain, the new nation suffered from a drastic imbalance between economic and political power. Under the Articles of Confederation, certain groups could not secure government rules or actions which they believed necessary for the protection of their economic interests and beneficial to their rapid development. Determined to correct what they regarded as an unjustifiable, dangerous imbalance between economic and political power, a relatively small number of men—Burgess' "natural leaders"—led the movement to overthrow the old political system.[56] That Beard essentially agreed with their appraisal of the post-Revolutionary situation is evident from his 1912 book on the Supreme Court:

The close of the Revolutionary struggle removed the *prime* cause for radical agitation and brought a new group of thinkers into prominence. When independence had been gained, the practical work to be done was the maintenance of social order, the payment of the public debt, the provision of a sound financial system, and the establishment of conditions favorable to the development of the economic resources of the new country. The men who were principally concerned in this work of peaceful enterprise were not the philosophers [of the Revolution], but men of business and property and the holders of public securities.[57]

---

56. In his first chapter, Beard stated this general proposition: "Inasmuch as the primary object of a government, beyond the mere repression of physical violence, is the making of the rules which determine the property relations of members of society, the dominant classes whose rights are thus to be determined must perforce obtain from the government such rules as are consonant with the larger interests necessary to the continuance of their economic processes, or they must themselves control the organs of government." In his third chapter, in effect, he invoked this proposition to explain "The Movement For The Constitution." *Ibid.*, 13, 52-63.

57. Charles A. Beard, *The Supreme Court and the Constitution* (New York, 1912), 79, and 75-76, 86-87. Characteristically, Beard was not entirely consistent on this point. In 1913, while questioning the accuracy of Fiske's "critical period" label for the years after 1783, he hinted that the Constitutional "political revolution" may not really have been necessary. *Economic Interpretation*, 47-48. However, he essentially argued that the Federalist leaders believed the "political revolution" was necessary to get on

As Beard described the process, the men who wanted to get on with "the practical work" were able to overcome widespread popular opposition, because they represented certain groups and possessed certain attributes. That is, the Federalist leaders secured power because they represented groups that: (1) had a high potential both for unity among themselves and for control of politics; (2) could realize their political potential because they had strong motives for acting and were well-informed.[58] Specifically, he identified seven attributes that contributed to the Federalists' success. I am not implying, however, that he believed every leader possessed every attribute, or that all leaders possessed any one to the same degree.[59]

c. *Seven Attributes of Successful Revolutionists.* As Beard depicted them, the men who led the revolutionary movement represented groups whose interests would benefit directly and immediately from the establishment of a strong, centralized government. Thus, their first attribute stemmed from the close relationships between the economic interests of their group and government action. Those relationships not only existed objectively, they could be easily seen; in other words, conscious self-interest describes their second attribute. The third was a function of the size, rather than the nature, of property holdings. Apart from the direct, perceived relationships that existed between government action and their interests, because of their relatively large property holdings, the pro-Constitutionalist groups would derive greater profits (or benefits) from such action than would the relatively poor defenders of the status quo.

The three attributes identified thus far are particularly rele-

---

with the "practical work" of the "new country." Beard's inconsistency here perhaps may be accounted for by observing that his head seemed to be with the Federalists, his heart with the Antifederalists.

58. Here I have adapted, for my own purposes, some provocative ideas suggested in Robert A. Dahl, "A Critique of the Ruling Elite Model," *American Political Science Review*, 52: 463-469 (June, 1958).

59. Beard did not present a systematic discussion of the attributes identified below; I have pulled together and reformulated comments scattered throughout the book, particularly those found in *Economic Interpretation*, 50-51, 61-62, 64, 100-114, 125-126, 152-154, 161, 251-252.

vant to the *content of opinion*. As quotations from Beard suggest, the next four are particularly relevant to the *capacity and power of men to make their opinions count*.

After offering several illustrations "to show how the demand for reform was being fostered and also the connection between the leaders in the agitation and the personnel of the public bodies which later achieved the great work of framing and ratifying the Constitution," Beard summarized his argument:

> By correspondence such as this just cited, by an increasing recognition of the desperate straights [sic] in which they were placed, a remarkable fusion of interested forces was effected. The wealth, the influence, and a major portion of the educated men of the country were drawn together in a compact group, "informed by a conscious solidarity of interests," as President Wilson has so tersely put it.[60]

The following dictum suggests the fourth attribute Beard assigned to Federalist leaders: In revolutionary situations, numbers count some but organization counts more. Disregarding their own differences, Federalist leaders organized to achieve one overriding, common objective. Although Beard explicitly described them as members of a "compact group" drawn together to achieve a common objective, he did not claim that they belonged to the same economic group.

Another attribute derived from the nature of their economic interests and occupations. "They resided for the most part in the towns, or the more thickly populated areas, and they could marshall their forces quickly and effectively."[61] That is, they were able to move about, communicate with each other, and get to the places where opinions were formed and decisions made, more easily and quickly than could their opponents.

The size and type of their property holdings (or the profitability and type of occupations in which they engaged) enabled Federalist leaders to secure disproportionate control of sources of information, e.g., newspapers, pamphlets, and public meetings. Apart from being able to rely upon their own money, talents,

---

60. *Ibid.*, 61.
61. *Ibid.*, 251.

and prestige "in the campaign of education" for a strong central government, they were in a strategic position to influence the "influentials," to use a present-day term. They commanded greater support from "the professional classes" (lawyers, editors, clergymen) than did their opponents. In Beard's words, their "influence over the press was tremendous, not only through ownership, but also through advertising and other patronage."[62]

Finally, personal ability and character probably constituted the Federalist leaders' seventh and most valuable attribute. Compared with their opponents, they were generally superior political organizers, better educated and informed, more articulate and persuasive, and commanded more prestige. As Beard depicted them, they possessed the necessary political talents for victory in a revolutionary situation. Thus, in referring to Pennsylvania political battles after 1789, he observed that the "dissenters against the Constitution . . . were at length, beaten, outgeneralled, and outclassed in all the arts of political management"—an observation equally applicable to his treatment of the movement for the Constitution.[63]

E.
Beard's Main Hypothesis: Summary Statement

Since I regard Beard's observation about "the arts of political management" as the key to his book, it is now possible to restate his main hypothesis. As I read him, he asserted seven sets of claims, which are closely related yet logically distinct.

1) During the 1780's, a relatively small group of men who were highly motivated and talented, well-organized, well-edu-

---

62. *Ibid.*, 51. In this connection, see the stimulating chapter, "Patterns of Influence: Local and Cosmopolitan Influentials," in Robert K. Merton, *Social Theory and Social Structure* (Glencoe, Ill., 1957, rev. ed.), 387-420.

63. Beard, *Economic Interpretation*, 233-234.

cated, and well-informed, led a revolutionary movement. Securing effective control of the apparatus of opinion-making and decision-making, they restored the balance between economic and political power. They succeeded because they represented groups whose position in American society gave them political influence disproportionate to their numbers, and because they possessed certain personal attributes most frequently found among members or representatives of those groups.

2) The Federalist leaders shared a common objective: non-violent overthrow of the weak, decentralized system of government, and its replacement by a strong central State possessing qualitatively different powers from those of its predecessor. In general, those powers were designed to: a) enable the State to foster national economic development, b) protect property and property rights from attack by popular majorities, and c) give direct aid to the economic groups represented by the revolutionary leaders.

3) The Federalist leaders represented a variety of economic groups whose interests conflicted in some respects, but who shared at least one attribute of crucial importance: each would benefit directly from the new State created by the Constitution.

4) Some groups would benefit from the new State more than others, as well as more directly and immediately. Because they were the chief beneficiaries, members or representatives of "substantial personalty interests," particularly the large holders of public securities, played the most "dynamic" roles in the revolutionary movement. Substantial personalty interests included men who, for the times, operated on a relatively large financial scale. They had "money at interest or capital seeking investment," or owned "state and continental securities," or had "manufacturing, shipping, trading, and commercial interests," or speculated "in Western Lands," or engaged in some combination of these different forms of enterprise.

5) The belief that the economic groups they represented would benefit directly and immediately from the Constitution impelled the Federalist leaders to action—as it did a large majority of the men they represented. But the Federalist leaders

did not represent all the individuals or groups favorable to the Constitution, and some men who favored it may have been influenced by motives that were not economic.

6) Opposition to the Constitution came primarily from poor rural and urban debtors, particularly from small debtor-farmers who lived in isolated or interior areas lacking good communication facilities (measured by the standards of the time). A preponderant majority of the adult free white males belonged to those groups, and a large majority of their *politically active members* opposed the Constitution. Partly because of their legal status, but mostly because of their position in the American social structure, the groups that opposed the Constitution failed to mobilize their members as effectively as the groups that favored it. As a result, despite their numerical superiority, they lost the battle for political control.

7) Like the Federalists, conscious self-interest determined the opinions of a large majority of the opposition. They wanted to retain the existing system of government because they believed their interests would suffer if the Constitution were adopted and a strong national State created.

Beard advanced other claims, of course. Some are excluded here on the ground that they are *irrelevant* to his main hypothesis; others are excluded on the ground that they only represent more detailed claims *consonant* with it (e.g., claims about developments in the several states, about specific governmental changes ushered in by the Constitution, about specific benefits that individual groups would derive from the changes). Still others are excluded because they essentially *contradict* the ones around which I have constructed his hypothesis. My reason for excluding them is that they run counter to the whole tenor of Beard's book; since they were not built into the logical structure of his main argument, their exclusion does not significantly alter it.

An example of exclusion on grounds of logical inconsistency is the statement that his purpose was not "to show that the Constitution was made for the personal benefit of the members of the Convention." Whatever that ambiguously-worded disavowal was intended to convey, its implications, at least, are irreconcilable with the burden of argument, both in the chapter where it appeared and in the book as a whole.

Excluded, also, are a set of claims that *are* logically consonant with those summarized above, but that represent unnecessary overstatements of Beard's main hypothesis. Explicitly or implicitly, they constitute extreme statements of his views and their exclusion modifies the form of his hypothesis without significantly altering its character.

For example, as noted previously, in the 1935 introduction, he conceded that he had originally overstated his views on "class-solidarity in historical conflicts." It seems reasonable, therefore, to modify his claims to read "a large majority" rather than "substantially all" members of a specified economic group held the same opinions and were impelled by the same considerations. Similarly, even in 1913, Beard treated Madison and Hamilton, his two most important Federalist leaders, as *representatives* of specified economic groups, not as men who were "immediately, directly, and personally interested in, and [who] derived economic advantages from, the establishment of the new system."[64] Thus, he was logically required only to assert and demonstrate that the Federalist leaders *represented groups* whose members generally "were immediately, directly, and personally interested in, and derived economic advantages from, the establishment of the new system." In other words, I have eliminated overstatements that at least implied that men necessarily possess the economic attributes of the groups they lead or represent politically.

Again, on the ground of unnecessary overstatement, I have toned down Beard's claim that the Fathers knew "the precise results which the new government that they were setting up was designed to attain."[65] Logically, Beard was required only to claim that they knew what they wanted in general, and, as restated here, his hypothesis asserts that.

---

64. *Ibid.*, 100-114, 125-126.
65. *Ibid.*, 151.

Finally, I have modified overstatements which resulted from his unsuccessful attempts to summarize material that he had presented at length. For example, one of his final "conclusions" reads: "In the ratification, it became manifest that the line of cleavage for and against the Constitution was between substantial personalty interests on the one hand and the small farming and debtor interests on the other."[66] Taken out of context, that ambiguously phrased sentence can be interpreted to mean this: No one but men who had "substantial personalty interests" favored the Constitution, no one but small farmers and debtors opposed it. In the context of his book as a whole, however, that interpretation is unwarranted. As I have restated his hypothesis, it claims only that the *main* line of cleavage was between the two sets of groups he specifically mentioned in his conclusion.

No doubt, as I suggest in an Epilogue to this essay, Beard's hypothesis can be restated so radically as to prune it of all economic determinist characteristics. But while we are appraising it, we are not justified in changing its character so radically. Had Beard not presented a hypothesis that largely, although by no means exclusively, derived from "the theory of economic determinism in politics," he would not have written the book that he did.

F.

Recent Critics' Versions of "Beard's Thesis"

As I have tried to show, a useful critique of Beard's work must first identify his questions and then restate his answers. In my opinion, his recent critics have not met those requirements.

---

66. *Ibid.*, 325.

I. ECONOMIC DETERMINISM IS NOT ECONOMIC INTERPRETATION

Almost immediately after Beard published his study in 1913, critical blasts began to be blown. But the first critique of book-length did not appear until 1956. Its author, Robert E. Brown, failed to recognize the dualism in Beard's thought and treated economic determinism and economic interpretation as the same theory of history, called by slightly different names:

> Before starting his survey of the origins of the Constitution, Beard wrote a chapter on historical interpretation in which he rejected previous schools of historical writing and then made a strong plea for economic determinism *or the economic interpretation of history* [italics added]. . . . Having rejected the old interpretations of history, Beard then presented a new hypothesis, the theory of economic determinism. The hypothesis that economic elements were the chief factors in political development had been little used, Beard declared, and until the theory of "economic determinism" had been tried, it could not be found wanting.[67]

Professor Brown's confusing the two theories of history led him to charge that Beard had omitted a "rather important" section of *Federalist* No. 10. That charge has previously been noted and appraised. But further appraisal of Brown's argu-

---

67. Brown, *Charles Beard*, 26. The conjecture seems reasonable that critical re-examination of Beard's ideas was delayed by the intellectual currents generated during the depression of the 1930's and the World War of the early 1940's. We need not subscribe to subjective relativism to observe that a hypothesis expressing the spirit of the Progressive era received its first effective challenge in the decade that produced the "New Conservatism." That observation does not imply that Beard's recent critics are New Conservatives; they may or may not be. My purpose is not to denigrate or praise their work by pinning political labels upon them, but to call attention to the different intellectual milieus in which Beard and his critics worked. Though this essay tries to show that the errors committed by Beard's critics vitiate their conclusions, it would be both ungenerous and mistaken to deny their contributions. Among other things, they have reminded American historians that intellectual liberty requires each generation to combat the tyranny imposed by ruling hypotheses. More specifically, Beard's critics have brought about a long overdue re-examination of traditional historical doctrines, just as Beard did in 1913, when he took a fresh look at old problems.

ment provides additional support for the view that Brown failed to recognize the differences between economic determinism and economic interpretation. His argument runs as follows:

When we examine No. 10, we find that the omission is rather important if we would understand Madison. What Madison said here was that the latent causes of faction are sown in the nature of man. Unfriendly passions and violent conflicts among men have been caused by zeal for different opinions on religion, government, and other things, by attachment to different leaders or others, and even by the most frivolous and fanciful distinctions. In short, it was necessary to omit this section from Madison's statement to make Madison an "economic determinist." It is quite true that Madison placed economic factors ahead of all others, but he did not rule out the non-economic either here or in his other writings and statements, as we shall see later.[68]

Apparently, Brown identifies a theory as "economic determinist," only if it rules out *all* non-economic factors. But it was not Madison's assessment of the relative significance of different factors that fixed the character of his theory; it was his fatalistic views about man's faculties and behavior, and his assumption that a one-to-one relationship existed between economic interests and political factions. Since that assumption is economic determinism in classic form, Beard cannot be said to have distorted Madison's views to make them conform to his own. Brown's theoretical confusion not only led him to make that unfounded charge, but kept him from undertaking an instructive critique of the claims that Beard actually advanced.

The same observation holds for Forrest McDonald, author of the second book-length critique of Beard. As the next chapter will show, Professor McDonald departed from Beard and based his "new system of categories of interest groups" on assumptions even more rigidly economic determinist than were Beard's. In other respects, he claimed to have faithfully copied Beard, but he did not recognize that a hypothesis cannot be tested by a logically fallacious design of proof:

---

68. *Ibid.*, 27-29.

The purpose of the present work is to examine Beard's thesis as history. To do so, I have followed a rather unorthodox method. For purposes of this book I have accepted, without qualification, Beard's system of interpretation and his system of testing it. His pages, he wrote, were "frankly fragmentary"; he sketched in broad outlines and left it for others to fill in the details. Insofar as possible, I have filled in the details.[69]

McDonald subtitled his book, *The Economic Origins of the Constitution*. But, in exploring the problem, he took the wrong road when, like Brown, he equated the theory of economic interpretation of history with the theory of economic determinism. He not only used the terms interchangeably,[70] but in his choice of categories he showed that he had a fundamentally erroneous conception of an "economic interpretation" of the Constitution. As we have seen, Beard did not present an economic interpretation. And as we shall see, his design of proof and his method of analysis did not permit him to test one. Thus, since Mc-Donald faithfully copied Beard, he, too, inevitably, failed to present or test an economic interpretation of the Constitution.

2. BROWN'S VERSION OF "BEARD'S THESIS"

Brown asserted that Beard advanced a "double-edged" thesis and described its two edges as follows:

1. Instead of being a document drawn up by *patriotic men* [italics added] for the protection of life, liberty, and the pursuit of happiness, the Constitution was the work of consolidated economic groups—personal property interests including money, public securities, manufacturers, and trade and shipping—groups that were personally interested in the outcome of their labors. . . .

2. Instead of being a document embodying democratic principles, the Constitution was put over in an undemocratic society by undemocratic methods for the express purpose of checking democratic majorities.[71]

---

69. McDonald, *We The People*, vii.
70. *Ibid.*, 7-8.
71. Brown, *Charles Beard*, 3-4.

Brown tended to paraphrase Beard, rather than to quote his actual words, often with unfortunate results. For example, his use of the phrase, "patriotic men," suggests that Beard condemned the Founding Fathers as "unpatriotic." Actually, in his *1912* book on the Supreme Court, Beard decried the "imbecilities of the Confederation" and eulogized the Fathers:

It was a truly remarkable assembly of men that gathered in Philadelphia on May 14, 1787, to undertake the work of reconstructing the American system of government. It is not merely patriotic pride that compels one to assert that never in the history of assemblies has there been a convention of men richer in political experience and in practical knowledge, or endowed with a profounder insight into the springs of human action and the intimate essence of government. It is indeed an astounding fact that at one time so many men skilled in statecraft could be found on the very frontier of civilization among a population numbering about four million whites. It is no less a cause for admiration that their instrument of government should have survived the trials and crises of a century that saw the wreck of more than a score of paper constitutions.[72]

But, in his book of 1913, Beard attempted to develop a "scientific" mode of analysis that would avoid such "moralistic epithets" as "imbecilities," "patriotic," and "unpatriotic." In reviving the charge that Beard stigmatized the Fathers as unpatriotic, Brown ignored Beard's statement in the preface to the 1935 edition:

. . . an economic analysis may be coldly neutral, and in the pages of this volume no words of condemnation are pronounced upon the men enlisted upon either side of the great controversy which accompanied the formation and adoption of the Constitution. Are the security holders who sought to collect principal and interest through the formation of a stronger government to be treated as guilty of impropriety or praised? That is a question to which the following inquiry is not addressed.[73]

It is true that Beard's "economic analysis" was not unambiguous. But it was not as ambiguous as Brown suggests.

---

72. Beard, *Supreme Court and the Constitution*, 76, 86-87.
73. Beard, *Economic Interpretation*, ix-x.

Brown's failure to state Beard's position accurately becomes evident when we examine this version of "Beard's thesis":

So to prove that the Constitution was "an economic document drawn with superb skill by men whose property interests were immediately at stake," Beard had to violate the concepts of the historical method in many ways. These ran the gamut from omission to outright misrepresentation of evidence, and included the drawing of conclusions from evidence that not only did not warrant the conclusions but actually refuted them. To say that the Constitution was designed in part to protect property is true; to say that it was designed only to protect property is false; and to say that it was designed only to protect *personalty* is preposterous.[74]

A harsh epithet, "preposterous."

At the end of a chapter which described in detail the heterogeneous coalition of pro-Constitutionists, Beard did say that "It [personalty] was, in short, the dynamic element in the movement for the new Constitution."[75] That, however, is not the same as saying that the disparate groups covered by the clumsy term, "personalty," were the *only ones* that favored the Constitution, or that no group other than "personal property interests including money, public securities, manufacturers, and trade and shipping," to quote Brown's summary of Beard's thesis, favored the Constitution.

In 1913, Beard described speculators in western lands as members of one group of "personalty interests." Moreover, he observed that southern planters, as well as urban artisans, mechanics, and "working-men" favored the Constitution. And, in his 1935 "memorandum of correction," he added leading New York "landed proprietors" to the coalition.[76] Actually, four pages before the passage quoted above, Brown revealed that his summary failed to present "Beard's thesis" accurately:

One key to an understanding of the Constitutional Convention was provided by Beard himself in his discussion of the control of commerce (p. 175). His earlier use of petitions signed by mechanics and manufacturers was evidence that these skilled artisans wanted

74. Brown, *Charles Beard*, 111.
75. Beard, *Economic Interpretation*, 51, 19-51.
76. *Ibid.*, xv-xvi, 25 n. 1, 29-30, 41-45.

protection from foreign competition just as does organized labor today. But his final sentence in the paragraph is the important one— that merchants and manufacturing interests achieved commercial benefits, but "they paid for their victory by large concessions to the slave-owning planters of the south." This is only one example of what is so evident to anyone who reads the *Records* [of the Convention] without preconceptions. There were a multitude of conflicting interests in the Convention, some economic and some not, and there simply had to be a great deal of compromising of interests for anything to be achieved.[77]

It is difficult to understand how Brown could cite Beard's explicit description of a heterogeneous coalition favorable to the Constitution, and simultaneously depict him as having said that the Constitution "was designed only to protect *personalty*. . . ."

Brown also depicted Beard as having claimed that *The Federalist* "appealed only to personalty interests." This assertion could be accurate only if "personalty" is defined to include southern slaveholders, a definition Brown rejected.[78] Beard did differentiate between slaveholders who "combined a wide range of personalty operations with their planting" and "the slave-holding planter as such." But he discussed both types under the heading, "Groups of Real Property Holders," and lined them both up on the pro-Constitution side.[79] In analyzing *The Federalist*, he wrote that "every fundamental appeal in it is to some material and substantial interest." Among those interests, he explicitly included the "slaveholding planter as such":

In considering the importance of defence against domestic insurrection, the authors of *The Federalist* do not overlook an appeal to the slave-holders' instinctive fear of a servile revolt. Naturally, it is Madison [previously described by Beard as "a descendant of one of the old landed families of Virginia whose wealth consisted principally of plantations and slaves, and whose personal property was relatively small in amount"] whose interest catches this point and drives it home, by appearing to discount it.[80]

---

77. Brown, *Charles Beard*, 107.
78. *Ibid.*, 92-94, 47-48.
79. Beard, *Economic Interpretation*, 29-30.
80. *Ibid.*, 174, 125-126, and 153-154.

The validity of Beard's claims is, of course, open to challenge. But little justification exists for Brown to summarize his "thesis" as though it asserted that the Constitution "was designed only to protect *personalty*. . . ."

Since Brown's misstatements stem from a fundamental misreading of Beard, they formed integral parts of his critique. When we recognize that he did not read and represent Beard accurately, the logical structure of his critique collapses. One does not discredit a hypothesis which asserts that southern planters and northern mechanics and working-men favored the Constitution by demonstrating that southern planters and northern mechanics and working-men favored the Constitution. For the most part, the evidence Brown presented to support his condemnation of Beard's thesis is relevant only if his summary of it is accepted.

3. MC DONALD'S VERSION OF "BEARD'S THESIS"

Like Brown, McDonald misread Beard and, therefore, directed his critique against a non-existent "thesis."

Following a short sketch of the "central points in the thesis advanced by Professor Beard," McDonald wrote:*

If from this tightly and skillfully woven system of ideas are extracted those parts which are essentially nonconjectural—which are susceptible, in other words, of a reasonable degree of validation or invalidation as historical facts, and upon which the interpretative superstructure is erected—three propositions come into clear focus, namely that:

1. The Constitution was essentially "an economic document drawn with superb skill" by a consolidated economic group "whose interests knew no state boundaries and were truly national in their scope." (pp. 188, 325)

2. "In the ratification, it became manifest that the line of cleavage for and against the Constitution was between substantial personalty interests [approximately identical to those which had been represented in the Philadelphia Convention] on the one hand and the small farming and debtor interests on the other." (p. 325)

3. "Inasmuch as so many leaders in the movement for ratifica-

---

* Remarks in brackets and parentheses are McDonald's.

tion were large [public] security holders [as were most members of the Philadelphia Convention], and inasmuch as securities constituted such a large proportion of personalty, this economic interest must have formed a very considerable dynamic element, if not the preponderating element, in bringing about the adoption of the new system. . . . Some holders of public securities are found among the opponents of the Constitution, but they are not numerous." (pp. 290, 291 n)[81]

Like Brown, McDonald failed to recognize that Beard depicted a conflict between two coalitions. Instead, he had Beard assert that the conflict over the Constitution was between two groups, "personalty" and "realty."[82] Several examples demon-

---

81. McDonald, *We The People*, 6-7.

82. See, for example, the chapter, "Economic Interests and Votes in the Convention." McDonald, ignoring Beard's actual claims, arbitrarily divides the delegates into "Personalty Group" and "Realty Group," and argues that "If the economic interests represented by the delegates were the dominating element, or even one of several dominating elements, in the making of the Constitution, one would expect to find an alignment inside the Convention along the above lines." Using dubious logic and evidence to support his conjectures, he then goes on to assert that "the voting patterns of the state delegations in the Convention by no means followed the lines of a basic economic cleavage into realty and personalty interests"; "that in so far as can be ascertained from the votes of individual delegates, no alignment of *personalty interests* versus *realty interests* existed in the Convention"; and concludes that the "facts" represent "insurmountable obstacles" to Beard's interpretation of the Convention. Similarly, in his chapter, "A Revaluation of the Beard Thesis of the Making of the Constitution," he insisted on the personalty-realty straw man, and argued that "Beard's essential error was in attempting to formulate a single set of generalizations that would apply to all the states."
Even if McDonald's data were accurate and his categories meaningful, his arguments and conclusions would be irrelevant to "Beard's thesis." The latter maintained that the Convention delegates, with few exceptions, represented different groups which all favored the Constitution, and tended to share a common outlook. "The south had many men who were rich in personalty, other than slaves, and it was this type, rather than the slaveholding planter as such, which was represented in the Convention that framed the Constitution. The majority of the southern delegates at Philadelphia in 1787 were from the towns or combined a wide range of personalty operations with their planting. On this account there was more identity of interest among Langdon of Portsmouth, Gerry of Boston, Hamilton of New York, Dayton of New Jersey, Robert Morris of Philadelphia, McHenry of Baltimore, Washington on the Potomac, Williamson of North Carolina, the Pinckneys of Charleston, and Pierce of Savan-

strate that McDonald's propositions do not faithfully summarize "Beard's thesis."

Proposition 1 had Beard maintain that the Constitution was the work of "a consolidated economic group." Early in the book[83] these words were not enclosed by quotation marks; they appeared as a paraphrase of Beard:

> 1. The Constitution was essentially "an economic document drawn with superb skill" by a consolidated economic group "whose interests knew no state boundaries and were truly national in their scope." (pp. 188, 325)

Later,[84] the same phrase undergoes a transmutation. There, it is presented as a quotation from Beard and is combined with another phrase, original with McDonald, but also attributed to Beard:

> It is clear [from McDonald's analysis of the "Economic Interests of the Delegates"] that Professor Beard's assertion that the members of the Convention were a "consolidated economic group" with an "identity of personalty interests" cannot be accepted without a large number of qualifications.

Still later,[85] McDonald again misplaces quotation marks and ellipses while summarizing Beard's conclusions:

> From his analysis of the Philadelphia Convention, Beard concluded that the Constitution was essentially an "economic document drawn with superb skill" by a "consolidated economic group . . . whose

nah than between these several men and their debt-burdened neighbors at the back door. Thus nationalism was created by a welding of economic interests that cut through state boundaries." And, in the very next paragraph, Beard explicitly added "the slaveholding planter as such" to the pro-Constitution coalition. He did claim that members of "personalty" groups played the most "dynamic" roles in the Constitutional revolution, but that is a far cry from saying *that they alone favored it*. No implication is intended that McDonald set out first to erect and then to knock down a straw man; nevertheless, that is what he did. Compare McDonald, *We The People*, 93-110, 349-357, with Beard, *Economic Interpretation*, 29-30, 50-51, 71-151, 253-291.

83. McDonald, *We The People*, 6.

84. *Ibid.*, 92.

85. *Ibid.*, 349.

property interests were immediately at stake"; that these interests "knew no state boundaries but were truly national in their scope."

And on the next page, Beard is again rewritten:

In the light of these and other facts presented in the foregoing chapters, it is impossible to justify Beard's interpretation of the Constitution as "an economic document" drawn by a "consolidated economic group whose property interests were immediately at stake."

Apart from other considerations discussed in later chapters, we cannot accept McDonald's appraisal of "Beard's interpretation," because Beard did not assert the claims or write the words attributed to him in any one of the four variants we have just reviewed. After an analysis designed to demonstrate the material benefits that the Constitution bestowed upon a *wide variety of groups*, Beard summarized his arguments as follows:

To carry the theory of the economic interpretation of the Constitution out into its ultimate details would require a monumental commentary, such as lies completely beyond the scope of this volume. But enough has been said to show that the concept of the Constitution as a piece of abstract legislation reflecting no group interests and recognizing no economic antagonisms is entirely false. It was an economic document drawn with superb skill by men whose property interests were immediately at stake; and as such it appealed directly and unerringly to identical interests in the country at large.[86]

And, in the last paragraph of his book Beard wrote:

The Constitution was not created by "the whole people" as the jurists have said; neither was it created by "the states" as Southern nullifiers long contended; but it was the work of a consolidated group whose interests knew no state boundaries and were truly national in their scope.[87]

In other words, Beard first observed that a heterogeneous coalition favored the Constitution. He then summarized his views by observing that the document appealed "to identical interests in the country at large"; he did not write "that the

---

86. Beard, *Economic Interpretation*, 188.
87. *Ibid.*, 325.

members of the Convention were a 'consolidated economic group' with an identity of personalty interests. . . ." Similarly, he first discussed the political effectiveness of the Federalist leaders, their ability to work closely together, and their successful campaign to secure control of the apparatus of opinion-making and decision-making. He then summarized his arguments against theories that held that the Constitution was created either by "the whole people" or by "the states." The Constitution, he wrote, "was the work of a consolidated group whose interests knew no state boundaries and were truly national in their scope."

"Economic," inserted into Beard's phrase, "consolidated group," does make it more plausible to read him as postulating a conflict between all "personalty" and all "realty" groups. But it also changes Beard's meaning and results in a summary of his thesis that has no basis in fact.

McDonald's misstatement of Beard was not confined to general propositions that allegedly summarized Beard's thesis. One example is his précis of Beard's analysis of opposition to the Constitution in Maryland, here quoted in its entirety:

Professor Beard, basing his observations on the earlier work of [Orin] Libby, concluded that "the opposition came from the rural districts and particularly from the paper money constituencies." The hordes of small farmer-debtors who had sought paper money as a cheap remedy for their indebtedness, Beard contended, opposed the Constitution because it cut off this fraudulent source of relief.[88]

McDonald then cites data, collected after 1913, allegedly demonstrating that "This theory has been pretty thoroughly exploded. . . ."

The details need not be discussed here, but McDonald stressed the argument that most of the leaders in the fight against ratification "had speculated heavily in the purchase of confiscated loyalist estates."[89] If true, this finding would actually tend to support Beard's main claim about opposition to the Constitution

---

88. McDonald, *We The People*, 153-154.
89. *Ibid.*, 154-155.

in Maryland. (This, however, will not be apparent to the reader unless he refers to the original.)

In the chapter entitled, "The Economics of the Vote on the Constitution," Beard devoted only two paragraphs to Maryland. The sentence that McDonald quoted comes from the first paragraph; the second paragraph reads as follows:

> But it should be noted that [in Maryland] we are now leaving the regions of small farms and of estates tilled by free labor and are coming into the districts where slavery and the plantation system dominate rural economy. *Indeed, the slave-holding plantations were so extensive and the small farming class so restricted that the paper money party would have been seriously weakened had it not been for the fact that their ranks were recruited from other sources* [italics added—compare with McDonald's "hordes of small farmer-debtors"]. A contemporary, speaking of the election of delegates to the convention, says: "Baltimore and Hartford counties alone are clearly anti-Federal, in which are many powerful and popular men who have speculated deeply in British confiscated property and for that reason are alarmed at shutting the door against state paper money. The same men, their relations and particular friends are more violently anti-Federal because they paid considerable sums into the treasury in depreciated continental currency and are scared at the sweeping clause . . . which may bring about a due execution of the treaty between Great Britain and America to their loss. [sic.][90]

McDonald also misstated Beard's claims about New Hampshire. He wrote:

> With respect to the Connecticut valley area [in New Hampshire], where about five-sixths of the towns voted for ratification, Beard follows Libby in the rather absurd assertion that the towns there were "commercial" by virtue of their location on the river and that it was as commercial communities that they supported ratification.[91]

Quotation of Beard's actual words seems sufficient comment:

> The third region in New Hampshire (whose representatives favored ratification) was "the Connecticut valley or border district" whose interests were akin to those of the sea towns because it had *commercial connection* [italics added] with the outside world through the Connecticut River. It was to this region particularly that Oliver

---

90. Beard, *Economic Interpretation*, 281-282.
91. McDonald, *We The People*, 245.

Ellsworth must have appealed in his open letter to the citizens of New Hampshire in which he said: "New York, the trading towns on the Connecticut River, and Boston are *the sources from which a great part of your foreign supplies will be obtained, and where your produce will be exposed for market* [italics added]. In all these places an import is collected, of which, as consumers, you pay a share without deriving any public benefit. You cannot expect any alteration in the private systems of these states unless effected by the proposed government."[92]

Having rejected the versions of "Beard's thesis" that Brown and McDonald presented, we can go on to appraise Beard's design of proof and his method of securing the data that he believed would bear out his hypothesis.

---

92. Beard, *Economic Interpretation,* 254-255.

Chapter Two

AN APPRAISAL
OF BEARD'S DESIGN
OF PROOF AND METHOD

❖❖

ALTHOUGH Beard's most acute insights relate to the unequal power of men to influence opinions and control decisions, he offered almost no evidence to support them. He asserted that men played different roles in the sequence of events that led to the adoption of the Constitution because they occupied different positions in the American social structure, but he did little more than sketch the sequence and suggest the attributes that gave them unequal power. For this set of claims, his treatment was not even "frankly fragmentary." Moreover, he did not indicate how they might be tested.

Beard's main preoccupation becomes evident when we recognize that his design of proof and his method apply only to his claims about the relationships between ideas and interests. They did not actually permit him to test those claims, however, for they both rest upon logically untenable assumptions.

A.
The Logical Fallacy in Beard's Design of Proof

Beard's design of proof required him to establish two variable relationships. That is, he proposed first to classify men "as economic beings dependent upon definite modes and processes of gaining a livelihood," and then to ascertain on which "side" of the Constitutional issue they "are to be found." To avoid misunderstanding, a quotation from Beard's first chapter will be repeated here: If men in the same economic group "were equally divided on the matter of adoption or rejection—it would then become apparent that the Constitution had no ascertainable relation to economic groups or classes, but was the product of some abstract causes remote from the chief business of life—gaining a livelihood." But, if "substantially all" members of "groups of personal property interests" and "their professional associates" were pro-Constitution, and "substantially all or the major portion of the opposition came from the non-slaveholding farmers and the debtors—would it not be pretty conclusively demonstrated that our fundamental law was not the product of an abstraction known as 'the whole people,' but of a group of economic interests which must have expected beneficial results from its adoption?" A short answer to that long question is—No.

1. SELF-INTEREST AND POLITICAL BEHAVIOR

Unless Beard had first demonstrated that perceived self-interest is the only determinant of political behavior, his design of proof was logically untenable. Apart from other considerations, it was logically untenable because it *assumed* what Beard proposed to *demonstrate*.

Beard had no basis for assuming that conscious self-interest is the only aspect of class position that influences political behavior. Apparently, the unresolved dualism in his thought led him to treat the direct effects of self-interest as though they were synonymous with the subtle, complicated, and indirect effects of men's being "dependent upon definite modes and processes of gaining a livelihood." In other words, he confused the concepts of "interest group" and "social class." Certainly, Seligman's version of the economic interpretation of history, which Beard regarded as "nearly axiomatic," did not postulate a direct, one-to-one relationship between self-interest and political behavior. As noted above, Seligman warned against the fallacies inherent in economic determinism and criticized Loria's "landed" application of it.[1] Thus, even if Beard's description of the divisions of opinion among groups on the Constitution were accurate, he was still logically required to offer additional evidence for his claims about men's motives; he could not infer them from the data required by his design of proof.

---

1. Beard apparently did not grasp the significance of Seligman's assertion that it would "be absurd to deny that individual men, like masses of men, are moved by ethical considerations. On the contrary, all progress consists in the attempt to realize the unattainable,—the ideal, the morally perfect. History is full of examples where nations, like individuals, have acted unselfishly and have followed the generous promptings of the higher life. The ethical and the religious teachers have not worked in vain. To trace the influence of the spiritual life in individual and social development would be as easy as it is unnecessary. What is generally forgotten, however, and what it is needful to emphasize again and again, is not only that the content of the conception of morality is a social product, but also that amid the complex social influences that cooperated to produce it, the economic factors have often been of chief significance—that pure ethical or religious idealism has made itself felt only within the limitations of existing economic conditions." *The Economic Interpretation of History* (New York, 1902), 126 and 112-134. Clearly, Seligman argued against the fallacy of making conscious self-interest the invariant, primary determinant of human behavior.

2. IS CLASS POSITION THE ONLY DETERMINANT
   OF POLITICAL BEHAVIOR?

The fallacious assumption that self-interest is the only aspect
of class position that influences political behavior does not warrant the further assumption that class position is the only determinant of political behavior. Beard revealed the fallacy in his
design of proof by making vague, scattered references to the
political effects of membership in ethnic and religious groups
and of partisan affiliations antedating the Constitutional conflict.[2] If class position were the only determinant of political
behavior in 1787-1788, other factors became entirely irrelevant
to his interpretation. But, for example, if men's opinions on the
Constitution were influenced by their membership in certain
ethnic groups, Beard could not test his hypothesis by restricting
his attention to their class position.

Stated in somewhat formal terms, Beard's design of proof
is logically fallacious because it assumes that the relationship
between two variables can be discovered without considering
the possible influence of other variables. Or, in positive terms, to
discover the relationships between opinion on the Constitution and economic class, it is necessary to consider the effect
of other variables (factors) that might also have influenced
opinion (e.g., membership in ethnic groups, membership—or
lack of it—in religious groups, previous partisan affiliations, level
of education). In short, spurious relationships *may* result if
attention is restricted to two variables. Two examples—one
hypothetical, one substantive—help to clarify the point.

a. A Potentially Verifiable Hypothesis. To be potentially
verifiable, a hypothesis must satisfy at least one set of data that
are logically relevant to its claims. (Of course, the likelihood
of verifying a hypothesis increases as we see that it satisfies
additional sets of relevant data.) In my opinion, voting behavior

---

2. See, for example, Charles A. Beard, *An Economic Interpretation of
the Constitution of the United States* (New York, 1935), 283, 310-312.

during the contests for delegates to the state ratifying conventions is the best indicator of men's opinions about the Constitution. Thus, we should regard Beard's hypothesis about why men favored, or opposed, the Constitution as potentially verifiable, if we find it consonant with voting statistics that have been systematically collected, organized, and analyzed.

Suppose we take New York as a test case. To support a judgment that Beard's hypothesis is potentially verifiable, we must show that members of the same class tended strongly to vote for the same party, despite their membership in groups identified by some other attribute than economic class, e.g., small debtor-farmers voted Antifederalist, even though they belonged to different ethnic groups such as Scotch-Irish, English, Dutch, and German. And, to take the same example, if we could show that small debtor-farmers voted Antifederalist irrespective of their membership in groups identified by *any* attribute other than economic class, we would increase the likelihood that Beard's hypothesis was verifiable. No matter how many attributes we consider, the logic of the procedure remains the same. To simplify the example, therefore, we can restrict attention to economic classes and ethnic groups and assume that we have the required data.

To test Beard's hypothesis, we would examine the data to learn the voting behavior of each economic class in each ethnic group, e.g., small debtor-farmers whose ancestry was English, Scotch-Irish, Dutch, and German. Put another way, depending upon the precise nature of our data, in each ethnic group, we would try to learn the voting behavior of men who belonged to the different classes, e.g., men of English ancestry who were small debtor-farmers, landed proprietors, large holders of personal property, merchants, mechanics.

To conclude that Beard's hypothesis was potentially verifiable, we must find a common voting pattern among members of each class. For example, we would not only have to find that most small debtor-farmers voted Antifederalist, but that roughly the same proportion of them tended to vote Antifederalist in each ethnic group. (To simplify the discussion, I am imposing the unrealistic requirement that members of a specified class vote alike in every ethnic group; this enables us to ignore the problem of deciding how much variation among ethnic groups is consonant with Beard's claims about class voting.) Similarly, we would have to find that, in each ethnic group, large holders of personal property gave overwhelming Federalist majorities. The hypothetical table below shows the kind of data that would support the conclusion that Beard's claims were potentially verifiable.

Hypothetical Table: Voting by Class and Ethnic Group, New York, 1788

	Scotch-Irish		English		Dutch		German	
	Fed. %	Anti. %	Fed. %	Anti. %	Fed. %	Anti. %	Fed. %	Anti. %
Debtor-Farmer	20	80	20	80	20	80	20	80
Landed Proprietor	40	60	40	60	40	60	40	60
Mechanic	75	25	75	25	75	25	75	25
Large Holder, Personal Property	85	15	85	15	85	15	85	15

Suppose we found, however, that small debtor-farmers of Scotch-Irish ancestry held opposite opinions on the Constitution from their English counterparts. And suppose we found that the Scotch-Irish voted strongly Antifederalist irrespective of class, the English voted strongly Federalist, also irrespective of class. Finally, let us suppose that the same homogeneous voting behavior characterized all ethnic groups, i.e., members of the group tended strongly to vote alike, irrespective of class position. We would then be forced to conclude that, insofar as we had tested it, Beard's hypothesis about why men favored or opposed the Constitution was invalid.

I have been trying to show that Beard could not test his hypothesis by restricting attention to the relationships between the two variables, opinion on the Constitution and economic class. *At the minimum*, he was logically required to consider the effects upon men's opinions of one other possible influence, such as their membership in ethnic groups.

Perhaps the logical fallacy in his design of proof is best pointed up by this paradox: We might have to conclude that his hypothesis was invalid, even though we found that most small debtor-farmers voted Antifederalist and most large holders of personal property voted Federalist. In discussing this paradox, let us assume that the following statements are true: The proportion of men who belonged to specified economic classes varied widely according to ethnic group, e.g., a large majority of the Scotch-Irish, but only a small minority of the English, were debtor-farmers. The reverse was true of large holders of personal property, i.e., they constituted a small minority of the Scotch-Irish, a large majority of the English. Irrespective of class, the Scotch-Irish voted strongly Antifederalist, the English voted strongly Federalist. Our final assumption: the large majority of small debtor-farmers were Scotch-Irish; in all other classes, the large majority were not Scotch-Irish.

Under those conditions, although it would be literally true to say that voting patterns showed class differences, it would be thoroughly misleading. For, despite their different class positions, members of the same ethnic group voted alike. Since most small debtor-farmers were Scotch-Irish, as a class they necessarily voted Antifederalist. But the spurious nature of the relationship becomes apparent when we realize that it seems to exist only because of the ethnic composition of the class. Voting behavior was not related to class but to ethnic group; the relationship between opinion and class was a spurious one because it disappeared when another factor (or variable) was considered.

Unfortunately, largely because Beard's design of proof has gone unchallenged to date, the information required by our hypothetical example has never been collected. Thus, to show that it may be possible to collect the information necessary to test his hypothesis about why men favored or opposed the Constitution, as well as to demonstrate further the fallacy in his design of proof, a substantive example from another period in American history will now be given.

b. Testing Claims about Economic Class and Voting Behavior. Following Beard's lead, historians of New York politics have claimed that party divisions in the state essentially followed class lines. To support their hypotheses, they also used a two-variable design of proof. But when I examined data about men's membership in groups defined by attributes other than class (e.g., ethnic and religious), with few exceptions, the alleged relationships became either non-existent or spurious.[3]

For example, in testing the claim that, during the, 1840's, urban workers in New York strongly supported the Democrats, I considered the possibility that the overwhelming majority of workers belonged to religious and ethnic groups whose members voted Democratic *independently of their economic class position.* Under those conditions, a strong, positive relationship between workers and the Democratic Party might turn out to be spurious, i.e., their affiliation with the Democrats would be related to their religious and ethnic affiliations, rather than to their class position. And, after the relevant data were collected, ordered, and analyzed, that is what I found. With few exceptions, in each economic class, voting tended to vary strongly with membership in ethnic and religious group, previous political allegiance, local conditions (and numerous other influences). One specific example illustrates the point.

In 1844, about 95 per cent of *Catholic* Irish workers voted Democratic and about 90 per cent of *Protestant* Irish workers voted Whig. Yet, because the religious and ethnic groups that voted overwhelmingly for the Democrats constituted so large a proportion of the urban workers, the statement that "most workers" voted Democratic is both literally true and completely misleading. They voted that way, not because they were workers, but because they were Irish Catholics (or members of certain other groups) and also happened to be workers. Contrary to the economic determinist interpretation that stemmed from Beard,

---

3. The material is reported in a book to be published in 1961 by the Princeton University Press; it is tentatively entitled, *The Concept of Jacksonian Democracy: New York as a Test Case.*

during the 1840's, political divisions in New York related more closely to ethnic and religious groupings than to economic class.

3. APPRAISING BEARD'S DESIGN OF PROOF

From the examples given above, we can see that neither an economic determinist nor an economic interpretation of politics can be tested by restricting attention to two variables. Beard's design of proof made it impossible for him, therefore, to draw any reasonable inferences about the relationships between class position and opinion on the Constitution. Even if he had devised an adequate system for classifying economic groups, and even if the data he required had been arranged systematically and accurately, it could only be said with confidence that his claims might be correct—and then again, they might not be. When we try to discover the relationships between any two variables, our design of proof must permit us to consider the possible influence of *at least* one other variable. And the more variables we consider, the greater the likelihood of our verifying, or discrediting, a hypothesis. (For convenience, the procedure outlined above will hereafter be referred to as *multivariate analysis*.)[4]

---

4. Historians, no doubt, will find its mathematical passages hard going, but I believe that they can profit considerably from the section, "Multivariate Analysis," in Paul F. Lazarsfeld and Morris Rosenberg, eds., *The Language of Social Research* (Glencoe, Ill., 1955), 109-199. As defined by Lazarsfeld and Rosenberg, multivariate analysis describes "*the study and interpretation of complex inter-relations among a multiplicity of characteristics.*" I do not intend to imply that historians should mechanically imitate procedures developed by non-historians. On the contrary, I have deliberately used a non-technical term, "relationship," instead of "correlation," to avoid the implication that historians must become statisticians in order to use quantitative methods. It is the *logic* of multivariate analysis, not its specific applications in other disciplines, that seems to me to have potential value for historiography.

Scholars who shy away from anything smacking of "scientific" and "statistical" procedures because of concern for literary values, might recall that T. S. Eliot developed the method of "objective correlatives," used so effectively by Ernest Hemingway. See Carlos Baker, *Hemingway: The Writer as Artist* (Princeton, N. J., 1956), 54-58. The "potentially verifiable" concept is discussed in Lee Benson, "Research Problems In American

A balanced appraisal of Beard's work, however, must take this consideration into account: In 1913, no useful models existed to inspire him as he tried to devise a design of proof for hypotheses about mass behavior. Here, as elsewhere, he contributed significantly to historiography by recognizing the existence of a problem and beginning the job of solving it. As American history demonstrates, in all fields of endeavor, it is usually the second or third wave of settlers who reap the harvest for which pioneers have broken the ground. And Beard, it is worth remembering, was a pioneer in what he then called "scientific history."

B.
The Logical Fallacy in Beard's Method

Now, if it were possible to have an economic biography of all those connected with its [the Constitution's] framing and adoption—perhaps about 160,000 men altogether,—the materials for scientific analysis and classification would be available.

Since he could not compile those biographies, Beard devised a method that he believed yielded the data required by his design of proof. He divided the 160,000 men into three types, depending upon the roles they played in the framing and adoption of the Constitution: 1) the few who actually framed the Constitution; 2) the somewhat larger number of delegates to the state ratifying conventions; 3) the mass of voters who elected the delegates. He assumed that in all three categories of political activity, men who belonged to the same economic class tended strongly to take the same position on the Constitution, e.g., that roughly the same proportion of large holders of personal property favored the Constitution, whether they were delegates to the Constitutional Convention, delegates to the state conventions,

Political Historiography," in Mirra Komarovsky, ed., *Common Frontiers of the Social Sciences* (Glencoe, Ill., 1957), 118-119.

or voters. Thus, according to Beard's assumption, if we learn the group divisions among the delegates to the Constitutional Convention, we can infer the group divisions among the voters.

In his most carefully developed chapter, Beard presented short "economic biographies"—admittedly sketchy and based largely on secondary sources—of the fifty-five delegates who attended the Philadelphia Convention. He conceded that a valid test of his claims also required collection of biographical data about men assigned to the other two categories of political activity. For example, in a later chapter, he observed that:

It would be fortunate if we had a description of each of the state [ratifying] conventions similar to that made [by him] of the Philadelphia Convention; but such a description would require a study of the private economy of several hundred men, with considerable scrutiny. And the results of such a search would be on the whole less fruitful than those secured by the study of the Philadelphia Convention, because so many members of the state-ratifying bodies were obscure persons of whom biography records nothing and whose property holdings do not appear in any of the documents that have come down to us.[5]

Having these data only for Pennsylvania, Beard attempted to buttress his findings with materials "drawn from incomplete sources." For the most part, the sources were secondary works influenced strongly by Turner's adaptation of Loria's "free land" theory of American (and world) history.[6]

Despite the obvious imprecision and fragmentary nature of the data, Beard concluded that collective biographies of the Founding Fathers at Philadelphia and of the delegates to the Pennsylvania ratifying convention—the only one that he studied—supported his claims about the framing and adoption of the Constitution. He based this conclusion on the assumption that

---

5. Beard, *Economic Interpretation*, 253-254. "For the purposes of a fine analysis of the economic forces in the ratifying process, it would be of the highest value to have the vote on delegates to the state conventions in each town and county throughout the whole country; but unfortunately no such figures are compiled and much of the original materials upon which the statistical tables could be based have doubtless disappeared." *Ibid.*, 243.

6. *Ibid.*, 254. See my essay on Loria, Part One of this book.

his method of compiling collective biographies of men appointed or elected to political assemblies enabled him to discover the class division of opinion. This assumption is logically fallacious. Even if he had compiled accurate and fairly complete collective biographies of delegates to the Constitutional and state ratifying conventions, and even if he had used what we have called multivariate analysis to discover the divisions of opinion among them, he would still have lacked justification for drawing inferences about the class divisions of opinion in the country at large.

1. DID MADISON INSPIRE THE COLLECTIVE BIOGRAPHY METHOD?

Where did Beard get the idea that the compilation of collective biographies of delegates to political assemblies would enable him to discover the divisions of opinion among groups or classes? I suggest that Madison's *Federalist* No. 10 inspired him. At any rate, he based the procedure of compiling collective biographies on the same assumptions that Madison made in the section of that paper dealing with "Legislation by Special Interests"—to use Beard's caption from his edition of *The Enduring Federalist.*

Madison warned that unless a well-designed government system were created to control the "effects" of faction, the will of "the most numerous party . . . must be expected to prevail" in legislative assemblies:

No man is allowed to be a judge in his own cause, because his interests would certainly bias his judgment, and, not improbably, corrupt his integrity. With equal, nay with greater reason, a body of men are unfit to be both judges and parties at the same time; yet what are many of the most important acts of legislation, but so many judicial determinations, not indeed concerning the rights of single persons, but concerning the rights of large bodies of citizens? *And what are the different classes of legislators but advocates and parties to the causes which they determine* [italics added]? Is a law proposed concerning private debts? It is a question to which the creditors are parties on one side and the debtors on the other. Justice ought to hold the balance between them. Yet the parties are, and must be, themselves the judges; and the most numerous party, or, in other words, the most powerful faction must be expected to prevail. [A number of similar examples follow.][7]

Whether or not Madison actually inspired Beard's method, their assumptions were identical. For, if it were true that "the different classes of legislators [are] but advocates and parties to the causes which they determine," class divisions of opinion in legislative assemblies might accurately reflect class divisions among the population at large. We have only to substitute the Philadelphia and state ratifying conventions for Madison's legislative assemblies and the parallels with Beard's assumptions and procedures become apparent. But, unless we accept the assumption of economic determinism that all members of the same social class hold the same opinion on issues that affect them, the collective biography method, as used by Beard and implied by Madison, is logically untenable.

b. Do Public Assemblies Represent the Electorate in Microcosm? Contrary to Madison, delegates (or legislators) belong simultaneously to many different groups (e.g., ethnic, religious, urban). And their ideas of "justice" do influence their opinions —at least to some extent on some occasions. Not all men who belong to the same class or group take the same position on an issue, even if they all perceive that it serves their individual interests. A Liberal Republic is not the same as a Corporate State, and men who belong to one class or group may represent men who belong to classes or groups other than their own. Failure to recognize this possibility, or to weigh it properly, led Beard to devise a method that can demonstrate only how members of public assemblies vote on issues.

The fallacy in Beard's method can be seen most clearly by examining his treatment of the Pennsylvania ratifying convention. Let us make three arbitrary assumptions: 1) membership

---

7. Quoted in Charles A. Beard, ed., *The Enduring Federalist* (Garden City, N. Y., 1948), 71. The conjecture that Beard derived the collective biography method from *Federalist* No. 10 is supported by his summarizing the passage quoted above as asserting that "The theories of government which men entertain are emotional reactions to their property interests." *Economic Interpretation*, 157.

in an economic group was the only factor that influenced opinion on the Constitution; 2) his system of economic classification was adequate; 3) his information about the delegates' economic interests was accurate and comprehensive. The convention voted 46 to 23 in favor of the Constitution and Beard believed he could accurately classify thirty-eight delegates who favored the Constitution and eighteen who opposed it. His table is given below:

[Pennsylvania Ratifying Convention—Vote by Economic Group]

	For the Constitution	Against
Merchants	4	1
Lawyers	8	1
Doctors	2	—
Clergymen	2	—
Farmers	10	13
Capitalists	12	3
Total Classifiable	38	18

Commenting upon his tabulation, Beard argued: "When all allowance for error [in the data] is made, the result is highly significant and bears out the general conclusion that the Constitution was a reflex of personalty rather than realty interests."[8] But that conclusion rests on the assumption that the Pennsylvania convention represented the electorate in microcosm, i.e., that the delegates accurately reflected the opinions of the groups to which Beard assigned them. Is that assumption warranted?

For example, can we assume that the five merchant delegates constituted a representative sample of *all* Pennsylvania merchants? Other considerations aside, the convention delegates

---

8. *Ibid.*, 273-281. Interestingly enough, members of the "Namier school" of English historiography have employed the collective biography to support conclusions about the absence of class divisions during the English Revolution. For example, see D. Brunton and D. H. Pennington, *Members of the Long Parliament* (London, 1954). I do not know whether Beard inspired the Namier school's use of the method; but, whether it is used to "prove" the presence or absence of class divisions in politics, it is logically fallacious.

were elected to represent *counties*, not *economic classes or interest groups*. Thus, men who happend to belong to the same economic class or group might have been elected to take different positions on the Constitution.

Beard, it should be noted, did not challenge Orin Libby's claim that the "delegates of all the Federal counties . . . [with one possible exception] clearly represented the sentiments of their constituents in their vote in the Convention," and that the "opposition [Antifederalist] section of Pennsylvania, as indicated by the votes of the delegates in convention, seems to have very generally coincided with the avowed sentiments of the majority of the people of the section."[9] If Libby is right, therefore, we do not discover anything about the class divisions of opinion when we learn that the Constitution was favored by 80 per cent of the "merchants" (four of five) at the Convention and by 43 per cent of the "farmers" (ten of twenty-three). It is possible that they reflected accurately the divisions of opinion among all Pennsylvania merchants and farmers; it is also possible that they did not. Since Pennsylvania was overwhelmingly agrarian, Beard's table indicates only that the proportion of delegates at the Convention who were not farmers exceeded their proportion in the population.

Even if we assumed that factors associated with membership in economic groups were the only determinants of opinion, it is still possible to conceive of instances in which Beard's tabulation would misrepresent group divisions on the issue.

Suppose that a small minority of merchants throughout the state favored the Constitution. But, suppose further, that those few merchants were joined by members of other groups favorable to the Constitution, and thus, together, they were able to elect the candidates whom they nominated. In that event, divisions among the mercantile delegates at the Pennsylvania ratifying convention would give a distorted picture of divisions among Pennsylvania merchants generally. For present purposes,

---

9. Orin G. Libby, *The Geographical Distribution of the Vote of the Thirteen States on the Federal Constitution, 1787-8* (Madison, Wisconsin, 1894), 82-84.

it does not matter whether this actually happened; the point is that it could have happened. We must demonstrate, not assume, that members of an elected or appointed public body form a representative sample of a population and accurately reflect its views. But once we know the group divisions of opinion among the population, compilation of the collective biographies of legislators becomes superfluous. At best, it can tell us only what we already know.

The same line of argument applies to the Philadelphia Convention. Beard may have been correct in claiming that the delegates identified themselves with particular economic groups, and that they acted as representatives and accurately reflected the views of those groups. It does not follow, of course, that all *representatives* of a group were actually *members* of that group. Moreover, they may have had diversified interests which made them difficult to classify by the criterion of their occupation or property. Historians are not entitled, therefore, to assume that the compilation of economic biographies automatically reveals which delegates represented what groups at Philadelphia (or at any other convention), or that divisions among delegates assigned by historians to one group, accurately reflected divisions among the members of that group. By following Beard's own line of argument about the process of gaining power, we can suppose that a small minority of a specified group may have been able to get its representatives appointed and thereby to prevent the view of the majority from being expressed at the Convention.

In summary: Even if we assume that nothing but conscious self-interest influenced opinions on the Constitution, Beard's method of collective biography cannot provide a short cut to the goal of discovering the group divisions of opinion—no matter how systematically and accurately it is followed.

And yet, it is only fair to say that Beard significantly contributed to the development and application of quantitative methods to historical materials. When we view his work in perspective, we can see that he was trying to find sampling techniques that would facilitate the systematic analysis of group behavior (of the kind discussed below, pages 200-202). Beard did not reach his goal, but pioneers rarely do.

3. RECENT CRITICISMS OF BEARD'S METHOD

Although, in recent years, historians have sharply criticized Beard's use of the method of collective biography, they have not advanced beyond him. Far from questioning his assumptions, they have accepted the essential validity of the method, as he used it. Taken together, they have criticized him on three grounds: 1) his data were inaccurate; 2) his categories of economic groups were inadequate; 3) most important of all, his method, properly used, yielded data that discredited his claims.

Since Forrest McDonald based his critique of Beard's thesis largely upon data gathered by the collective biography method, his assessments of Beard's findings and procedures can illustrate recent criticisms in their most developed and detailed form.[10]

a. Interest Groups and Voting Behavior. As I read Beard, he wanted to locate men in the social and cultural structure that resulted from the "modes and processes" by which men gained their "livelihood[s]" during the 1780's. To achieve his objective, he tried to devise an index of social class based upon the criteria of wealth, occupation, status, and geographic location.

Convinced that Beard's system of identifying and grouping men was inadequate, Professor McDonald proposed to replace

---

10. Of course, Beard's critics are legion. But I am concerned here with the four who have specifically employed his method to discredit his conclusions. To my knowledge, the first study of this kind was William C. Pool, "An Economic Interpretation of the Ratification of the Federal Constitution in North Carolina," *North Carolina Historical Review*, 27: 119-141, 289-313, 437-461 (April, July, October 1950). It was followed by Robert E. Thomas, "The Virginia Convention of 1788: A Criticism of Beard's *An Economic Interpretation of the Constitution*," *Journal of Southern History*, 19: 63-72 (February 1953); Robert E. Brown, *Charles Beard and the Constitution* (Princeton, N. J., 1956), and Forrest McDonald, *We The People: The Economic Origins of the Constitution* (Chicago, Ill., 1958). For an illuminating, wide-ranging review of the literature, see Richard B. Morris, "The Confederation Period and the American Historian," *William and Mary Quarterly*, 3rd ser., 13: 139-156 (April 1956).

it with a "new system of categories of interest groups," composed of "at least twenty basic occupational groups" and "six basic forms of capital." McDonald would carry the process of atomizing American society even further, for "most of the occupational groups and all the forms of capital may be divided into two to seventy-five subdivisions." Once the requisite data were brought "within the framework of the new system of categories of interest groups presented here [in his book], some assessment may be made of the role of economic forces in the contest over the Constitution."[11] But, in my opinion, if historians abandoned Beard's inadequate system, only to accept the one proposed by McDonald, they still would not be able to assess "the role of economic forces in the contest over the Constitution."

As we have already seen, McDonald accepted Beard's design of proof which rests upon economic determinist assumptions. And, to understate the case, when he proposes to arrange men in an extremely large number of groups with extremely narrow interests, McDonald comes no closer than Beard to a system of classification that would help historians to discover the relationships between social class and political opinion. His "new system," designed to sharpen the theory of economic interpretation, would actually distort it into a theory of atomistic egoism. For McDonald's system derives from the crude version of economic determinism that assumes men behave primarily as members of interest groups that keep a profit-and-loss account of their feelings and calculate the cash value of their political actions.

Conceivably, in the study of some types of political problems, a system similar to the one proposed by McDonald might be appropriate. For example, it might be used to study the history of a tariff bill which directly, immediately, and seriously affected a wide range of narrowly-based interest groups, e.g., producers of beet sugar, pottery, steel.[12] From my own work in the politics of railroad regulation, however, I am inclined to believe

---

11. McDonald, *We The People*, 398-399, and 358-399.

12. See, for example, the use made of such interest group categories, in E. E. Schattschneider's famous study, *Politics, Pressures and the Tariff* (New York, 1935).

that, even under those conditions, cash value calculations would at best determine the voting behavior of only a substantial minority of the rank and file members of those groups. On the other hand, such calculations might determine the voting behavior of most of the leaders of those groups.[13] In dealing with problems of this type, therefore, we could profitably use the kind of system that McDonald proposed.

But, whether they are violent or "peaceable," political revolutions are radically different from battles by pressure groups over tariffs and railroad regulation. Thus, the large number and specific kinds of categories of interest groups, which might be used to study the Smoot-Hawley Tariff and the Interstate Commerce Act, would be grossly inappropriate in a study of the Constitutional revolution.[14] When the system of government of a country is at stake, when fundamental ideas about what constitutes the Good State in the Good Society are in conflict, economic self-interest is only one of many considerations that influence men's opinions and actions. In short, historians can regard ideology as a direct product of self-interest, only by clinging to economic determinist fallacies which, at this late date, need no further exposure.

Ideology always cuts across the lines of interest groups, particularly in a crisis. As a result, some men whose "interests" sharply conflict find themselves in agreement on matters more important to them, or united against other men with whom they have more fundamental conflicts, or both. In studying the battle over the Constitution, we are likely to progress further if we group men, not according to their "economic interests," but according to their social and cultural characteristics (defined by such criteria as class, ethnic group, religious group,

---

13. See the discussion in Lee Benson, *Merchants, Farmers, & Railroads: Railroad Regulation and New York Politics* (Cambridge, Mass., 1955), 55-114, 204-246.

14. My thinking about the general problem of devising systems of classification has benefitted considerably from Paul F. Lazarsfeld and Allen H. Barton, "Qualitative Measurement in the Social Sciences: Classification, Typologies, and Indices," in Daniel Lerner and Harold D. Lasswell, eds., *The Policy Sciences* (Stanford, Cal., 1951), 155-192.

residence, education), their formal and informal organizations (e.g., Masonic Order, Order of Cincinnati, political factions), their values, their beliefs, their symbols, their sense of identity. In general, during the 1780's, with whom did men identify? With whom did they regard themselves as being in conflict? In other words, which side were men for? Which side were they against? With whom were they identified by others? When we learn the answers to these questions, when we learn whom men referred to when they spoke of "us" and "them," we have excellent criteria for classification.

The argument can be summarized briefly: In studying the Constitutional revolution, the problem is not to devise a system of classification based primarily on narrow interest groups that can be precisely defined. The problem is to devise one based on the "broad symbolic groups"—to borrow Daniel Bell's illuminating phrase[15]—that the men of the 1780's knew existed, even though they would have not been able to define them precisely or say exactly whom they included.

As a solution to the problem, Beard's system was seriously inadequate. Yet, with all its deficiencies in conception and execution, it at least pointed in the right direction; that is, it was based upon broad symbolic groups, such as inland "small farmers" and large-scale "landed proprietors." In contrast, the system advocated by his critic would lead historians astray. For if they followed McDonald and used narrowly-based interest groups as guide lines to study the Constitutional revolution, they would march backwards and resume the search for "Economic Man."

  b. Did McDonald Advance Beyond Beard? Critical of Beard's categories of delegates to the Philadelphia and state conventions, McDonald proposed new ones and set about gathering the data needed to fill them out. Fortunately for our purposes, his analysis of the Pennsylvania ratifying convention compares directly with Beard's use of the collective biography. McDonald's table, reproduced below, summarized his discussion of "how the dele-

---

15. My ideas have been clarified by discussions with Daniel Bell. The "broad symbolic group" concept will be treated in detail in his forthcoming study, *Communism and the American Labor Movement.*

[Pennsylvania Ratifying Convention—Voting by Interest Groups]

Economic Classification	Voting Yea		Voting Nay	
	No.	Per Cent	No.	Per Cent
Occupation:				
Merchant	1	2.2	1	4.3
Tradesman	4	8.7	1	4.3
Manufacturing Capitalist	6	13.0	7	30.4
Lawyer	6	13.0	1	4.3
Physician	2	4.3	—	—
Clergyman	2	4.3	1	4.3
Miscellaneous	9	19.6	6	26.0
Farmer	16	34.8	6	26.0
Total	46	100.0	23	100.0
Investments in:				
Commerce	6	13.0	2	8.7
Manufacturing	8	17.4	8	34.8
Vacant Lands	11	23.9	8	34.8
Securities	23	50.0	17	73.9
One or more of the above	39	84.7	21	91.3
Security holdings:	[dollars]		[dollars]	
Combined, all delegates	67,666		70,852	
Average per holder	2,942		4,167	
Mean per holder	846		1,460	
Average, all delegates	1,471		3,080	

gates lined up for and against ratification, considered from the point of view of their occupations and from the point of view of their investments and security holdings."[16]

Anyone who has compiled the collective biography of a public assembly will appreciate how much work that short table represents, as well as the tremendous amount of work that must have gone into all of McDonald's tables for the Philadelphia and state conventions. Arguing that his categories were more realistic and his data more accurate than Beard's, he claimed to have discredited Beard's findings about the group divisions of opinion in Pennsylvania. Far from dividing along economic lines, "the delegates on the two sides held about the same

16. McDonald, *We The People*, 181.

amounts of the same kinds of property, and they were engaged in similar occupations." According to McDonald, Pennsylvania was not a unique case, and, he believed, his data for all the conventions demonstrated that "on all counts, then, Beard's thesis is entirely incompatible with the facts."[17]

But once it is recognized that public assemblies cannot be treated as the electorate in microcosm, it becomes clear that McDonald's data no more discredited Beard's claims than Beard's data had originally supported them. Suppose we ignore McDonald's commitment to the assumption that only self-interest influences opinion. If we learn that *literally* one out of two, rather than four out of five, merchants at the Pennsylvania convention voted for the Constitution, can we then conclude that, as a group, the merchants of the state were equally divided on the issue? Can we credibly conclude from the table that 80 per cent of the *members* of his "Tradesman" category favored the Constitution and 20 per cent opposed it? To ask these questions is to answer them. Like his predecessors who had essentially copied Beard's method while trying to discredit his study, McDonald did an enormous amount of work which, because of the logical fallacy on which the method rests, could not yield the data needed to test Beard's claims about the divisions of political opinion among groups.[18]

Failing to recognize the logical fallacies in the design of proof and the method that he copied from Beard, McDonald wound up his book as though its alleged refutation of "Beard's thesis" entitled him to render this judgment:

. . . the whole idea (expounded by Beard and many others) of beginning [historical] research with a system of interpretation and basis of selection, or with a hypothesis, or even with a question, breaks down. However it might be evaluated in terms of philosophy and pure logic, the fact is that it was developed largely for practical reasons, and it is precisely from the practical standpoint that it is weakest. If one guesses wrong, if one investigates a phenomenon in terms of a system of interpretation and selection which proves

---

17. *Ibid.*, 181-182, 349-357.

18. McDonald's use of evidence is discussed in the Appendix to Part Three.

to be unworkable, all one's efforts may be wasted. An equal amount of effort, applied inductively, might have covered less ground, but it would at least have brought the investigator to a stage at which a more tenable system of interpretation could be induced from the body of particulars, and would *at least have taught him to ask meaningful questions* [italics added].[19]

The errors in that back-to-induction manifesto have long been recognized and exposed. "No systematic thought," A. N. Whitehead observes, "has made progress apart from some adequately general working hypothesis, adapted to its special topic. Such an hypothesis directs observation, and decides upon the mutual relevance of various types of evidence. In short, it prescribes method. To venture upon productive thought without such an explicit theory is to abandon oneself to the doctrines derived from one's grandfather."[20]

Scholars like McDonald who fail to venture forth with theories, hypotheses, and questions, fail to recognize that good research designs permit investigators to explore problems by checking, modifying, or abandoning hypotheses and developing new ones as they proceed. Ideally, such designs are not biased in favor of confirming ideas tentatively advanced during the early stages of work. True, the ideal is seldom attained. Time and energy are usually wasted even in well-designed studies that start with interesting questions, hypotheses, and interpretative systems. It is also true that, once committed to a hypothesis or line of investigation, researchers tend to resist recognition of error. "I was wrong," is perhaps the most difficult phrase scholars are ever called upon to pronounce. But this only shows that, in the domain of scholarship and science, as in most others, man has not yet attained perfection.[21]

---

19. McDonald, *We The People*, 414, 411-414.
20. Alfred N. Whitehead, *Adventures of Ideas* (New York, 1933), 286.
21. A personal note is relevant. The original design of the study which resulted in the present essay called for the compilation of legislative collective biographies. Considerable time and energy was devoted to compiling the requisite data before I became aware of the method's logical fallacy. In fact, in a preliminary paper written in 1954, I confidently asserted that "Beard's main contribution . . . [to American historiography] was not interpretative but methodological. Few would deny that the pro-

McDonald to the contrary, perhaps Beard contributed most significantly to American historiography by explicitly rejecting the notion that researchers should venture forth unguided by theory or hypothesis. He recognized that "many pitfalls . . . beset" travellers on the tricky road to interpretation, but he recognized also that Baconian Rules of Induction provide little guidance to historians seeking to avoid those pitfalls. Historians concerned with the "proximate or remote causes and relations" of phenomena, Beard argued, were more likely to reach their goals if they consciously adopted or formulated a theory and a hypothesis than if they set out uncommitted—but blind.[22] That the specific theory he adopted and the specific hypothesis he formulated may be untenable neither discredits his general approach nor detracts from his contribution. After the appearance in 1913 of Beard's book, it was never so easy again for an American historian to ignore theory or hypothesis and proceed to pile up a mountain of "facts," in the hope that, somehow, the mountain itself would move and reveal the truth.

---

cedure he outlined and partially demonstrated, constituted a major advance in the investigation of historical problems." Contrary to McDonald's inductionist argument, however, use of a systematic research design eventually helped me to discover the error in my procedures.

22. Beard, *Economic Interpretation*, 3-4.

Chapter Three

AN APPRAISAL
OF BEARD'S HYPOTHESIS

◇◇

FORTY-SEVEN YEARS after Beard published his brilliant pioneering book, we still cannot confidently appraise his main hypothesis. At present, we can say only that a convincing case has yet to be made, for or against it.

Beard's claims about the sequence of events that led to the framing and adoption of the Constitution require data that are not yet available. For example, they require us to know the divisions of opinion among groups in the several states. Since we do not have this information, a Scot's verdict on Beard's hypothesis is mandatory: "Not Proven" or "Not Disproven."

Nevertheless, with existing data we can make a highly tentative appraisal. For our purposes, a tentative appraisal of a few claims is sufficient; what we want to decide is not whether Beard's hypothesis has been proven or disproven, but whether it has plausibility.

Since Beard's hypothesis consists of a number of closely related, but logically distinct, sets of claims, we shall examine them separately. Proceeding from the simple to the complex, we begin with his claims about the numerical divisions of opinion, go on to those that deal with men's motives, and conclude with his claims about men's ability to control the processes of opinion-making and decision-making.

A.
Numerical Divisions of Opinion

Beard's claims about the numerical divisions of opinion on the Constitution fall into two categories: 1) the number of men who expressed their opinions by voting for delegates to the ratifying conventions; 2) of those who voted, the number who favored, and the number who opposed, the Constitution.

1. VOTERS AND NON-VOTERS

Beard conceded that the available voting data were fragmentary; nevertheless, he thought it possible and useful "to put together several related facts bearing on the matter." Having examined those "facts," he went on to observe: "It seems a safe guess to say that not more than 5 per cent of the population in general, or in round numbers, 160,000 voters, expressed an opinion one way or another on the Constitution. In other words, it is highly probable that not more than one-fourth or one-fifth of the adult white males took part in the election of delegates to the state conventions. If anything, this estimate is high." When he wrote his "Conclusions," he had settled on "one-fourth" as the percentage of adult white male participants.[1] Since the number of men who voted was 160,000, this gives us a figure of 640,000 for the adult free white males. (He referred briefly to indentured servants, but apparently did not include them in his estimates.)

Writing more than four decades later, Professor Brown did not offer any estimates of his own about the number and percentage of men who took part in the ratification of the Constitution. Throughout his book, however, he criticized Beard for his misleading use of evidence, unwarranted conclusions from evidence, and guesses unsupported by evidence:

Given all this discussion [by Beard], we can only conclude that Beard's estimates of the total vote on the Constitution are mere guesses (p. 250). Since we do not know how many people voted, we are not justified in saying that 100,000 voted for it and 60,000 voted against it.[2]

Brown's use of evidence will be examined later, but it is appropriate to cite McDonald's appraisal in 1958 of Beard's "mere guesses" of 1913.

Perhaps because he believed that Beard's thesis could be reduced to the three "propositions" quoted in Chapter Two, McDonald did not comment in detail upon his findings about voting which must have required a great amount of work. But, evidently, he does not share Brown's low opinion of Beard's estimates, for he praised them highly:

Using ingenious calculations as a means of projecting a paucity of known facts into a larger estimate, Beard conjectures that about 160,000 persons voted in the election of delegates to the several state ratifying conventions, and that of these not more than 100,000 favored ratification.[11]

Note 11 reads:

After a survey based on tabulations from all discoverable voting records preserved in the archives of the thirteen states and of all

---

1. Charles Beard, *An Economic Interpretation of the Constitution of the United States* (New York, 1935), 239-251, 325.

2. Robert E. Brown, *Charles Beard and the Constitution* (Princeton, N. J., 1956), 164, 61-72, 149-170.

votes recorded in extant newspapers of the period, it is my conclusion that Beard's estimate of the total vote was remarkably accurate.[3]

And later in the book, although he was not then referring to Beard's estimate, McDonald discussed the "600,000 free adult white males who were entitled to express themselves on political questions. This figure takes no account of those few who were disfranchised by law."[4] Beard's figure—640,000—was slightly higher, but it included men disfranchised by law, who, by his estimate, made up roughly one-quarter of the total. (Claims about disfranchisement will be discussed below.)

I am not suggesting that McDonald's findings are conclusive, particularly since he did not report his data in detailed form. But he did not tend to accept Beard's views uncritically. It seems reasonable to say, therefore, that as far as they have been tested, Beard's claims about the turnout of voters appear valid.

a. Involuntary Non-voters. In his second chapter, Beard identified "four groups whose economic status had a definite legal expression: the slaves, the indentured servants, the mass of men who could not qualify for voting under the property tests imposed by the state constitutions and laws, and women, disfranchised and subjected to the discriminations of the common law." After noting that these groups were "not represented in the Convention which drafted the Constitution," he wrote: "How extensive the disfranchisement really was cannot be determined."[5]

Read in context, the last sentence refers to adult free white males. Yet Brown interprets it as a "startling confession" by Beard that his thesis was untenable:

First Beard discussed the disfranchised, and here appeared the initial statement of the second part of the Beard thesis—that the Constitution was put over undemocratically in an undemocratic society. His classification of the disfranchised—slaves, indentured servants,

---

3. Forrest McDonald, *We The People: The Economic Origins of the Constitution* (Chicago, Ill., 1958), 14 and n. 11.

4. *Ibid.,* 359 n. 1.

5. Beard, *Economic Interpretation,* 24.

women, and the "mass of men" who could not qualify for voting because of property qualifications—is misleading. If slaves and women had to vote before there was democracy in this country, we did not have democracy until 1920. Actually the only group which concerned Beard in the remainder of the book was the *free adult white men who were disfranchised by property qualifications* [italics added]. Half of the Beard thesis, that the Constitution was put over undemocratically in an undemocratic society, must therefore depend on proof that a "mass of men" were disfranchised by these property qualifications.

By his own statement, this second half of the Beard thesis should have been discarded on page 24. After saying that "the mass of men" were disfranchised, a phrase having the connotation of large numbers, and that these disfranchised were not represented in the Convention, Beard made this startling confession: "How extensive the disfranchisement really was cannot be determined." But of course determining the extent of disfranchisement is absolutely fundamental to half of the Beard thesis. We *must* determine the extent of disfranchisement before we can state that "the mass of men" were disfranchised and that the Constitution was put over in an undemocratic society. If Beard did not have the evidence, and if the problem cannot be solved, he did not have a valid interpretation.[6]

These two paragraphs could be criticized on a number of counts, but, for our purposes, to show that nothing in Beard's book justifies Brown's discovery of a "startling confession," is sufficient.

In his second chapter, "A Survey of Economic Interests in 1787," Beard wrote that certain people who lived in the United States were not then entitled to vote in public elections and, therefore, were not represented by the delegates appointed to the Constitutional Convention by state legislatures. This short, factual statement was not related to his claims about the ability of Federalist leaders to secure political power. Brown's comments, which implied that the statement was part of "Beard's thesis," are misleading and irrelevant. For, as Brown observed, "the only group which concerned Beard in the remainder of the book was the free adult white men who were disfranchised by property qualifications."

On the same page,[7] Beard noted that the proportion of dis-

---

6. Brown, *Charles Beard*, 34-35. See also *ibid.*, 66-68.
7. Beard, *Economic Interpretation*, 24.

franchised adult white males could not be *precisely* determined. Contrary to Brown, however, he neither said nor implied that *rough estimates* were impossible, and, in the appropriate chapter (IX), "The Popular Vote On The Constitution," he presented them.

After a sketchy survey (Chapter IV) of the effects of property qualifications for suffrage in the several states (we still do not have an adequate study of their effects), Beard summarized his views in Chapter IX:

It is impossible to say just what proportion of the adult [free white] males twenty-one years of age was disfranchised by these qualifications. When it is remembered that only about 3 per cent of the population dwelt in towns of over 8000 inhabitants in 1790, and that freeholds were widely distributed, especially in New England, it will become apparent that nothing like the same proportion was disfranchised as would be today under similar qualifications. Dr. [J. F.] Jameson estimates that probably one-fifth of the adult males were shut out in Massachusetts, *and it would probably be safe to say that nowhere were more than one-third of the adult [free white] males disfranchised by the property qualifications* [italics added].

Far more were disfranchised through apathy and lack of understanding of the significance of politics.[8]

That Brown failed to take the italicized clause into account is the more noteworthy, since he commented upon the one immediately preceding it, and quoted the sentence immediately following it.[9] Had Brown accurately summarized what Beard said on this page (and elsewhere), he could not have sustained his argument that Beard claimed it was impossible to estimate the proportion of men disfranchised by property qualifications.

Though stated imprecisely, Beard's estimate set an upper limit, "nowhere . . . more than one-third . . ."; a figure he thought reasonably accurate for New York.[10] Since he observed that freeholders were particularly numerous in New England, his citation of Jameson's estimate for Massachusetts suggests a lower limit of 20 per cent for the nine states in which freehold

---

8. *Ibid.,* 241-242, 64-72.
9. Brown, *Charles Beard,* 69, 159.
10. Beard, *Economic Interpretation,* 67-68, 242.

suffrage qualifications existed.[11] In the four other states (Georgia, New Hampshire, New Jersey, Pennsylvania), it is difficult to infer what proportion of adult free white males he thought disfranchised by the requirements of property or payment of taxes. But it seems possible to strike a rough balance. A reasonably faithful translation of his imprecise statements about the extent of disfranchisement yields an estimate of 25 per cent for the country as a whole. Taking 25 per cent as his estimate of the proportion of involuntary non-voters, we can go on to a different kind of problem—the appraisal of the estimate's validity. Here McDonald joins Brown and dissents from Beard.

We have seen that McDonald noted that his own calculations took "no account of those few [free adult males] who were disfranchised by law."[12] We assume that "few" meant far fewer than 25 per cent; but he failed to present data to support his estimate. Brown, on the other hand, devoted a great deal of attention to the issue and cited data purporting to show that the estimated percentage of eligible voters among adult males in Massachusetts "should be revised upward into the high 90's," and that almost no adult white males were disfranchised anywhere in the country. "If ninety per cent or more of the men were freeholders and voters, and if merchants and mechanics voted in eight or nine states, where did the 'mass of men' who were disfranchised come from?"[13]

To understand how Brown arrived at his estimate of disfranchisement, it is necessary to examine his estimate of the distribution of property in the United States. As he alternatively phrased it, "American society was predominantly middle-class

---

11. We do not yet have a credible, systematic account of the impact of suffrage restrictions over time. A brief survey of the 1780's is given in Dudley O. McGovney, *The American Suffrage Medley* (Chicago, Ill., 1949), 11-25, but it clearly was not based upon detailed research. Richard P. McCormick is currently engaged in studying this problem and his work may answer the questions with which historians have long but sporadically grappled.

12. McDonald, *We The People*, 359 n. 1.

13. Brown, *Charles Beard*, 34-45, 61-72, 100-106, 157-170. The quotations are from pp. 161 and 39, respectively.

in 1787 . . . there were few extremes of wealth and poverty, and . . . most men owned property"; "most men were middle-class farmers who owned realty. . . ."[14] "Middle-class" is an extraordinarily elastic term. It can mean, and has meant, remarkably different things to different historians. Brown made a number of statements, however, that permit us to translate his definition into quantitative terms applicable throughout the country.

After asking what Beard's state-by-state summary of property qualifications "for the suffrage and for holding [public] office" actually showed, Brown wrote:

In New Hampshire, apparently most men could vote and a *very small amount of property* [italics added] qualified a man for office. The £ 200 freehold for senators and £ 100, half to be freehold, for representatives favored *realty*, not *personalty*, and, as I have shown elsewhere [i.e., in his book on Massachusetts], a *£ 200 freehold was a very small farm indeed* [italics added]. . . . Beard said that the New York Senate represented property, but it was *realty*, not *personalty*, for a senator had to be a freeholder and electors of senators had *to own freeholds worth £ 100—a small holding* [italics added].

The same situation existed in the Southern states. In Maryland:

The £ 500 and £ 1000 current money requirements for representatives and senators should have restricted officeholding *to average small farmers at least* [italics added] . . .

Farther South:

South Carolina demanded a settled estate and freehold worth £ 2000 currency for senators and £ 1000 for representatives, *which would probably have cut out the smallest farmers* [italics added].[15]

Thus, to Brown, a £ 200 freehold was relatively a "very small farm," "average small farmers" were worth about £ 500, and only the "smallest farmers" probably could not satisfy a £ 1000 freehold requirement. Fortunately, McDonald has provided a

---

14. *Ibid.*, 42-43, 197. See also, 20-21, 156, 197-200.
15. *Ibid.*, 62, 63, 65, respectively.

table of exchange rates which shows what the pound was worth in the various states in 1787. One pound was valued at $3.33 in New Hampshire, $2.50 in New York, $2.67 in Maryland, and $4.28 in South Carolina.[16] Even if we take the lowest figure, in 1787, according to Brown, the *average small farmer* in the United States owned a farm worth about $1250.

Though Brown acknowledged that he had not studied the distribution of property in any state other than Massachusetts, he assumed that "detailed research" would yield similar results in the other states.[17] That estimate, however, is so far off for New York that I doubt its accuracy for any state.

Brown did not use the data and conclusions reported in the well-known monograph by E. Wilder Spaulding, *New York in the Critical Period: 1783-1789*. Nonetheless, to maintain that a £ 200 freehold was "a very small farm indeed," and that a £ 100 freehold was "a small holding" in New York, Brown had to discredit Spaulding's data which showed that under the state Constitution of 1777:

Qualifications for the suffrage were intricate, varied, and restrictive. All £ 20 freeholders or renters of tenements worth 40 shillings a year, if they paid their taxes, might vote; as well as all the [138] freemen of the cities of Albany and New York. The 24 freeholders who composed the Senate were chosen for four years by £ 100 freeholders only; and the governor, himself a freeholder, by the same limited electorate. Under these restrictions there were in 1790 some 57,600 electors in the state, nearly 17 per cent of the whole population. Of these electors *just one-third could qualify under the £ 100 freehold clause that enabled them to vote for governor or senators. Two-fifths of the total were £ 20, but not £ 100, freeholders. One-quarter were not freeholders at all, but forty-shilling men* [italics added.][18]

The italicized figures, it will be noted, are for the restricted electorate, not for all adult white males. Spaulding estimated

16. McDonald, *We The People*, 385.

17. Brown, *Charles Beard*, 71-72.

18. E. Wilder Spaulding, *New York in the Critical Period: 1783-1789* (New York: 1932), 90-91.

that from 25 per cent to 40 per cent of the latter were disfranchised by property qualifications;[19] Beard, it will be recalled, put the figure at "one-third."

If Spaulding was correct in accepting as reasonably accurate the statistics of the 1790 New York State Census, *then substantially less than one-third* of the adult white males in the state possessed even "a very small farm indeed," as characterized by Brown. This conclusion follows for two reasons: first, only one-third of the restricted electorate possessed freeholds worth at least £ 100, and surely not all of them were worth £ 200; second, Spaulding's impressionistic data suggest that about one-quarter of the tenant farmers did not ordinarily meet the minimum property qualifications for voting, and some adult white males in New York stood even farther down on the economic ladder. In other words, if a £ 200 freehold is set as the lower economic limit of middle-class status, then the overwhelming majority of adult white males in New York did not qualify for membership in that class; if the lower limit is set at £ 100, more than two-thirds of them still failed to qualify. (No doubt, some non-freeholders owned other property worth more than £ 100, but there is no reason to suppose that they were very numerous.)

Nearly fifty years after Beard called attention to the problem, we still do not have a sound, detailed description of social stratification in the United States during the 1780's. So far as they go, however, the New York data cited by Spaulding tend strongly to discredit Brown's estimate that the *average* small farmer owned a freehold worth as much as £ 500. If the distribution of property in other states even loosely resembled that in New York, his thesis about "middle-class America" has no basis in fact. In any case, Spaulding's study lends considerable support to Beard's claim that the property requirements for voting *and officeholding* had the effect of disfranchising a significant proportion of the adult white males.

Though Brown was mistaken about the distribution of prop-

---

19. *Ibid.,* 200-201.

erty in New York in 1787, it might still be said that my last conclusion is unjustified for at least two reasons: first, these property qualifications for *voting* might work to disfranchise men, but property qualifications for officeholding would not. Second, all such qualifications might be considered irrelevant to the political conflict over the Constitution in New York. Brown expressed the second point in these words: "In the end, all these figures, generalizations, and estimates for New York add up to nothing, anyway, for as Beard said (p. 67), the ratifying convention in New York was elected under the universal manhood suffrage rule."[20] Yet in this sentence, Brown reveals another crucial weakness in his criticism of Beard; he substitutes legal formality for political reality. Here, as elsewhere, he attempted to grind Beard between the dull millstones of formalism and literalism.

The penetrating comment upon this formal view of the political process was made long ago and its point is still sharp, despite frequent use. "The law in its majestic equality," Anatole France observed, "forbids the rich as well as the poor to sleep under bridges, to beg in the streets, and to steal bread."

It is true that the New York Legislature suspended long-established voting qualifications and allowed universal manhood suffrage during the election of delegates to the state ratifying convention. (No other state, it will be recalled, enacted such a provision.) It is true that officeholding qualifications did not formally affect men's legal right to vote. But, as informed students of American politics have long known, many subtle *extra*-legal considerations affect participation in the political process. In saying that Beard's observations about disfranchisement in New York "add up to nothing," because the extraordinary step was taken of suspending the traditional rules, Brown was applying an anti-historical conception of human behavior; it prevented him from understanding the behavior of men who ordinarily were either "shut out" of politics or had only limited voting privileges and were debarred from holding certain offices.

---

20. Brown, *Charles Beard*, 64.

b. Voluntary Non-voters. Some of Beard's most acute observations, though stated ambiguously, dealt with the behavior of men who could vote but failed to do so. Some men were disfranchised by law, he noted, but:

Far more were disfranchised through apathy and lack of understanding of the significance of politics. It is a noteworthy fact that only a small proportion of the population entitled to vote took the trouble to go to the polls until the hot political contests of the Jeffersonian era. Where voting was *viva voce* at the town hall or the county seat, the journey to the polls and the delays at elections were very troublesome.[21]

Literally and formally, of course, no one entitled to vote is disfranchised. But Spaulding's conclusions about the campaign in New York give evidence that Beard was perceptive in fact, if imprecise in form.

The campaign for the election of delegates to the state convention exhibited at the same time a surprising amount of indifference upon the part of the voters and an amazing amount of controversy in the press and among those who relished politics. Despite the extension of the franchise, most of those who had never been accustomed to go to the polls remained away as usual in 1788. But those who were experienced in the use of the ballot evinced an amount of interest that often bordered upon the fanatical. Those versed in public affairs appreciated the momentous character of the issue.[22]

Spaulding's observations need not be the last word on the subject. Yet, Brown, to sustain his argument that New York's long-established property qualifications for voting and office-holding meant "nothing" in the battle over the Constitution, was required to discredit them. Surely, the habitual behavior patterns of men would continue to affect their actions, even after the lifting of traditional legal restraints, especially when they were lifted suddenly and quietly. As Spaulding has observed, "Contemporaries were strangely silent concerning the reasons for extending the suffrage. . . ."[23] Under those condi-

---

21. Beard, *Economic Interpretation*, 242, and 252.
22. Spaulding, *New York in Critical Period*, 205.
23. *Ibid.*, 199-200.

tions, many men may not have been aware that the privileges of suffrage had been temporarily bestowed upon them. It is probable, also, that men who were accustomed only to limited voting privileges, who were debarred from major offices, and who were reminded of their inferior legal status every time they took part in an election, would tend to be less active in politics than men who suffered no such discrimination. But Brown's literal, formalistic view of the political process prevented him from appreciating Beard's insights:

Actually, Beard confused the issue [of participation] by his statement that "far more were disfranchised through apathy and lack of understanding of the significance of politics" (p. 242). In the first place, a man is not "disfranchised" if he has the right to vote but does not use it. The term disfranchised means that he has been deprived of the right, not that he simply failed to exercise his right. In the second place, the problems of whether a man *can* vote, but does not, are quite different from those of whether he *cannot* vote, but wants to. . . . When we stop talking about the "mass of men" who *could not* vote on the Constitution and start talking about the "mass of men" who *could* vote but did not bother to do so, then, and only then, will we understand the Constitution and its adoption.

Beard unwittingly gave the answer to this political apathy. On page 242 he implied that the journey to the polls and delays at elections were troublesome, thus accounting for the smallness of the vote. *This had little to do with the problem* [italics added]. The governing factor was whether or not there was an issue, or whether the people thought there was an issue, and how important it was. Beard gave figures to show that few people in Massachusetts voted in 1786, before Shays' Rebellion, but that in 1787, after Shays' Rebellion, the number trebled. This is correct, and anyone can chart the importance of the issues of the day by checking on the vote. In other words, the people exercised their right to vote when they thought something was at stake, and failed to vote when they were not particularly interested.[24]

It is surprising that a close student of American political history believes that the *conditions* under which elections were held "had little to do with the problem" of participation in the campaigns for delegates to the state ratifying conventions. Is

---

24. Brown, *Charles Beard*, 159-160.

it really necessary to debate the issue that the location of polling places, the time of elections, the ability of men to get to the right place at the right time, and similar considerations have influenced political conflicts from the eighteenth century to the present day? Richard P. McCormick's excellent study of voting in New Jersey during the eighteenth century helps us to appraise the contradictory positions taken by Beard and Brown:

> There were other factors not associated with suffrage qualifications that influenced voting. Perhaps of major importance was the accessibility of the polling place. Although the regulatory act of 1725 permitted the poll to be moved around the county with the consent of the candidates, it was the usual practice to hold the election in one place. Consequently, electors might have to travel as much as sixty miles to give their vote. Even though the polls were kept open for several days, one would have had to be especially zealous or interested to undertake the trouble and expense of voting under such conditions.[25]

McCormick cuts the ground from under Brown's formalist position. For Brown carried formalism to its illogical extreme when he argued, in effect, that the electoral law was the same for well-to-do members of "personalty groups" who lived at the county seat and for debtor-farmers who had to spend days getting to and from the polling place. What does the greater than normal turnout of eligible Massachusetts voters, under the extraordinary pressures generated by an armed rebellion, actually demonstrate? To answer that question, we must avoid such vague terms as "the people," and find out *who* normally voted and *who* normally did not. If a different class or group pattern of political behavior existed during the 1780's, and certain classes or groups turned out only under extraordinary pressures, then Beard can hardly be faulted for emphasizing the impact of extra-legal considerations upon men's ability to take part in the political process.

Aside from extra-legal considerations affecting men's ability

---

25. Richard P. McCormick, *The History of Voting in New Jersey* (New Brunswick, N. J., 1953), 62-63, *passim*.

to vote, we must consider, as students of American politics
have long done, the "disfranchisement" that occurs because of
"apathy and lack of understanding of the significance of politics"—to use Beard's early formulation. Like Beard, these scholars
recognize that to discover who does, and who does not, vote is
indispensable to an analysis of political contests. And their findings agree with his claim that differences in turnout closely
corresponded to differences in socioeconomic status, i.e., a much
larger proportion of the members of groups that were well-to-
do and well-informed took part in the Constitutional conflict
than did members of groups that were poor and poorly-
informed. Thus, an outstanding recent book summarizes the
results of many studies of twentieth-century voting behavior:

> Perhaps the most significant differentials in voting participation are
> those associated with economic status, educational level, and occu-
> pation. The body of participating electors consists disproportionately
> of persons in the upper half of the economic spectrum, of persons
> who have completed high school, and of persons in the so-called
> higher occupations. Contrariwise, the poor, those of little education,
> the unskilled and manual worker participate in elections in lesser
> degree. The extent of the differentials between these groups is great.[26]

Appropriately paraphrased, this statement might have been written by Beard to describe participation in the Constitutional
contest. Of course, even if we grant their accuracy and com-
prehensiveness, findings for twentieth-century elections are not
necessarily applicable to the eighteenth century. But they testify
to Beard's perceptiveness in raising the question whether class
differences existed in political participation during the 1780's.[27]
That question has not yet been answered by systematic research, but McDonald's impressionistic observations suggest
that research of this type would support Beard's claims:

> A large portion of the New Hampshire population was character-
> ized by an uninformed lethargy combined with an intense and
> narrow localism. The hard work that attends rural life in a cold,

---

26. V. O. Key, Jr., *Politics, Parties, and Pressure Groups* (New York,
1953, third ed.), 573 and 564-581.
27. Beard, *Economic Interpretation*, 251-252.

mountainous country, the closed-in environment, and the absence of social or economic stimuli made the majority of the citizenry almost unbelievably apathetic toward all political matters except those immediately concerning the towns in which they lived or their neighboring communities.[28]

Similarly, in commenting upon the political behavior of "subsistence farmers" who lived along "the stony ridges of New England," McDonald observed:

These farmers joined with other groups in insurrectionary movements in New Hampshire, Massachusetts, and Connecticut in 1786, all as a protest against the excessive tax burden on real property and polls [i.e., poll taxes]. In general, however, they often did not bother to participate in political affairs at all, not even to the extent of holding annual town meetings to vote for state officers.[29]

Historians concerned solely or mainly with legal formalities may criticize Beard for asserting that "Far more [men] were disfranchised through apathy and lack of understanding of the significance of politics"; historians concerned with political realities can be grateful to him for insights that students of American political behavior have been documenting since 1913.

2. DIVISIONS AMONG VOTERS

Beard estimated that the men who voted for delegates to the ratifying conventions divided about 100,000 in favor of the Constitution to 60,000 against. But he believed that these crude figures actually exaggerated the extent of popular support. "Indeed, it may very well be that a majority of those who voted were against the adoption of the Constitution as it then stood.

---

28. McDonald, *We The People*, 239. That quotation also serves to illustrate McDonald's failure to recognize the crucial differences between economic interpretation and economic determinism. Though he clearly was following Beard's lead and offering a *socioeconomic interpretation of political apathy* in New Hampshire, the sentence preceding the passage quoted in the text reads: "Economic factors seem to have had very little weight with most voters in New Hampshire, *except perhaps* [italics added] as ultimate causes of symptomatic conditions, as the fundamental characteristics and the immediate postwar history of the state attest."

29. *Ibid.,* 360-361, n. 5.

Such a conjecture can be based on the frank statement of no less an authority than the great Chief Justice Marshall who took a prominent part in the movement which led to the formation and ratification of the new instrument of government."[30]

Because Beard's most detailed statistics were for New York, it can again serve as a test case for his claims. Using fragmentary data, he estimated that the New York Antifederalists won a large majority of the delegates to the state ratifying convention—forty-one to twenty-three for their opponents—and a smaller majority of the popular vote in the seven counties for which he had statistics. Moreover, based upon the "ratio of delegates to population," he estimated that the Federalist counties were considerably over-represented in the convention.[31]

In his 1932 monograph, Spaulding slightly revised Beard's estimates but did not significantly alter them. He increased the Antifederalist majority to forty-six of the sixty-five delegates, gave the popular vote for an additional county, and noted that the Antifederalists won by majorities of two to one in two other counties. One of Spaulding's findings, however, did contradict Beard's argument about the impact of disfranchisement. Suspension of property restrictions for voting on delegates to the ratifying convention resulted in a total somewhat larger than that cast for assemblymen (the elections were held simultaneously), but the proportion of the vote for the parties remained almost unchanged. That is, in a particular county the Federalist candidates for convention delegate received about the same percentage as did the Federalist candidates for assemblyman.[32] But, Spaulding supported Beard's critically important conclusion "that the distribution of representation in the convention was grossly unequal and decidedly unfavorable to the Antifederalists":[33]

---

30. Beard, *Economic Interpretation*, 251.

31. *Ibid.*, 244-246. His table gave the Antifederalists 340 votes in Orange County; none were listed for the Federalists. Since it seems unlikely that the latter did not get a single vote in Orange, I have not included it among the counties for which Beard had statistics of the popular vote.

32. Spaulding, *New York in Critical Period*, 200-204.

33. Beard, *Economic Interpretation*, 244.

Delegates to the convention were to be apportioned among the counties exactly as their representatives to the Assembly were apportioned. This is important, for it worked some injustice to the Antifederalists . . . if the counties had had the number of their delegates strictly apportioned according to the population, the Antifederalists would have come off even better [in delegates], and the state might well have rejected the Constitution. Professor Beard has shown that 7 of the 9 Antifederal counties were underrepresented in the Assembly and convention as compared with all four Federal counties, and that the other 2, Suffolk and Washington, were underrepresented as compared with Kings and Richmond. If the ratio between the number of delegates and the population had been corrected, the Federalists would have obtained 6 less, or 13 delegates, in a total of 65. The state was clearly overwhelmingly opposed to the Constitution, with less than a quarter of its population within the Hamiltonian camp.[34]

Overlooking Spaulding's monograph once again, Brown castigated Beard:

The [Beard's] tables (pp. 244-45) on the Federalist and Antifederalist vote *mean very little as they now stand* [italics added]. The only thing they show is that except for Suffolk and Washington counties, the Federalist counties had fewer people per delegate than did the Antifederalist counties. Other than that, the tables merely raise questions. Given the fact that many people in other states were undecided and many delegates to the ratifying conventions went uninstructed, we would want to know whether New York's delegates were instructed, and if so, how, or whether they were merely to use their own judgment. Beard's figures on the vote are obviously incomplete and practically worthless, yet without the popular vote, we cannot say that the people of New York were overwhelmingly against ratification. It [if] we accept the figures in the tables at face value, the Constitution was defeated 41 to 23 in spite of inequitable representation. What we need to know is why it was ratified 30 to 27 [after weeks of debate at the Convention], and this Beard did not explain.[35]

It is true that, as Beard was the first to point out, "what we need to know is why it was ratified 30 to 27," and that he did not know the answer. It is also true that, down to the present,

---

34. Spaulding, *New York in Critical Period*, 201.
35. Brown, *Charles Beard*, 162-163.

no other historian has known the answer. But does Beard's inability to answer the question he raised justify the assertion that his tables on the vote "mean very little as they now stand?" Other considerations aside, those tables did not "stand" alone when Brown's book was published in 1956. By then, Spaulding's monograph, which amplified them while supporting their essential accuracy, had been available for twenty-four years. Brown's implied argument from silence carries no weight, particularly since two recent studies strongly support the view that he had no tenable basis for challenging Beard's estimate as amended by Spaulding.

No one familiar with Broadus Mitchell's biography of Alexander Hamilton is likely to characterize its author as a partisan of Beard. And no one is likely to characterize Hamilton as uninformed about the contest in New York or eager to exaggerate the Antifederalist strength. Both points underscore the significance of Mitchell's report that "When he knew the results of the elections Hamilton was surprised at the size of the Anti-Federal victory—a majority of two-thirds in the convention and, as best as he could judge, of four-sevenths in the state at large."[36] As we might expect, Hamilton apparently underestimated the Antifederalist majorities. According to McDonald:

The elections resulted in a smashing defeat for the Federalists. Anti-ratificationist candidates received more than 14,000 of the known votes as against only 6,500 for the Federalists. Federalists carried only the City and County of New York and three other counties with a total of nineteen delegates; their opponents carried nine counties with a total of forty-six delegates. The popular mandate was clear.

Indeed, while speculating about the results in counties where he had been unable to obtain the statistics on popular voting, McDonald suggested that "these facts would seem to indicate that the total vote gave the anti-Federalists an even greater majority of the popular vote, probably about 16,000 as against 7,000 for the Federalists."[37]

---

36. Broadus Mitchell, *Alexander Hamilton* (New York, 1957), 1: 428.
37. McDonald, *We The People*, 286 and n. 121.

McDonald, it will be recalled, characterized Beard's numerical totals for the country as "remarkably accurate." But his figures for New York show an even larger Antifederalist majority than did Beard's and therefore lend support to the latter's conjecture that "a majority of those who voted [actually] were against the adoption of the Constitution as it then stood." Whether or not systematic, detailed research will verify his conjecture, the New York data support Beard's minimum claim that, of the estimated 160,000 participants, "not more than 100,000 men favored the adoption of the Constitution at the time it was put into effect. . . ."

B.
Group Divisions among Voters

As we have noted, in attempting to appraise Beard's claims, it is difficult to determine who he included in his vaguely defined groups, the approximate percentages of specified groups that he assigned to each side, and whether the same divisions were supposed to hold in states, such as Delaware, Georgia, and New Jersey, which ratified the Constitution so quickly that any political contest was precluded (Connecticut might also fall into this class). Since his categories overlapped, men might simultaneously belong to groups that, according to him, tended to hold opposite opinions, e.g., Northern farmers who owned public securities. An arbitrary solution would be to classify men according to their major interest; that is, granted the validity of Beard's assumptions, did they stand to gain most from supporting the Constitution or from opposing it? Similarly, it might be possible to exclude from consideration those states in which, as he put it, "The absence of any contest of course contributes to obscuring the economic forces which may have been at work."[38]

---

38. Beard, *Economic Interpretation*, 265-273, 290.

But even if we adopted such arbitrary measures, Beard's claims about the popular vote would still have to be tested by multivariate analysis, not by his procedure which restricts attention to the relationships between economic class and voting behavior. For the present, because multivariate analysis requires collection and ordering of non-economic data on a town, parish, or county basis, and because the requisite data are not available, our appraisal of his claims must be highly tentative.

Once again New York can serve as a test case. Aside from its being a state for which county election returns are now available, several other characteristics make it worth examination: County voting patterns were distinct enough for us to draw inferences about the relationships between opinion and membership in specified economic groups; the long, intense campaign permitted the Federalists and Antifederalists to mobilize supporters; the heterogeneous character of the state permits us to examine the divisions of opinion among a wide variety of non-economic groups. New York, therefore, seems a good place to study "the economic forces which may have been at work" (although this does not imply, of course, that findings for New York are necessarily valid for other places.)

1. NEW YORK VOTING PATTERNS

Because McDonald did not present his voting statistics for New York, it is necessary to use Spaulding's earlier table.[39] Unless the table is grossly inaccurate, the county percentages reveal a sharp rural-urban cleavage. New York City (identical with the county) formed the core of the Federalist party. The Federalists won majorities in only three other counties clustered around Manhattan Island and their strength tended to diminish with distance from the urban center. (Available voting returns also show overwhelming Federalist majorities in urban areas all along the seaboard.)[40] Spaulding reports that, in

---

39. Spaulding, *New York in Critical Period*, 202-203.
40. Beard, *Economic Interpretation*, 245-246; McDonald, *We The People*, 129-130 n. 24, 164-165, 203.

addition to New York City, "the larger towns, especially Hudson, Albany, Lansingburgh . . . were generally Federalist, [and] the struggle might be called one of city against country . . ."[41] Because we have the returns only on a county basis, we cannot tell whether, in each county, the larger towns voted Federalist and the rural communities voted Antifederalist. Therefore, the best way to learn whether a rural-urban cleavage existed, is to examine the strongest and weakest Federalist counties.

Just as New York City formed the core of the Federalist strength and gave it 95.3 per cent of its vote, Ulster formed the core of the opposition, and gave 95.2 per cent of its votes to the Antifederalists. Birthplace and longtime political stronghold of George Clinton, the state's Antifederalist governor, Ulster was overwhelmingly an agricultural county. And, if Spaulding is correct, its population was composed mostly of independent freeholders; "the Ulster farmers, unlike the patroons of Westchester, Dutchess and Albany counties, usually worked their own fields and milled their own flour."[42]

Fortunately, a wide variety of ethnic and religious groups populated both New York and Ulster counties. Since both counties supported their favorite parties almost unanimously, it seems reasonable to infer that factors associated with ethnic or religious attributes had relatively little impact in either county —unless voting was confined to members of one group, a pos-

---

41. Spaulding, *New York in Critical Period*, 220. Quoting Spaulding more fully emphasizes the need to use multivariate analysis of political behavior: "No one formula will explain the party divisions of the spring of 1788. Geographically, the contest was to be of North against South, New York City and its neighbors against Ulster and its neighbors. And since the larger towns, especially Hudson, Albany, Lansingburgh and New York City were generally Federalist, the struggle might be called one of city against country; or, since all these towns were on navigable rivers, seaboard against countryside, merchant against farmer. It has also been labelled a contest of Tory against Whig, of 'ins' against 'outs,' of debtor against creditor, of plutocrat against democrat, of intelligence against stolidity, or of Episcopalian against non-Episcopalian."

42. *Ibid.*, 51-52; E. Wilder Spaulding, *His Excellency George Clinton* (New York, 1938), 10.

sibility for which there is no evidence. We can infer, therefore, that men who belonged to the same ethnic or religious group voted for opposite parties, their choice depending upon whether they lived in Ulster or New York.

Since voting in both counties apparently was not significantly related to ethnic and religious attributes, and since Ulster was agrarian and New York was urban, their diametrically opposed patterns—95.2 per cent Antifederalist, 95.3 per cent Federalist—suggests a sharp political cleavage between agrarians and non-agrarians. More precisely, it suggests that, as far as we have tested the relationship, a sharp political cleavage existed between men who lived in urban and agrarian communities. Our inference about the strong relationships between agrarianism and Antifederalism and urbanism and Federalism is supported by the available voting statistics; they indicate that the more remote from New York City, the more strongly the agrarian communities supported the Antifederalists.

I am not implying that exactly the same relationships between voting and type of community existed all throughout the state. Undoubtedly, factors other than residence in a particular type of community influenced men's opinions on the Constitution and party choices. But the available data suggest that the voting patterns of Ulster and New York counties typified the patterns that predominated in the state; namely, a sharp political cleavage between the inhabitants of agrarian and urban communities.

"Agrarians" and "non-agrarians" are neither elegant nor precise terms, but they do significantly differentiate men who lived in communities "dependent upon definite modes and processes of gaining a livelihood." Thus, although the inferred voting patterns in New York do not permit us to appraise Beard's claims about certain specialized groups, e.g., western land speculators and Hudson Valley landed proprietors, they do tend to support his general description of the conflict in the state. For example, from the nearly unanimous party votes in New York and Ulster counties, it seems reasonable to infer that men engaged in foreign and domestic commerce, in manufactures (broadly defined to include mechanics and artisans), and in professions and service industries associated with urban areas (broadly defined to include large towns), overwhelmingly voted Federalist, and that interior "small farmers" overwhelmingly voted Antifederalist. But the same data that support one of Beard's claims cast doubt upon another claim to which he attached great importance:

Inasmuch as so many leaders in the movement for ratification were large security holders, and inasmuch as securities constituted such a large proportion of personalty, this economic interest must have formed a very considerable dynamic element, if not the preponderant element, in bringing about the adoption of the new system.

In that statement, Beard was referring to "large security holders," but he went on to say that possession of *any* amount of securities turned men to Federalism. "The point, it may be repeated, is not the amount but the practical information derived from holding even one certificate of the nominal value of $10."[43]

Beard may have attached such great importance to security-holding because it represented his only significant research contribution to Constitutional historiography. His preface called attention to "The records of the Treasury Department at Washington, now used for the first time in connection with a study of the formation of the Constitution. . . ."[44] Not the first or last historian to exaggerate the importance of hitherto unused sources, Beard may have wanted to demonstrate that he was not entirely dependent upon secondary works. Whether or not this is so, Beard seems to have considerably exaggerated the importance of security-holding in the movement for the Constitution. Thus, in 1950, while praising him for destroying forever "the myth of a Constitution written by moral supermen in an economic vacuum," Irving Brant observed that he had "put far too much emphasis on ownership of public securi-

43. Beard, *Economic Interpretation,* 290 and 272 n. 1.
44. *Ibid.,* xix.

ties. . . ."[45] The voting data for New York support Brant's judgment.

In 1786, the Clintonians enacted a program beneficial to the state's five thousand security holders. Moreover, all of Ulster County's delegates to the 1788 ratifying Convention were Antifederalists, and all four, whose economic interests are known (they include George and James Clinton), owned public securities.[46] Taken together, these facts suggest that ownership of public securities was not rare in Ulster. And yet, of the county's 1,440 votes, only 68 were cast for the Federalists.[47] In the absence of precise data, let us assume that the county had something like its proportionate share of the relatively large number of men who owned public securities in New York. It follows, then, that possession of public securities did not convert men to Federalism. Contrary to Beard's claim, the 1786 Clintonian financial program, the 1788 voting data, and the fact that Ulster delegates owned securities all support McDonald's conjecture that "Probably a majority of the five thousand small security holders who had benefitted from the funding-assumption plan of 1786 followed Clinton in opposing the Constitu-

---

45. Irving Brant, *James Madison: Father of the Constitution* (Bobbs-Merrill Company, Inc., 1950), 60.

46. McDonald, *We The People*, 293-294, 305, 306, 307, 308. The Ulster County delegates whose economic interests have been ascertained by McDonald were George Clinton, James Clinton, Cornelius Schoonmaker, and Dirck Wyncoop. He was unable to compile an economic biography for Ebenezer Clark and John Cantine, but noted that the latter held a very small amount of continental securities. It should be observed that McDonald followed Beard in assuming that men who appeared on the funding books of the new government held public securities in 1787. Brown has challenged that assumption on the ground that men *could* have bought securities *after* 1787. This is true, but in the absence of *positive* evidence to the contrary, it seems reasonable to accept the assumption made by Beard and McDonald that *most* men who appeared on the funding books had not engaged in post-1787 speculation. Discussing the members of the Constitutional Convention, Beard dismissed the idea "that many of them would sink to the level of mere speculators." Compare, Beard, *Economic Interpretation*, 75 n. 3, and Brown, *Charles Beard*, 74.

47. Spaulding, *New York in Critical Period*, 203.

tion."[48] In other words, no significant relationships existed between owning public securities and opinions on the Constitution.

2. SOME IMPLICATIONS OF VOTING PATTERNS IN NEW YORK

From this short review of the available data on voting in New York, it seems clear that Beard's claim about the divisions of opinion among groups must be appraised separately, state by state. Although most of his claims for New York seem valid, the one to which he attached the greatest importance does not. It is also clear that to identify who voted for whom requires much more systematic and detailed information than has yet been collected; at present, even the elementary data (voting statistics) are not generally available for counties.

My own studies of nineteenth-century political behavior have persuaded me that before we can make sound estimates of the group divisions of opinion on the Constitution, we must collect on a town (or similar unit) basis, such data as voting statistics over time, and the economic, ethnic, and religious composition of the electorate. Once these data are collected and ordered, we should be able to learn who voted for whom. For example, as the New York and Ulster examples were designed to suggest, we can learn whether voting was more closely related to residence in certain types of communities than to membership in certain ethnic and religious groups. Of course, since we must rely upon data for political units (e.g., towns), we will not be able to identify precisely who voted for whom. But we do not have to. In order to appraise Beard's claims, we need only substantiate such statements as these: farming towns in New York tended to vote strongly Antifederalist, urban wards tended to vote strongly Federalist; farming towns, roughly similar in ethnic and religious composition, tended to vote more strongly Antifederalist as they were more remote from New York City.[49]

---

48. McDonald, *We The People,* 300.

49. The present study reports upon one aspect of a research project in political historiography which I have been conducting for several

Some of Beard's claims, however, concerned groups whose voting patterns cannot be inferred from the data for political units. For example, to learn whether "large holders of personal property," "Western land speculators," and "landed proprietors" voted strongly Federalist, we must collect information about individuals; it is highly unlikely that members of such specialized groups made up a significant proportion of the electorate in any town or ward.

Ideally, before appraising Beard's claims, we would know how every member of a group voted. But that is not only impossible, it is unnecessary. If we draw up an adequate, representative sample of the group and collect the data with a reasonable degree of completeness, we can infer the voting behavior of its members. For reasons already discussed, the individuals studied cannot consist exclusively, or predominantly, of men elected as delegates to the Constitutional Convention, or to the state ratifying conventions. In this respect, the method of collective biography suggested here differs significantly from the one Beard used. While it seeks to learn how the members of a group voted by studying how a relatively small number of men voted, it does not assume that members of public assemblies represent the electorate in microcosm.

American historians, of course, have long used sampling techniques, e.g., certain newspapers are used to represent the views of certain groups. But our argument is that, because we are dealing here with individuals, for the collective biography method to be successful, we must take particular care to see that we are studying *representative* men.

For example, if we compile a collective biography of "large holders of personal property," we must include, among others,

years. See Lee Benson, "Research Problems in American Political Historiography," in Mirra Komarovsky, ed., *Common Frontiers of the Social Sciences* (Glencoe, Ill., 1957), 113-181. See also, Paul Lazarsfeld and Morris Rosenberg, eds., *The Language of Social Research* (Glencoe, Ill., 1955), 290-296; Paul F. Lazarsfeld and Herbert Menzel, "On The Relation Between Individual and Collective Properties," in Amitai Etzioni, ed., *Reader in Organizational Analysis* (in press); Rudolph Heberle, *Social Movements* (New York, 1951), 211-217.

men who belonged to different ethnic and religious groups, who belonged to different political factions before 1787, who lived in different types of communities, and, ideally, each in ratio to their number in the population. In short, we must be sure that the men we study do *not* include a disproportionate number of any one group that is likely to hold similar views on a political issue. Otherwise, we may infer relationships that turn out to be spurious when we consider the influence of men's membership in a variety of groups.

C.
Content of Opinion

Since we do not yet have the necessary data, e.g., voting statistics, we do not know what happened during the political conflict over the Constitution, much less which groups held what opinion. It follows, therefore, that we are poorly prepared to appraise Beard's claims about the content of opinion. How can we hope to learn why men acted, for example, if we do not know who (what groups) held what opinions? But, though we know little about *group* opinions, we know a good deal about the opinions of such individuals as Madison and Hamilton. Analysis of their motives, and of the arguments they employed in *The Federalist* to win support for the Constitution, suggests that Beard's economic determinist claims about men's motives form the weakest part of his hypothesis.

1. BEARD'S INTERPRETATION OF WHY MEN ACTED

As restated here, Beard's hypothesis claims that, whether the Federalist leaders acted for themselves or as representatives for others, they were impelled by the belief that their own economic groups would directly and immediately benefit from the adoption of the Constitution. He ascribed similar motives to the

Antifederalists, but it is necessary to examine only one set of claims.

Beard's interpretation of why men acted was based upon three logically-related ideas: 1) As a result of the modes and processes by which livelihoods were gained during the 1780's, men belonged to different economic groups. 2) If they belonged to certain groups, they saw that their economic interests would either be aided or harmed by the Constitution; if they belonged to other groups, they failed to see that it would affect their interests. 3) Calculations of direct, immediate self-interest determined whether men supported, opposed, or were indifferent to the Constitution. Particularly as Beard related them to each other, those ideas derive, not from economic interpretation, but from economic determinism.

2. WHY DID MADISON AND HAMILTON ACT?

Referring to Madison as one of "the profoundest thinkers of the period," Beard depicted him as representing the "slave-holding planter as such." In other words, Madison represented the slaveholder who did *not* combine "personalty operations" with his planting, and who wanted a strong national government capable of guaranteeing the maintenance of "order against slave revolts." To support his interpretation, he cited Madison's *Federalist* No. 43 and claimed that it reflected "the slave-holders' instinctive fear of a servile revolt."[50]

As we have seen, Irving Brant applauded Beard's recognition that the Constitution was not framed "in an economic vacuum." Brant neither challenged Beard's description of Madison as a representative of Southern planters, nor denied that group and sectional interests influenced Madison's attitudes and opinions concerning the most desirable form of government. But he parted with Beard when he argued, in effect, that Madison was also influenced strongly by his conviction that adoption

---

50. Beard, *Economic Interpretation*, 29-30, 125-126, 174-175.

of the Constitution would lead to "the advancement of general welfare" and help to preserve "justice" in a liberal republic.

Aware of the "compulsions and clashes of economic interest," Brant, after examining the Constitution critically, found that his conclusions "do not diminish the economic motivation of the framers, but they build up the accompanying devotion to liberty. . . . No greater error can be made than to say that the Constitution was written either in a spirit of blind self-interest or of hostility to democracy." He argued that patriotic convictions greatly influenced Madison's opinions on the Constitutional issue. But, like Beard, he recognized that such a statement is meaningless unless it also accounts for Madison's particular conception of patriotism. Thus, he felt bound to explain why Madison "saw only one issue—'the simple one of whether the Union shall or shall not be continued,'" why "Madison's outlook was fundamentally national and totally unselfish" in "sharp contrast" to the parochialism and egoism of another Virginian, Patrick Henry.[51]

Brant evidently contends that Madison's membership in a certain economic group and his views about its interests significantly influenced his opinions. But, Brant also pointed to other significant influences: the convictions Madison had derived from studies in political science and history, his continuous public service during and after the Revolution, his familiarity with contemporary developments in Europe, and his personal experiences that contributed to a cosmopolitan outlook. Support for Brant's argument is found in Beard's matured views, which altered fundamentally the explanation he had advanced in 1913.

In 1948, in the preface to his edition of *The Enduring Federalist*, Beard emphasized that other factors besides group or sectional interests influenced Madison's conception of the Good State.

. . . Madison [like Hamilton and John Jay] was also active in the public service from 1780 to 1787. During this period he was a mem-

---

51. Brant, *James Madison*, 55-70, 158-160, 188-194.

ber of the Congress, a member and leader of the Virginia assembly, a member of the Annapolis convention, and again a member of Congress. While he was learning at first hand the arts of politics, Madison was engrossed in the study of history and government. He wrote to his friend Thomas Jefferson in Paris and asked him to supply books on the constitutions and public laws "of the several confederacies which have existed," and he dedicated toilsome days and nights to mastering the history of the great experiments in federal government from remote antiquity to his own time. With good reason Madison may be placed among the ablest "scholars in politics" in the history of the United States. He knew the weaknesses and proclivities of the old Congress, for he had served in it. He was acquainted with the propensities and activities of state legislatures, for he had served in the Virginia legislature. *Attached to his native state, he was nevertheless as much at home in New York or Philadelphia, as on his plantation in Virginia* [italics added]. In all the land Hamilton could have found no man so well fitted by study, knowledge, and public service to take part in the work of writing *The Federalist*.[52]

Had Beard not been handicapped by his Progressivist view of reality and his partial adherence to economic determinism in 1913, he might have recognized then that Madison, in *Federalist* No. 10, explicitly argued that the Constitution would promote "the advancement of general welfare" and secure "justice." Beard's failure to recognize this point, however, may have stemmed also from the fundamental contradiction between Madisons' theory of politics and his argument for the Constitution.

Since Madison was educated to view certain assumptions of Aristotelian political science as axioms and was convinced that history had demonstrated their soundness, he assumed that egoism controlled political behavior.[53] In *Federalist* No. 10, therefore, he sketched an economic determinist theory of politics.

52. Charles A. Beard, *The Enduring Federalist* (Garden City, N. Y., 1948), 23-24.

53. He bears no responsibility for the particular formulation here, of course, but my understanding of these matters has benefitted considerably from Douglass Adair's perceptive comments on an earlier draft of the present essay, and from study of two unpublished papers by him: "The Use of History by the Founding Fathers: The Historical Pessimism of A. Hamilton," "G. Morris on Alexander Hamilton as a Statesman."

But his practice belied his theory. For, in the same paper, in seeking support for the Constitution, he appealed to men's altruism, not to their egoism—and thus demonstrated the inadequacies of economic determinism, both as an explanation of human behavior and as an instrument of ideological warfare.

Immediately after giving a number of examples designed to show how a majority "might trample on the rules of justice" and disregard "the good of the whole"—every example involved economic interests—Madison maintained that the function of government was to prevent such calamities.

If a faction consists of less than a majority, relief is supplied by the republican principle, which enables the majority to defeat its *sinister* [italics added] views by regular vote. It may clog the administration, it may convulse the society; but it will be unable to execute and mask its violence under the forms of the Constitution. When a majority is included in a faction, the form of popular government, on the other hand, enables it to sacrifice to its ruling passion or interest *both the public good and the rights of other citizens* [italics added]. To secure the public good and private rights against the danger of such a faction, and at the same time to preserve the spirit and the form of popular government, is then the great object to which our inquiries are directed. Let me add that it is the great desideratum by which this form of government can be rescued from the opprobrium under which it has so long labored, and be recommended to the esteem and adoption of mankind.[54]

Clearly, Madison did not argue that property interests should be put beyond the reach of majority action; he argued that property interests—and by extension, all interests—should be protected against *unjust* majority action. Similarly, he urged protection of the Commonwealth against *harmful* majority actions, i.e., actions that might serve the *immediate* interests of the majority but would hurt their long-run interests. In short, Madison advocated the establishment of a Good State that would advance the general welfare, dispense justice, maintain liberty, and thereby earn its citizens the esteem of mankind.

True, Madison did not deal convincingly with the crucial

---

54. Quoted in Beard, *Enduring Federalist*, 71-72.

consideration that the same system of government, avowedly
designed to thwart unjust and ill-considered actions by the
majority, could be so controlled and operated by a strategically-
located minority as to thwart majority actions of an altogether
different character (e.g., presidential vetoes could rain down
upon the just and the unjust alike).[55] But that observation does
not alter the fact that Madison ignored his theoretical assumptions and *appealed to the public* to support the Constitution on
grounds other than self-interest, nor does it weaken Brant's
conclusion that Madison was impelled to act by considerations
other than group and sectional interests.

In his 1913 work, Beard placed more emphasis upon Hamilton's role in the Constitutional revolution than upon Madison's.
The famous chapter on "The Economic Interests of the Members Of The Convention" gave one and one-half pages to Madison and fourteen pages "to the colossal genius of the new
system, Alexander Hamilton."[56] In my opinion, the relative
space given these two Founding Fathers reflected Beard's estimate of the relative importance of groups in the Constitutional
revolution. Madison was depicted as representing certain "slave-
holders," Hamilton as representing three different sets of groups:
creditors (financiers, bankers, money lenders), merchants and
manufacturers, and "land speculators and promoters."

To say that Hamilton was depicted as representing these
three groups is justified only in the context of Beard's entire
book. Actually, the pages specifically devoted to the "colossal
genius of the new system" portrayed him as a man "swayed
throughout the period of the formation of the Constitution by

55. We need not accept Beard's description of the Constitution as
"essentially an economic document" to recognize the force of his argument that, under the system of government it established: "Property interests may, through their superior weight in power and intelligence, secure
advantageous legislation whenever necessary, and they may at the same
time obtain immunity from control by parliamentary majorities." *Economic Interpretation*, 159-161, *passim*. In 1913, Beard failed to recognize
that the Constitution was much more than "an economic document," but
American historians have profited from, and documented, his insights
concerning the nature and use of power in the American political system.

56. *Ibid.*, 100-114, 125-126.

large policies of government. . . ." If I interpret Beard correctly, he believed that the creation and maintenance of a strong national government was Hamilton's primary objective. To achieve this objective, Hamilton *used* certain groups. By helping them discover what they wanted, and then helping them get it, he succeeded in "attaching them to the federal government." Whether or not that interpretation is a correct reading of the Beard of 1913, it is essentially the interpretation convincingly presented in Mitchell's biography of Hamilton, as summarized in this sentence: "The exertion [by Hamilton, Madison, and Jay] to promote the Constitution was not covert, for a class, but *pro patria*."[57] Since Beard took virtually the same position in 1948 in his edition of *The Federalist*,[58] it is not necessary to cite further support here for Mitchell's views.[59] But it is worth emphasizing that neither Mitchell nor Beard contented themselves with saying that men supported the Constitution because they were patriotic; they tried to explain why men came to believe that patriotism required them to lead the Constitutional revolution.

3. TO WHAT MOTIVES DID *The Federalist* APPEAL?

If Madison and Hamilton (and Jay) were primarily impelled to act, not by considerations of direct, immediate group interests, but "by large policies of government," it seems reasonable to suppose that other men had similar motives. That hypothesis is supported by examining *The Federalist*.

We have noted that in 1913, Beard assumed that the arguments made in *The Federalist* papers indicated the motives that

---

57. Mitchell, *Alexander Hamilton*, 1: 421-422.

58. Beard, *Enduring Federalist*, 20-25.

59. The most recent biography of Hamilton appeared shortly before this essay went to press, but a hasty reading indicates that it offers essentially the same interpretation. However, it tends to give somewhat greater weight to personal ambition, i.e., to Hamilton's desire to influence "the shaping of the American future. . . ." John C. Miller, *Alexander Hamilton: Portrait in Paradox* (New York, 1959), 131-183.

led men to support the Constitution. Contending that its authors attempted "to convince large economic groups that safety and strength . . . [lay] in the adoption of the new system," he declared unequivocally that "every fundamental appeal in it is to some material and substantial interest." He dismissed its "discussion of the details of the new frame-work of government" as a discussion of "incidental matters when compared with the sound basis upon which the superstructure rested."[60] By 1948, however, Beard had arrived at a different appreciation of *The Federalist*. We are not concerned here with why he changed; the point is that his later reading is more consonant with a systematic analysis of its contents.

Perhaps the simplest way to indicate the weakness in the claims Beard made in *1913* is to note the questions that in *1948* he believed *The Federalist* illuminated:

To enumerate all the features of *The Federalist* that commend it to citizens concerned with government and liberty in the United States or the world would be to repeat many pages and numbers of the work. But, in brief, it may be safely said that there is scarcely a problem or aspect of government which excites contemporary interest that is left untouched in this great work.

Is it a question of government by discussion and reason or government by violence? . . . Is it a question of war, militarism, and civil liberty? . . . Is it a question of the circumstances and the kind of politics that lead to the suppression of liberty and the triumph of the tyrant or dictator? . . . Is it a question of class representation in the legislature or the representation of the people without reference to class distinctions? . . . Is it a question of the conduct of foreign relations and the dangers that may arise from the diplomacy of secret agreements—dangers of corruption and destructive commitments? . . . Is it a question of the power of Congress to protect the integrity of the Federal government by the regulation of elections in the State? . . . Is the conception of the United States as a "great power" in the world an invention of superior thinkers in our own time? . . .

Finally, to cut short this enumeration, is it a question of civic education in the first principles of the American system, of shaking ourselves loose from the partisan passions and hatreds which so

60. Beard, *Economic Interpretation*, 153-154.

often distort discussion of that system, and of trying to take a judicial view of it?[61]

Beard, writing in 1948, makes a convincing witness against Beard, writing in 1913. True, the *Federalist* papers were aimed at the educated public. But they appealed to men to support the Constitution for many different reasons. Contrary to what Beard believed in 1913, they did not appeal exclusively or predominantly to direct, immediate, economic interests.

D.
Translating Ideas into Action

Just as the biographies by Brant and Mitchell tend to discredit Beard's claims about men's motives, they tend to support his claims about the ability of Federalist leaders to put their ideas into effect. The operative words are "tend to support." For, although a long time has elapsed since Beard presented his ideas about the "peaceable" revolution, we still lack detailed knowledge of how the Federalist leaders proceeded and why they succeeded.

Because Brant and Mitchell wrote biographies, not histories, they gave hero's-eye views of events in Virginia and New York during the climactic stage of the Constitutional revolution, the ratification by state conventions. Nevertheless, though more rounded studies are necessary before we can make firm judgments, their biographies support Beard's argument that the Antifederalists were "beaten, outgeneralled, and outclassed in all the arts of political management."

In effect, two quotations from Brant's and Mitchell's accounts enable us to summarize their views.

To cap a detailed description of how Madison's strategy, tactics, and activities achieved "Victory in Virginia," Brant wrote:

---

61. Beard, *Enduring Federalist*, 17-19.

In guiding the Constitution to victory, Madison won the greatest forensic battle of his life, over the most formidable adversary [Patrick Henry] he ever faced, for the greatest stakes in national welfare. His leadership was not measured by his own work on the floor, extensive and effective as it was. Except for the arguments of [Edmund] Pendleton and [John] Marshall on the judiciary, virtually every affirmative utterance from any source bore the stamp of Madison's thought, previously expressed in the convention, in letters or in *The Federalist*. Superior reasoning was not enough. He had to pile up an extraordinary margin of logic to cancel the opposing eloquence.[62]

Mitchell was equally enthusiastic about Hamilton's accomplishments. In fact, he contended that to achieve victory, Hamilton had much greater obstacles to overcome in New York than did Madison in Virginia. That contention is easily accepted because, among other things, the popular elections had given the Federalists in Virginia a much larger proportion of the ratifying convention delegates than in New York. Mitchell makes a good case for his claim that Hamilton played a leading role in the "Victory Against Odds" won by the New York Federalists, but his assessment seems somewhat extravagant:

Hamilton's leading part in persuading the New York State convention to ratify the Constitution was his foremost political exploit. His agency in the Annapolis Convention, in turning frustration to new resolve, was an act of accumulated purpose ably timed. The element of surprise assisted him in nerving the disconsolate delegates to demand of Congress that it summon the states to a survey of the structure of the Union. His work in the Philadelphia Convention contributed to give the Constitution national, as opposed to federative, features, and strength in the central government which the plan would have lacked without him. . . .

His *Federalist* papers, aimed at the deliberations to take place at Poughkeepsie [site of state convention], were ancillary to his achievement there . . . in the New York ratifying convention circumstances that favored his other feats were notably absent. Granted that he had perfectly briefed himself as far as previous thought and experience permitted. However, at Poughkeepsie he met a hostile overwhelming majority ably led. . . .

---

62. Brant, *James Madison*, 227.

In a sense it is meaningless to say that he won the convention to the Constitution by sheer will power, for this is resolvable, as the record shows, into particular words and decisions at particular times in the course of weeks of debate. Yet it is the truth, for his will held not only determination, but readiness to sacrifice much to the main result. Never one to keep back his reserves, at this time more than others he threw himself with all he had into the fateful contest.[63]

If we reformulate Mitchell's estimate to say that Hamilton brilliantly led his party and brilliantly exploited the advantages inherent in the circumstances in which the battle over the Constitution was fought, it seems convincing. It then agrees with Spaulding's estimate of the Federalist victory in New York—and Spaulding was a warm admirer of Clinton and the Antifederalists. Without going into the details of the particular "circumstances" that Spaulding believes enabled the Federalists to win,[64] we can make the point by this quotation:

Although the superiority of the Federalist advocates [at the Convention] was so marked that a contemporary called their reasoning and eloquence "irresistible," Hamilton himself admitted that their "arguments confound but do not convince." Indeed the arguments were nothing but what had already been filling the papers for ten months' time. What, then, did convince, and what was responsible for the ultimate Federalist victory? It was perhaps the constant work of the parties outside the convention: the activities of the Federalist leaders, Hamilton, Livingston, and Jay, in singling out individuals among the Clintonians, talking and arguing with them.[65]

---

63. Mitchell, *Alexander Hamilton*, 1: 430-431, 441-465.

64. As yet, no historian has presented a credible, systematic account of the sequence of events that resulted in the Federalists' convention victory in New York, despite their overwhelming defeat at the polls. One example makes the point. In 1898, Paul L. Ford asserted that it was due to New York City's threat to secede from the state unless the Constitution was adopted. In 1932, Spaulding gave heavy weight to that factor, and in 1958, McDonald observed that Ford, "declares that only the threat of secession forced New York to ratify. I agree with this view." It is possible that they are right, but, in my opinion, the scanty, impressionistic evidence they cite is unconvincing and leaves many critical questions either untouched or unanswered. Paul L. Ford, *The Federalist* (New York, 1898), 37-38 n. 1; Spaulding, *New York in the Critical Period*, 253-256; McDonald, *We The People*, 288 notes 124 and 125.

65. Spaulding, *New York in the Critical Period*, 253.

At present, we can not draw firm conclusions. But the Federalist victory in New York against heavy odds supports Beard. For, as restated here, he made these claims: 1) Even in a liberal republic, loosely-organized majorities are not likely to win decisions. 2) A minority, welded together by powerful motives and tight organization and brilliant leadership, outgeneralled its opponents, translated its ideas into effective action, and brought about the Constitutional revolution.

EPILOGUE

THE ARGUMENT thus far can be summarized in two sentences: Not even the elementary data (e.g., voting statistics) necessary to test Beard's main hypothesis have been systematically collected. The data now available indicate that some of Beard's claims are potentially verifiable and that some are not.

If this position is sound, then Professor McDonald's conclusion, "economic interpretation of the Constitution' does not work,"[1] is, at best, premature. McDonald to the contrary, we have a long way to go before we can firmly appraise Beard's

---

1. Forrest McDonald, *We The People* (Chicago, 1958), vii.

interpretation. But we need not take refuge in non-committal statements of what remains to be done and how it might be done. Instead, we can make a tentative appraisal that may contribute to further thought and research: When adequately tested, the *economic determinist* parts of Beard's main hypothesis will "not work," but, restated, some of his claims can be incorporated into a *social interpretation* of the Constitution that may "work."

Although the crudely stated interpretation sketched below satisfies the available data, further research will undoubtedly show that it requires drastic revision. But, to paraphrase Whitehead, if we begin with a crude interpretation, we are more likely to understand the Constitutional "revolution" eventually than if we begin with no interpretation.

A.
A Social Interpretation of the Constitution of the United States

Most Americans of the 1780's probably gave little sustained thought to the question of what constituted the Good Society. But, as Douglass Adair has brilliantly shown, this was not true of the leaders of the new nation; they purposefully studied the past to prepare themselves to control the present and shape the future.[2] Given the social and cultural structure of the United States during the 1780's, we can deduce that men differed radically over what constitutes the Good Society. No doubt, reality was more complex than our terms suggest, but we can say that partisans of the *Agrarian Society* and the *Commercial Society* fought the main intellectual battles. For convenience, we can

2. The extent to which the Founding Fathers derived their views from historical models is discussed in Adair's unpublished paper, "The Use of History by the Founding Fathers: The Historical Pessimism of A. Hamilton" (read before the American Historical Association in 1955).

oversimplify further and call the men who held these rival ideas, *agrarian-minded* and *commercial-minded*. The terms do not denote classes, socioeconómic status groups, or occupations —they denote ways of thinking. Thus, farmers with no intention or prospect of changing their occupation may have been commercial-minded, and men not engaged in farming may have been agrarian-minded. In short, our terms suggest the philosophy and ethos that men wanted to prevail in the United States.

1. THE AGRARIAN SOCIETY

Broadly, the Agrarian Society was Arcadia. Sparsely-settled, stable, localistic, self-contained, Arcadia would be populated and dominated in Jefferson's words, by "Those who labor in the earth" and by those who superintend their labor. Of course, such a society could not dispense with commerce, trade, and small-scale manufacturing and crafts which would supply local markets or fill specialized demands. Merchants, for example, were necessary to dispose of agricultural surpluses and to import goods from abroad. Moreover, merchants, shippers, tradesmen, mechanics, artisans, and members of the liberal professions had their proper place in any complete and interesting society. But their proper place was a subordinate place. As "handmaids" to agriculture, they could not set the tone for Arcadia. The following quotation gives us a keen analysis of Jefferson's outlook:

Commerce had a crucial place in his attitude. He did, however, deprecate the greedy and aggressive spirit which so frequently accompanied commercial enterprise and excessive commercial ambition: Merchants are often deficient in virtue and *amor patriae*. Unless kept within rein, they promote a heady fashion of gambling. It was this moralistic view that has been misinterpreted as opposition to commerce and commercial development.[3]

Less cosmopolitan than Jefferson, a Virginia planter-aristocrat who simultaneously favored and feared commerce, George Clin-

---

3. Joseph Dorfman, *The Economic Mind in American Civilization: 1606-1865* (New York, 1946), 1: 435.

ton, leader of the "yeomanry" of the New York "agricultural upcountry," clung to a more doctrinaire and extreme version of the agrarian philosophy. He believed that only an agricultural civilization could remain sound and virtuous because "the progress of a commercial society begets luxury, the parent of inequality, the foe to virtue, and the enemy to restraint."[4]

2. THE COMMERCIAL SOCIETY

As envisioned during the 1780's, the Commercial Society would contain a substantial majority of farmers. But the yeast of commerce would leaven what would otherwise be an agrarian lump. "Commerce is the great civilizing force," declared Tom Paine—who never profited from it, lived precariously, and died in poverty. "Paine," according to Joseph Dorfman, "succinctly summed up his economic philosophy when he said in *Agrarian Justice:* 'I am a friend of Riches,' and in *The Rights of Man:* 'In all my publications, whenever the matter would admit, I have been an advocate of commerce.' "[5]

Men who shared Paine's faith in the civilizing force of commerce believed that active participation in world markets would stimulate all forms of enterprise, permit dynamic development of the vast American potential, and foster a cosmopolitan society that would free men from parochial thinking, provincial allegiances, and petty jealousies. Specifically, it would enlarge the money economy, benefit agriculture, domestic trade, and industrial production, and would improve transportation and communication facilities. All this would unify the country, speed its expansion, elevate men's vision, and enable them to see distant and foreign horizons. Rich urban communities would flourish, and with them, the liberal professions and arts. Put another way, the envisioned commercial society would heighten the level of aspiration, provide scope for ambition and talent, create a variegated, exciting urban culture, give rise to a great nation, and earn for its citizens the esteem of mankind.

---

4. Quoted in E. Wilder Spaulding, *His Excellency George Clinton* (New York, 1938), 174.

5. Dorfman, *Economic Mind in American Civilization*, 1: 454, 459.

A century and a half later, during the 1920's and 1930's, it would have been difficult to find reasoned opposition to a Commercial Society in the United States. Perhaps the "Southern Agrarians" provide the proverbial exception, but even they were primarily opposed to industrialism rather than to commercialism. During the early twentieth-century decades, it seems safe to say, most men hostile to the ethos expressed in the slogan, "The business of America is business," would have tended to regard the Southern Agrarians as, at best, anachronistic romantics, and at worst, dangerous reactionaries. During the 1780's, however, the Agrarian Society as the Good Society was anything but an anachronistic dogma preached by southern intellectuals who refused to accept the American Universe as it had been shaped by history.

3. IDEOLOGICAL CONFLICTS AND THE CONSTITUTION

To paraphrase and extend Beard, during the formative years after the American Revolution, agrarian-minded and commercial-minded men waged an ideological conflict of great intensity. In part, the conflict stemmed from, and was shaped by, different views of the "lessons of history" and different exposures to past and present developments. But, in large part, it stemmed from the "modes and processes of gaining a livelihood" which produced a social and cultural structure capable of stimulating and harboring conflicting views of the Good Society.

As I see it, this is a social interpretation of the ideological conflict that wracked the new nation—and it may work. But it is the kind of interpretation that has been so thoroughly absorbed by American historians since Beard published his book in 1913 that it may seem to state the obvious. It may be denigrated as "trivial" because it asserts "what everybody knows." We can draw some conclusions from it, however, that are not so "obvious," and that may help us reconstruct the battle over the Constitution.

B.

The Good State as the Instrument of the Good Society

Government plays a powerful role in realizing or preventing the realization of the Good Society. We can deduce, therefore, that, during the 1780's, the conflict over the Good Society was reflected and expressed in the conflict over the Good State. I am not saying that the one *created* the other; the relations were reciprocal.

Within a liberal republic, the logical corollary of "agrarianism" (as defined above) was a system that allocated to the State relatively slight, widely-dispersed, strictly limited powers and located those powers "close to the people." Not that logic controlled all, of course, but I assume that the characteristics that predisposed men to agrarianism tended also to predispose them to distrust the State.

Agrarian-minded men tended strongly to hold these ideas: Montesquieu was right in postulating that republics can flourish only in small, homogeneous territories; liberty is best preserved if governmental power diminishes with distance from the locality and is centered in officials easily accessible to the people and directly responsible to them; history generally demonstrates that power lodged anywhere in the framework of government always potentially menaces liberty; and the developments that led to the Revolution specifically demonstrated that strong central governments inevitably become despotic; it follows, therefore, that the new nation should be a decentralized, loose confederation of the several independent states.

Men who subscribed to these general ideas differed over how far to carry the confederation principle. Some wanted a State Rights Confederation in which the "general government" would be primarily an agent, not a political entity in its own right. Others wanted a system of divided sovereignty which would give some power to the general government. But these were divisions within one main camp, for, as Merrill Jensen has pointed out, contemporaries primarily distinguished between a "federal" and a "national" government.[6] It seems reasonable, therefore, to follow their lead and say that the Articles of Confederation embodied the idea of "federalism."

Again, within a liberal republic, the logical corollary of "commercialism" was a system derived from the proposition that the State could function as a creative, powerful instrument for realizing the Good Society. Cosmopolitan commercialists, I assume, had a more positive and optimistic view of State power than localistic agrarians. Close to its center and confident that they could influence it, they did not fear the State per se, they feared the tyranny of petty parochialism. To function creatively, advance the general welfare, and dispense justice, they believed, the State must be strong and centralized. Moreover, it must have both positive powers to enlarge opportunities and coercive powers to prevent groups and localities from indulging their own interests, passions, and errors at the expense of the Commonwealth. This was the idea of "nationalism," which found limited expression in the system governed by the Constitution. (It is true that the nationalists, like the federalists, divided among themselves on the issue of democracy. But, for our purposes, the conflicts on this issue need not be discussed.)

To say that positive relationships existed between ideas of the Good Society and the Good State does not imply that contemporaries actually saw the relationships, or that all agrarians were federalists and all commercialists, nationalists. Particularly after the War of Independence, which had shaken even if it had not revolutionized American society, many factors had worked against the development of close relationships

---

6. Merrill Jensen, *The New Nation* (New York, 1950), xiii-xiv, *passim*. Though I do not agree with Professor Jensen in all respects, I have profited from his analysis of what once was known as the "critical period."

between men's social and political ideas. The following list suggests some of them: Attitudes towards the War of Independence, and activities and experiences during it; membership in certain economic groups; membership in certain ethnic and religious groups; personal and political friendships, loyalties and associations; personal and family history; residence in communities and states with particular historical traditions or particular needs; amount and type of education; long-established intellectual commitments; degree of receptivity to ideas from abroad.

I am not suggesting that an exact or near-perfect correspondence existed between men's social and political ideas; I am suggesting that a marked tendency existed for agrarians to be federalists and for commercialists to be nationalists. (It does not seem necessary to try to define "marked tendency" more precisely.)

Suppose data were available that enabled us to locate men along an ideological line ranging from "pure agrarianism" to "pure commercialism." And suppose we could simultaneously rank them according to intensity of conviction. If such data were available, I believe we would find that men who had strong, unambiguous convictions about the Good Society also tended to have the idea about the Good State that was logically related to it, and that the tendency would weaken as we moved towards the midpoint of the ideological line and the bottom of the intensity scale.

A concrete example: George Clinton typifies the intense, pure agrarian; Thomas Jefferson, the conflicted, agrarian-commercialist; Alexander Hamilton, the intense, pure commercialist. Clinton maintained an extreme federalist position before and after adoption of the Constitution (although by one of those ironies that delight and confound historians, his side took the name "Antifederalist"); Jefferson oscillated between moderate nationalism and moderate federalism that occasionally gave way to strong nationalism; Hamilton consistently maintained an extreme nationalist position.

C.

The Good Society, the Good State, and the Constitution

We can carry this line of reasoning a step further to deduce that a positive, marked relationship existed between the social and political ideologies of men and their opinions on the specific issue of replacing the Articles of Confederation with the Constitution. As always, many factors worked to prevent men from behaving with perfect consistency, including: prior political associations; experiences under the Articles of Confederation; the circumstances under which the issue arose and those which existed in 1787-88; the conduct of the political campaigns in the several states; specific provisions contained in, or excluded from, the Constitution; men's beliefs about the impact of the Constitution upon their interests (economic *and* noneconomic), as well as upon the interests of groups or communities of which they were members or with which they identified. A concrete example may make the point more clearly.

Almost immediately after the Founding Fathers ended their deliberations, three "small states," Delaware, Georgia, and New Jersey, called conventions and unanimously ratified the Constitution. Since their history after 1787 rules out the possibility that they were singularly free from social and political conflicts, special factors that did not influence the country at large must have operated in those states to cause them to deviate so strongly from the national pattern.

Excluding states in which special factors produced near-unanimity, my hypothesis claims that a marked tendency existed for agrarian federalists to oppose, and for commercial nationalists to favor, the Constitution. It claims also that the tendency increased in proportion to the purity and intensity of ideological convictions. Finally, it claims that commercialists who held the political idea that was logically inconsistent (federalism) tended strongly to resolve the conflict in favor of their idea of the Good Society and voted for the Constitution, and that agrarians in the same position divided more evenly. (Since the hypothesis refers to central tendencies, i.e., what most men did, citation of prominent exceptions does not discredit it.) The last claim is based upon one logical and one empirical assumption. Logically, I assume that the opinions of men tend to be influenced more by their views concerning the social order than by their views concerning a particular institution, such as the State, that helps to shape the social order. Empirically, I assume that the pro-Constitution party waged a more effective political campaign than did its opponents.

1. WHO HELD OPPOSING IDEAS OF THE GOOD SOCIETY?

From the line of reasoning employed thus far, our central problem is to identify the men most likely to hold opposing ideas of the Good Society. The hypothesis claims that social environment and position in the American social structure mainly determined men's ideologies, and, in turn, their ideologies mainly determined their opinions on the Constitution.

In less abstract terms, the hypothesis claims that, directly and indirectly, social ideologies and opinions on the Constitution were mainly determined by the combined effects of three related, somewhat overlapping factors: 1) men's roles within the existing economic structure which strongly influenced their roles within the social structure; 2) the degree of urbanization of the areas in which they lived; 3) the ties which linked their communities with seaboard cities and interior large towns. These ties, or patterns of interaction, were affected more by transportation and communication facilities than by distance. Concrete examples again can substitute for detailed discussion.

Belief in the Commercial Society and support for the Constitution were more likely to be found among New York City merchants who exported American commodities and imported European luxury items than among Ulster County farmers who took part only infrequently in the commercial network and who did not require specialized knowledge of market conditions. Similarly, planters located in communities with close ties to Charleston were more likely to be commercial-minded and pro-Constitution than Carolinians who owned the same number of acres and slaves and the same amount of other property, but who lived in areas relatively distant from the seaport.

I am emphasizing the nature of men's participation in the economy and the character of their over-all social environment; I do not dismiss as irrelevant to ideology and opinion the amount and kind of property owned and occupation held, but regard them as less influential. Of course, some kinds of property and some occupations almost automatically fixed the character of men's social environment, e.g., shipowners and exporting-importing merchants did not tend to live in isolated rural areas. But many types of property were held, and many occupations were practiced, in environments that differed radically.

Planters who lived in communities closely linked to southern seaports did not function in the same social environment as planters who lived in areas remote from urban influences and contacts. Similarly, shoemakers who plied their trade in New York City and in Ulster County villages can be assigned to the same group only in a formal sense, and only by accepting technological determinism and banishing social reality and social process from history. A shoemaker is a shoemaker, but a shoemaker in New York City is not a shoemaker in Shawangunk, Ulster County—particularly during the 1780's.

From the discussion it should be clear that the social interpretation presented here attempts to modify and extend Beard's ideas. Instead of studying men during the 1780's as "economic beings dependent upon definite modes and processes of gaining a livelihood," it proposes to study them as members of groups that occupied particular roles in the American social structure, lived in particular social environments, and were influenced by history and contemporary developments.

I do not assume that men's *views* of the most desirable social order are a direct function of their *places* in the existing social order. That is, men's ideas of the Good Society are not automatic products of calculated self-interest, or rationalizations veiling "rough and sordid reality." On the other hand, I do not deny that men have a healthy concern—frequently an unhealthy concern—for their own interests and for those of groups to which they belong, or with which they identify. "The human understanding," Francis Bacon long ago observed, "is no dry light, but receives an infusion from the will and affections. . . ." That astute observation, however, does not force us to conclude that men are egoistic, hedonistic, calculating creatures, unmoved by considerations other than their own (or their group's) interests and impervious to influences other than those likely to advance them.[7]

I make the following assumptions: The nature of life in society more or less disposes human beings to want to be good, to do good, and to live in a good social order. Inextricably entangled in a "web of kinship" from the time they are born until the time they die, human beings inevitably develop a desire and a need, as Edward Shils has expressed it, "for incorporation into something which transcends and transfigures their concrete individual existence. They have a need to be in contact with symbols of an order which is larger in its dimensions than their own bodies and more central in the 'ultimate' structure of reality than is their routine everyday life."[8] Depending upon conditions and experiences, the desire and need develop in different degrees and forms. Thus, altruism is a varying function

---

7. For a perceptive, provocative analysis of "The Sociology of Knowledge," see Robert K. Merton, *Social Theory and Social Structure* (Glencoe, Ill., 1957, rev. ed.), 456-508.

8. They bear no responsibility for the particular formulation here, but my understanding of these points has benefitted from discussions with Meyer Fortes and Edward Shils at the Center for Advanced Study in the Behavioral Sciences. Some of their ideas are discussed in Fortes, *The Web of Kinship among the Tallensi* (London, 1949), vii-viii, 337-347; Shils, "The Macrosociological Problem: Consensus and Dissensus in the Larger Society" (Center for Advanced Study in the Behavioral Sciences, 1959, multilithed). The observation that human behavior is influenced not only by groups to which men belong, but by groups to which they do *not* belong, has led to the development of the theory of reference group behavior. See, Merton, *Social Theory and Social Structure*, 225-386.

of human society, not an invariant function of human biology.

Again depending upon conditions and experiences, the desire and need of men to express their altruism more or less influences their ideals and their behavior. But, among other reasons why men tend to express their altruism in different ways, they are not equally exposed to competing ideals. Not only does information about contending ideals tend to vary with position in the social structure and in the local environment, many other influences subtly affect the processes of absorption and selection, particularly the following: 1) The ideals affirmed and pursued by the elites in certain groups and communities of which individuals are members, or with which they identify. ("Elites" are defined here as holders of authoritative positions in the group or community.) 2) The extent to which competing ideals are seen as compatible with individual experiences and individual interests.

The argument can be briefly summarized: The fiction of "Economic Man" may prove useful in studying certain kinds of human behavior, including certain kinds of interest group politics. But, in the study of the "natural history" of ideology, or the politics of ideology, or the politics of fundamental social change, it distorts rather than illuminates the behavior of men in society.

2. WHY DID THE FEDERALISTS WIN?

In addition to asking how men arrived at their ideas about the Constitution, Beard asked how men translated their ideas into action. Since I tend to agree with him and have discussed the problem elsewhere in the essay, a short discussion is all that is needed here.

Beard did not develop the point in his book, but he evidently believed that an instructive study of the framing and ratification of the Constitution cannot treat developments in each state as equally important. Historians, he implied, cannot avoid assessing the relative importance of specific decisions and actions in the sequence of events. For example, it seems clear that success or failure of the Constitutional revolution depended more on decisions and actions taken in Pennsylvania, Massachusetts, Virginia, and New York than in New Jersey, Delaware, and Georgia. In dealing with the problem of how men translated their ideas on the Constitution into action, we therefore must pay particular attention to the effectiveness of the strategy, tactics, and timing of Federalist and Antifederalist leaders in the decisive states; we cannot assume that men in all states played equally important roles in bringing about, or defeating, the "great political transformation."

According to the interpretation, or hypothesis, advanced here, men who strongly favored a Commercial Society were also likely to possess the personal and social attributes needed to win political power. Moreover, they operated in a particular historical situation which gave them a great advantage; it enabled them to join forces, not only with men who were agrarian-commercialists, but with some who were inclined to agrarianism. In large part, this *mésalliance* came about because the post-Revolutionary crisis induced some leading non-commercialists to take a nationalist position.

For example, Madison was not as devoted to commercialism as Hamilton—to employ understatement. And yet, during the turbulent period in which the new nation seemed to be struggling for survival and *before* a new social equilibrium had evolved, the Virginian devoted himself as zealously as did the New Yorker to the nationalist, pro-Constitution cause. Madison's subsequent course of action, however, supports the conclusion that agrarianism and nationalism were an unnatural combination, unlikely to hold together except in certain kinds of historical situations. After national and social stability had been achieved, he, like Jefferson, went over to federalism and led the State Rights party against Hamiltonian nationalism.

One individual case does not support a generalization, of course. But the over-all pattern of events during the 1780's and 1790's supports the argument that political behavior is influenced more strongly by ideas of the Good Society than by ideas of the Good State. The argument can be broken down into three parts: 1) The behavior of men is determined more by the ends they seek than by the means they use to achieve those ends; specifically, men favored the Constitution largely because they favored a Commercial Society, they opposed the Constitution largely because they favored an Agrarian Society. 2) The ends men choose are positively related to the "modes and processes" by which they gain their livelihoods, the social environments in which they live, the social roles they occupy, the groups with whom they identify, and the groups with whom they regard themselves in conflict. 3) In certain historical situations, men who choose certain ends are more likely than their opponents to possess the qualities and resources needed for victory; specifically, in the United States during the 1780's, commercial-minded men like Hamilton possessed the qualities and resources needed to defeat agrarian-minded men like Clinton.

Translated into appropriate terms, these general propositions extend Beard's original ideas and may provide a sound basis for a social interpretation of the framing and adoption of the Constitution of the United States.

Appendix to Part Three

McDONALD'S USE OF DATA

◇◇

SINCE SILENCE might imply agreement, it seems best to state explicitly that I have reservations concerning Forrest Mc-Donald's collection, ordering, and use of data. Aside from the logical fallacy in the collective biography method as he used it, I question the factual basis of his conclusions. Several examples suggest the character of his data and the use he made of them.

In effect, Beard claimed that the delegates assembled at Philadelphia did not accurately represent the American people as a whole; instead, with few exceptions, he depicted them as representing only those groups that favored "the movement

for the new Constitution. . . ."[1] To discredit Beard, McDonald
cited evidence purporting to show that the Convention delegates "constituted an almost complete cross-section of the
geographical areas and shades of political opinion existing in the
United States in 1787."[2] His evidence, I believe, cannot be
accepted at face value.

For one thing, in appraising the Convention's representative
character, McDonald failed to distinguish between the seventy-
four delegates elected, or appointed, to the Convention and the
fifty-five who attended. Moreover, he failed to distinguish
among the delegates who attended briefly and registered opposition to the proposed Constitution, the delegates who remained
for the duration, and the thirty-nine who actually signed the
document. But those distinctions must be made if we are to examine the representative character of the men who drafted the
Constitution.

Apart from failing to make the distinction suggested above,
McDonald arbitrarily assigned men to represent areas, groups,
and political factions which, in fact, they did not represent. For
example, he made Rufus King simultaneously represent two
considerably different Massachusetts areas; the Newburyport-
Merrimac area and the "District of Maine." Is it justifiable to
depict King of commercial, coastal Newburyport as the representative of frontier Maine because he had been *born* in the
latter place? Is it justifiable to depict William Blount, a North
Carolina tidewater planter who owned thirty slaves and who
engaged in large-scale western land speculation, as "a sympathetic representative of [frontier] Tennessee?"[3]

Similar questions concerning McDonald's use of evidence
arise from his treatment of the New York delegation. "All three
delegates elected from New York sat in the Convention," he

---

1. Charles A. Beard, *An Economic Interpretation of the Constitution*
(New York, 1935), 64-72, *passim*.

2. Forrest McDonald, *We The People: The Economic Origins of the
Constitution* (Chicago, Illinois, 1958), 21-37.

3. *Ibid.*, 24, 34.

writes, "though none of them attended full time. . . ." True, but Robert Yates and John Lansing permanently withdrew from the Convention on July 5, 1787, in order to oppose the Constitutional movement more effectively; in contrast, Alexander Hamilton *temporarily* withdrew in order to work more effectively for the movement, and later returned to Philadelphia to participate again in the Convention's deliberations. McDonald's phrase, "though none of them attended full time," is less than adequate in a chapter attempting to demonstrate that, contrary to Beard, the Convention functioned as a representative body.[4]

Doubts also arise about McDonald's use of evidence when we examine his treatment of the state ratifying conventions. For example, his analysis of the "occupations and economic interests of the 355 members of the [Massachusetts] ratifying convention" purported to discredit Beard's claims concerning the class basis of opposition to the Constitution. But, in brief notes, McDonald admitted that he could not ascertain the "occupations of thirty-nine of the [187] delegates favoring ratification," and that the "occupations of eighty-nine [of 168] delegates opposing ratification were not ascertained because of the lack of local histories and town records."[5] In other words, he only found some data about the occupations of 64 per cent of the delegates to the Massachusetts convention. But he failed to comment upon the significance of his finding that the "unknowns" were not evenly divided among supporters and opponents of the Constitution. Only 20 per cent of the ratificationists fell into the "unknown" category, compared to 53 per cent for the anti-ratificationists. The logical inference is that the delegates for whom McDonald could not find data in local histories and town records tended to belong to low status occupational groups. Thus, when we take the "unknowns" into account, McDonald's conclusions about Massachusetts become highly dubious—even if we ig-

---

4. Compare *ibid.*, p. 26 with Broadus Mitchell, *Alexander Hamilton* (New York, 1957), 389-413; and John C. Miller, *Alexander Hamilton* (New York, 1959), 150-83.

5. *We The People*, 191, 195, 199.

nore the logical fallacy in his use of the collective biography method.

Among other things, McDonald criticized Beard for not recognizing that ratification was speedy or slow depending upon the size and "strength" of the several states. For example, to support his argument, he emphasized that the five "pitifully weak" states speedily ratified the Constitution.[6] But his analysis rests on unjustified, arbitrary assumptions concerning the several states' "strength." What justification exists for depicting Maryland and Connecticut, which speedily ratified, as "weaker" than North Carolina and Rhode Island, which did not ratify the Constitution until after the new government went into effect?

The final example illustrates McDonald's tendency to substitute assertion for evidence. Discussing developments in North Carolina, he writes:

The campaign of the anti-Federalists was a peculiar one. Some of them tried to keep the arguments on a sane level, deploring the lack of a bill of rights, predicting exploitation of the South by shrewd Yankees, and warning debtors of British merchants that the federal courts would be opened to suits for debts. *More common and more effective, however* [italics added], were such fantasies as that of Baptist minister Burkitt in Hertford County. That divine told his illiterate flock that the clause in the Constitution providing for what was to become the District of Columbia was a provision for a walled city that would house thousands of soldiers who would be privileged to plunder the country. Anti-Federalist leaders based their appeal on ignorance, the Federalists based theirs on reason. The anti-Federalists won by a landslide.[7]

Perhaps no better illustration could be found of what Beard called the "doctrinaire position" of regarding the "struggle over the Constitution. . .[as] a simple contest between the straight-thinking men and narrower and local men of the respective sections. . . ."[8] Even if the story of "Baptist minister Burkitt" were factual, how does McDonald know that such "fantasies"

6. *Ibid.*, 114-15.
7. *Ibid.*, 311.
8. Beard, *Economic Interpretation*, x.

were "more common and more effective" than appeals to "reason"? To justify that claim, he was required to make a systematic analysis of the North Carolina campaign and demonstrate the extent and impact of Antifederalist and Federalist appeals to "ignorance" and "reason." But he made no such analysis, nor is one to be found in the sources he cited. "Proof" by selective quotation is unconvincing.

INDEX